VIEWS FROM BEYOND HEART MOUNTAIN

VIEWS FROM BEYOND HEART MOUNTAIN

ALAN O'HASHI

Copyright and Disclaimers

This memoir is a work of nonfiction that represents the author's personal experiences, reflections, and recollections. The author portrays the events described to the best of their memory. However, the author may have unintentionally altered, omitted, or embellished some details because memories can fade.

The opinions expressed in this book are solely those of the author and do not necessarily reflect the views of any organizations, employers, or individuals mentioned. The author assumes no responsibility or liability for any errors or omissions in the content of this book.

We advise readers that this memoir may include content some might find triggering or distressing. We advise readers to exercise discretion.

Prowritingaid and Grammarly provided editing assistance. Cover design by Canva

First Printing, 2026

Dedication

To my parents Frank O'Hashi and Sumiko Sakata-O'Hashi,
grandparents Jusaburo "Joe" and Toki Sakata
Toichi "George" and Natsu "Mary" Ohashi
And to all the Issei and Nisei who came before

Contents

Forward: Superman's American Way

Views from Beyond Heart Mountain is my memoir about how civility can help us reimagine Superman's American Way by balancing individual needs with those of the wider community, with everyone's acceptance based on who they are and success measured by collaboration and sharing.

The American Way is the path we follow to realize our American Dream. What if collective action drives social change, with individuals interacting in neighborhoods, neighborhoods joining together in local communities, and cities and towns working together to improve lives at the national level?

It's hard work.

Social change refers to major changes in personal behavior patterns, cultural values and norms, social institutions, and social structures over time. My book examines economic variations, political movements, social policies, cultural transformations, and personal interactions that have brought us to where we are today.

Society ingrains Superman's American Way in us from the moment we pop out of the womb. Our parents teach us to pursue material success, rugged "I-can-do-it-myself" individualism, and assimilation by exclusion. These constructs exclude and marginalize many people who society did not allow to benefit from the American Way.

I published a coffee-table book, *Nishigawa Neighborhood*, and a memoir, *Beyond Heart Mountain*, with old family photos and my recollections as a Japanese American Baby Boomer, first in my hometown of Cheyenne, Wyoming, after World War II, then in Laramie, Gillette, and Lander.

I expanded both books into *Views from Beyond Heart Mountain*, which, in addition to personal memories and reflections, offers ways we can all help span cultural divides. The backdrop of the story is the overt and subtle racial discrimination my family and I faced after the Empire of Japan bombed Pearl Harbor on December 7, 1941.

After the attack, authorities rounded up 125,000 Japanese Americans, mainly on the West Coast, processed their paperwork, and then transported them to War Incarceration Camps during World War II. The repercussions continue to this day.

The U.S. government spared Japanese families, like mine, living in the interior of the United States from the Camp experience. Still, for safety, we took refuge in the heart of the Japanese community in the 500 and 400 blocks of West 17th Street in Cheyenne, Wyoming.

****

Historians cite 1525 as the first year Spaniards kidnapped tribal members from Africa and transported them to America as an inexpensive enslaved labor force to drive the new and expanding economy. Between 1525 and President Lincoln's 1863 Emancipation Proclamation, 338 years had elapsed, 340 counting the two years it took for Union troops to arrive in Galveston Bay, Texas, on Juneteenth with the news that enslavement had ended.

Compare that to the years since June 19, 1865. America has existed for 159 years longer with a history of oppression than with one of equality. There have been legal remedies, such as the 13th Amendment to the U.S. Constitution, which abolished slavery and involuntary servitude. The 15th Amendment gave African American men the right to vote, followed by the 19th Amendment, which gave women the right to vote.

President Lyndon Baines Johnson (LBJ) signed the Civil Rights Act in 1964. Yet from then to the present, social divisions stemming from discrimination against dark-skinned residents and immigrants arriving from Asia, Africa, and Latin America have persisted.

America's culture hasn't yet caught up to its laws.

My book offers cultural competency strategies to help improve societal conditions, promote social justice, and address social issues.

My parents suppressed our Japanese heritage in favor of living by the tenets of Superman's American Way, which left me confused. I heard on the radio yesterday that there's a term for that: bicultural straddling.

****

Superman arrived on Earth in 1938, but I knew the Man of Steel from the TV series *The Adventures of Superman* (1952 - 1958), set in the fictional city of Metropolis. At the start of the show, the narrator establishes the backstory. Superman possessed powers such as X-ray vision and bulletproof strength. He could stop a fast-moving train on the tracks and leap over skyscrapers.

Jor-El and Lara rocket their infant son, Kal-El, from their home planet, Krypton, as it nears destruction. The spaceship crashes on Jonathan and Martha Kent's farm near Smallville, Kansas.

They rescue Kal-El and name their undocumented immigrant son Clark. His adoptive parents soon learn that their son has superpowers and teach him to harness them for the greater good. Clark grows up concealing his secret identity as Superboy and later Superman.

After college, Clark moves to Metropolis and works as a reporter for the Daily Planet. He learns about crimes in progress from news tips. Clark transforms into Superman when duty calls him to "fight a never-ending battle for truth, justice, and the American Way."

Superman's American Way supports a world founded on competition, rugged individualism, and acceptance through assimilation and exclusion. What if we could reimagine Superman's American Way as a more civil, collaborative, and accepting path toward our American Dream?

****

My book project started with a survey of Japanese residents and business owners who lived and worked on the 500 and 400 blocks of West 17th Street on the western edge of Cheyenne, Wyoming, from the 1920s to the 1970s.

I became curious about how the dominant culture first expanded into the New World and enslaved African tribal members as laborers to fuel a growing economy. European immigrants seeking better lives moved westward and conquered lands that Native Americans believed belonged to all with no ownership.

"Many Native tribes once lived on these lands," says the convener at the beginning of a public meeting. The convener invariably omits the fact that the dominant culture stole tribal lands and that the laws and institutions it established have primarily benefited the conquerors.

My family's roots in the United States exemplify Superman's American Way. Both sets of my grandparents, typical émigrés from Japan, sought better lives, starting their American adventures in Washington state. They followed different paths to Cheyenne, Wyoming, but met in the West 17th Street Japanese neighborhood.

Researching Japanese history in Cheyenne prompted me to reflect on how World War II molded my upbringing and life in Wyoming. I became a Wyomingite through and through. I'll explain my experiences in the context of the histories of the United States, Wyoming, Cheyenne, and its Japanese neighborhood.

I grew up in Cheyenne during the Cold War in the 1950s and 1960s. My family uprooted and moved to Laramie during my sophomore year at Hastings College. I worked my first job in Gillette during the coal boom and another in Lander during the uranium bust. I continued my journey of self-identity while working for the Northern Arapaho Tribe on the Wind River Reservation. I circled back to my Cheyenne roots with this writing project in 2019.

****

My parents expected me to act as an American citizen in specific ways: to stand and remove my hat when the flag passed in a parade and to recite the Pledge of Allegiance in school. I always struggled with my place in the American Way because my teachers and classmates viewed me as different, despite my efforts to be like everybody else.

The future of the past is the present.

What if we draw on past outcomes, learn from the Japanese World War II incarceration experience, and apply a new vision for how excluded communities can reimagine the American Way?

I address race and ethnicity in this book. Racial and ethnic oppression founded America and has widened all social and cultural schisms. These include sexual orientation, gender identity, and general inequality.

The World War II Japanese roundup, the 9/11 backlash against Muslims, and immigrants flooding the southern border between the United States and Mexico are different yet similar. The roots of racism stem from the same dominant culture's drive for social homogeneity, dating back to colonial times in America, whether you are in San Francisco, Cheyenne, Chicago, or Midtown Manhattan.

As an adult in my twilight years, it's taken me a lifetime to recognize the effect assimilation has had on me. Despite how well I learned to fit in with the American Way and to straddle two worlds, I am still isolated from my Japanese roots and continually becoming lost in the dominant culture.

Growing up, I had a large, close-knit extended family, no stranger to living in close quarters and on top of one another. That experience set me up to get off the couch and SHARE. The secret sauce I've poured over my life has essential ingredients that I'll touch on in the book:

Socialize: Get to know the people in your inner circle and beyond. If we hope to form stronger relationships, we have to get out and meet our neighbors. How can we learn about people unlike ourselves?

Help: Lend a hand. Be intentional when assisting people who need an up or a handout. Not only should we be charitable and helpful during the holiday giving season at the end of each year, but what about the other 50 calendar weeks?

Accept: Include others without judgment. Deciding about someone based on inaccurate or incomplete information is stereotyping. How did your socialization as a youth shape your view of people who may differ from you today?

Reach Out: Meet people different from yourself with respect and dignity. How can we break out of our comfort zone?

Engage: Help save the world by doing good, doing no harm, and being friendly. How do we set aside disagreements and personal biases to bridge cultural and social divides?

Although I'm mostly used up, I'm doing what I can to foster greater civility, as an individual and as a member of various groups in my neighborhood and across the country. I believe the world would be saved by now if each of us had more spare time.

Alan O'Hashi

Boulder, Colorado

PS: I apologize for all the acronyms. The U.S. government spent millions of dollars over four years, combining and redefining the roles of multiple agencies to contain 125,000 Japanese during World War II. An abbreviation key appears at the end of the book.

1

The Days the Earth Stood Still

Japanese Americans served in the U.S. military long before the bombing of Pearl Harbor on December 7, 1941. The number of Americans who remember the attack is dwindling. My Auntie Hisako passed away in 1995, but her story is one I'll never forget.

In his 1969 book Nisei, author Bill Hosokawa writes that in 1941 the military stationed several recently inducted Japanese American soldiers at Fort Frances E. Warren (Fort Warren) on the outskirts of Cheyenne, Wyoming.

Hisako worked there as the base chaplain's secretary. She arranged passes for the Nisei GIs to attend a dance on December 7th at the Japanese community hall in Downtown Cheyenne.

The local Japanese community prepared a spread of traditional food for the soldiers and arranged for a record player, not a common living room amenity at the time, to provide music and accompany dancing.

Earlier that Sunday, the Empire of Japan attacked the U.S. Naval base at Pearl Harbor near Honolulu. Despite all the planning, nobody wanted to dance or enjoy the fancy dinner. Everyone returned to the base and listened to President Franklin Delano Roosevelt (FDR) declare war on Japan over the radio the next day.

Over the years, Hisako became more culturally competent. She realized that society considered her and her family, who later became my family, inferior, so she worked exceptionally hard to become the first college graduate.

When she moved to Washington, DC, she drew on her Wyoming experience as an advocate for the Japanese community and worked on civil rights issues at the national level.

My future mother and father hadn't yet imagined they'd have a son. Even after I came into the world, I have no recollection of my parents discussing Pearl Harbor or World War II during my childhood in Cheyenne, Wyoming, my hometown. The War had a traumatic effect on my parents and our family.

Then 9/11 happened and became my mega-memory.

****

No explanation is necessary for what happened on September 11, 2001, other than that it became another day when the Earth stood still.

I called my mom a few days after three weaponized commercial passenger jets careened into the World Trade Center in New York City and the Pentagon in Washington, DC. A fourth plane crashed into a field in Pennsylvania.

We exchanged a few pleasantries and condolences about the tragedy. By then, news sources had reported that the *al-Qaeda* terrorist group had taken responsibility for the carnage.

"Thank God no Asians were involved," she said.

"Yeah, Americans have been shooting at Asians since the '40s," I responded, citing World War II, the Korean War in the '50s, and Vietnam, which ended in 1975.

"I feel for Muslims, but now they'll be watching all of us," Mom said.

"What do you mean?"

"Now, anyone with brown skin will be watched. You be good. You'll be noticed if you aren't," Mom warned me. "That's the way it's always been. Don't draw attention to yourself. Anything good you do won't be noticed. Anything negative will reflect badly not only on us but on all Asians."

"We'll be lumped in with the Muslims," I surmised. In 1998, I completed the *Visiones* Advanced Leadership Training, led by my friend and colleague, Daniel Escalante. The curriculum introduced me to the dynamics of dominant cultural power and to principles of cultural competency.

****

Sparks flew when Japan bombed Pearl Harbor, drawing the United States into World War II. FDR signed EO 9066 in February 1942. The FDR administration feared that the Empire of Japan might have embedded spies among the general citizenry. U.S. military efforts to uproot Japanese residents had a legal basis.

The Western Defense Command (WDC), along with the 4th Army, issued Civil Exclusion Orders (CEOs) that removed Japanese Americans living in militarily restricted Exclusion Zones on the West Coast from their homes and businesses.

Military Area 1 included the western halves of California, Oregon, Washington, and southern Arizona. Military Area 2 included the remaining portions of these states.

In 1942, the CEOs forced Japanese Americans to leave their homes and businesses and report to one of 15 temporary Assembly Centers. The WDC also established the Wartime Civil Control Administration (WCCA), a civilian affairs branch responsible for building and administering those Centers.

The relocation effort encouraged voluntary compliance to minimize military involvement. The WCCA quickly retrofitted county fairgrounds into 15 Assembly Centers, where it sorted and detained prisoners to ensure they wouldn't leave the Exclusion Zone while awaiting completion of the 10 Relocation Centers.

The terms "relocation" and "center" are misnomers and an example of doublespeak. Tall barbed-wire fences and guard towers encircled the 10 compounds scattered across the U.S. interior, where armed soldiers kept watch.

Based on conversations with my parents and their contemporaries, I learned that they referred to the relocation centers as "camps." Ten thousand incarcerees lived at the Heart Mountain Camp until the end of the War in 1945.

While researching this story, I found sources that refer to the relocation centers as "concentration" or "incarceration" camps and to the internees as "prisoners" or "incarcerees."

I use incarcerees and incarceration camps.

That said, the Casper Star Tribune (CST) reported in late 1942 that a group of incarcerees protested the barbed-wire fence and guard towers, stating in a petition to the WRA, "We are not prisoners of war" (PoW).

Prisoners waited for months or years before the WCCA transferred them by rail or bus to 10 remote incarceration camps in the interior of the United States, including one near Heart Mountain in northwestern Wyoming.

Several hundred Japanese volunteers arrived a month ahead of schedule to prepare for the first incarcerees. The WCCA initially herded them into California Assembly Centers in Sacramento, Pinedale, and Marysville, as well as at the Pomona and Salinas Fairgrounds.

My paternal grandfather, Toichi "George" Ohashi, and his eldest son, George, happened to be living in Ventura, California, sourcing vegetables in the Central Valley when FDR signed EO 9066. The WCCA confiscated their truck and transferred Grandpa to the Tulare Center and Uncle George to the Puyallup Center.

The WCCA built Centers at the Tanforan Racetrack near San Francisco; Manzanar in Independence; Santa Anita Racetrack in Arcadia; Fresno Fairgrounds; Riverside Fairgrounds; Puyallup Fairgrounds; Central Washington Fairgrounds in Toppenish, Washington; the Gila River Reservation in Arizona; Jerome, Idaho (not to be confused with Jerome, Arkansas); and Portland, Oregon.

Most WCCA administrators transferred from the Works Progress Administration (WPA). FDR established various agencies, including the WPA, as part of his "New Deal" shortly after his 1933 inauguration, employing millions of Americans who had lost their jobs during the Great Depression. Projects included road construction and the construction of public buildings, and the WPA made a smooth transition to the War effort.

EO 9102 established the War Relocation Authority (WRA) in March 1942, initially as an independent agency directly under the President's Executive Office. The WRA assumed day-to-day operations of the Japanese relocation from the WCCA. The 3,000-employee WRA spent an estimated $160 million by the end of World War II.

In February 1944, the President transferred the WRA to the Department of the Interior (DoI), a transfer that remained in effect until the camps and the Authority closed at the end of the War.

****

My aunt's experience at Fort Warren after Pearl Harbor reminded me of a family connection to 9/11. On that day, American Airlines (AA) scheduled Flight 11, a Boeing 767, to depart from Boston's Logan International Airport (BOS) en route to Los Angeles' LAX.

A flight attendant, Betty Ong, and my cousin Leonard's fiancée had scheduled herself on AA Flight 11 to meet her sister in Los Angeles for a Hawaiian vacation.

The aircraft could hold 158 passengers, but on September 11th, AA had sold about half of the seats.

After five passengers hijacked the plane, Betty made an Airfone call, a system that transmitted calls over radio frequencies. MCI developed the technology, enabling passengers to make in-flight calls for about four dollars. MCI discontinued the Airfone service in 2006 because of low usage.

Betty contacted the AA operations center in Raleigh, North Carolina. She told the center supervisor that five hijackers had taken control of her aircraft and provided the hijackers' seat assignments, which later helped investigators identify them.

Mohamed Atta, Abdulaziz al-Omari, and Suqami sat in business class, while Waleed al-Shehri and Wail al-Shehri secured first-class seats.

Flight Attendant Betty Ong became a heroine on AA Flight 11. She perished along with 91 passengers that morning.

****

After Pearl Harbor, Asian shopkeepers on the West Coast feared reprisal and posted signs in their storefront windows reading "No Japs Here." Shortly after the 9/11 attacks, history repeated itself, and South and Southeast Asian businesses posted signs reading "No Muslims Here."

I had no idea that the indelible, generational 9/11 attack on American soil by a foreign adversary had occurred. I fell behind schedule and didn't bother to turn on the *Today Show* or *Morning Edition* on KUNC public radio while getting ready to commute to work in Denver.

I walked to the convenience store for a cup of coffee before catching my Regional Transportation District (RTD) bus to Denver.

"Looks like it's going to be a good one out there." I don't think the clerk understood my comment about the glorious weather predicted for the day. He grinned and handed me my change. I clunked a couple of cents into the plastic leave-a-penny/take-a-penny tray on the counter, then cut through the gas pumps to the bus stop.

Living near the corner of Valmont Road and 28th Street, I could walk to the liquor store and the Asian market. A developer had converted Eden East, a 1970s-era apartment building, into condos.

Across Goose Creek, the vintage plumbing store Rayback stocked ancient brass fittings for minor maintenance projects.

The 205 bus pulled up en route to the RTD Walnut Street station in downtown Boulder. A few passengers waited to catch the B Express bus from the downtown Boulder bus station to Denver. Rather than drive to a Park n Ride, I didn't mind taking a local bus to get a good seat.

I walked to the rear and took a primo aisle seat with extra legroom near the middle of the cabin, a couple of rows ahead of where wheelchairs park, similar to the exit-row seats on an airplane.

By the time we reached the last Boulder stop at the Table Mesa Park-N-Ride, commuters filled most of the seats, rattling their morning papers, cramming for college classes at the Auraria campus, reading books, listening to music on iPods, and catching up on sleep.

Personal computers, internet hotspots, and smartphones didn't exist. I had a Kyocera cell phone, the size of two stacked regular Hershey bars, with a built-in personal digital assistant (PDA).

"Did you hear what happened in New York?" the guy beside me asked. When I said I hadn't, he replied, "An airplane crashed into one of the Twin Towers."

He shrugged when I asked him about the type of plane, but other passengers murmured about the news, and I overheard someone say, "It was a small plane, like a Cessna." Hmm, a small plane. Nothing to see here, folks. Soon we all returned to being immersed in ourselves.

The bus pulled up to a stop at Market Street Station. We disembarked and made our way up the stairs and escalators to the 16th Street Mall. I waited at the stop for the eastbound RTD 20 bus, which dropped me off near my work, a converted single-family home in an older neighborhood.

I walked up the steps and creaked open the wrought-iron screen door, then wound my way up the staircase toward my office at Project Safeguard, a domestic violence (DV) legal advocacy organization.

"You can go home if you want," my boss, Sharon, said from the top of the stairs, leaning over the railing. "Two planes hit the World Trade Center. There isn't much more information, but all air traffic is grounded."

My colleagues had all gone home. I had the longest commute from Boulder. I returned to the bus station and noticed the eerily quiet streets: no car engines, no airplane noise, and only a few pedestrians. When I stood waiting for the light at Broadway and the 16th Street Mall, I glanced up at the Denver World Trade Center. I later learned that two planes had careened into targets similar to their namesake in Lower Manhattan.

I didn't engage in any of the buzz on the ride back to Boulder.

What's your 9/11 memory?

****

The U.S. government didn't always prop up a xenophobic culture. The U.S. military withdrew from Vietnam in 1975, leaving the country in the capable hands of the Communists. Afterward, thousands of Vietnamese "boat people" traveled to the free world, including the United States. The military established detention camps at several U.S. Army bases to temporarily house Vietnamese refugees.

The week before Saigon, now Ho Chi Minh City, fell, U.S. Navy ships and the Air Force evacuated 95,000 South Vietnamese. U.S. military bases in the Philippines and Guam received another 125,000 refugees before the U.S. government transferred them to other domestic installations, where they lived while preparing for permanent resettlement.

At the beginning of the mass exodus, Americans didn't have a strong consensus on admitting refugees to the United States.

Despite the split public opinion, the U.S. Congress approved the Indochina Migration and Refugee Assistance Act, which President Gerald Ford signed into law in May 1975. The President also allowed Vietnamese refugees to enter the United States under a special status and provided $405 million in resettlement aid.

Today, corruption and violence in Central and South America have forced thousands of people to flee and seek asylum in the United States. Political gridlock over preserving American racial and ethnic homogeneity has meant that no permanent solutions to controlling immigration are in sight.

The Earth continues to stand still.

2

Tossed Salad and Civility Dressing

Superman burst into a homogeneous world, not exactly the epitome of multiculturalism, in *Action Comics* #1. In 1938, he lived in isolation with his adoptive parents in Smallville, Kansas. That didn't stop him from battling racism on his radio show, *The Adventures of Superman*.

One notable story arc aired in 1946. The narrative raised awareness but offered no mechanism for social change. Superman takes on a White supremacist organization, exposing its hateful practices and promoting tolerance and equality. The storyline countered the rise of racism and anti-Semitism in post-World War II America, using Superman's popularity to reach a broad audience with an anti-racist message.

****

What if we could reimagine Superman's American Way to reflect the United States' multicultural nature, promote civility, and strive for truth and justice through collaboration, consensus-based decisions that value the opinions of the few, and acceptance of everyone for who they are?

The U.S. Census Bureau projects that by 2045, the United States will become a "majority-minority" country, in which no single racial or ethnic group will constitute a majority of the population. The projection is based on trends in birth rates, immigration, and demographic change.

Some Caucasians feel that the demographic shift threatens their cultural dominance and the traditional values they associate with America. The growing desire among more brown-skinned people for a share of the American Way has led some White people to fear they may lose socio-political influence and economic opportunities.

Others view greater diversity as an opportunity to build an equitable society in which diverse cultures contribute to a collective American identity. New values prompt debates about Caucasian national identity and what it means to be American. The shift exacerbates longstanding social and racial tensions.

Demographic changes threaten white nationalist groups, leading to conflict and resistance. As groups compete for representation and resources, what can we do to avoid polarized political landscapes?

Civility is more than politeness. It begins with each of us taking on the daunting task of revisiting our pasts and recognizing how our experiences and upbringings shape who we are. It's also about disagreeing respectfully and finding common ground rather than entrenching ourselves in unwavering personal beliefs.

The hard work begins as we change our perspectives and view the world through our own eyes and through the eyes of others who may differ from ourselves.

During the 18th century, pundits metaphorically described the United States as a "melting pot" in which races and ethnicities would learn English and assimilate into a homogeneous America.

"He is an American, who, leaving behind him all his ancient prejudices and manners, receives new ones from the new mode of life he has embraced, the new government he obeys, and the new rank he holds," wrote T.J. Hector St. John de Crevecoeur in his *Letters from an American Farmer* (1782).

That might have been true when the pot contained white cheeses such as Swiss, Edam, Gouda, Parmesan, and Feta, which melted into a single pot of white cheese. The world expanded westward. Explorers and settlers encountered native peoples, as well as those who migrated northward from what is now Mexico and eastward from Asia.

Over time, European immigrants looked forward to the benefits of Superman's American Way after they learned English and easily blended into the dominant American cultural pot of white cheeses that melted on the East Coast stove, stoked by founding fathers and mothers from Europe.

America became more diverse. Other immigrant groups didn't enjoy the same social and cultural benefits because of public policies that restricted and prohibited immigration, particularly from Asian countries.

During World War II, authorities rousted West Coast Japanese from their homes and whisked them to incarceration camps. Meanwhile, Germans and Italians did not pose domestic threats because they had blended into White Cheese America.

However, during the first three months of 1942, German submarines entered United States coastal waters. They sank more than 100 merchant ships off North America's East Coast, in the Gulf of Mexico, and in the Caribbean.

The American public and government viewed Germans and Italians differently from how they viewed the Japanese. The dominant culture in America held stronger, more widespread anti-Japanese sentiments, fueled by historical racial prejudices and exacerbated by the attack on Pearl Harbor.

When the U.S. entered World War II, German and Italian Americans held important positions in industry, politics, the military, and professional sports. Interning large numbers of prominent Caucasian people would have had social, economic, and political repercussions.

Instead of mass internment, the U.S. government adopted a targeted approach for Germans and Italians. The FBI and other agencies investigated and arrested those suspected of posing security threats. The U.S. interned approximately 140,000 people. This total included 125,000 Japanese Americans who underwent mass internment and 11,000 German Americans and 3,000 Italian Americans who experienced selective internment, together accounting for 10 percent of the total.

During the War, authorities did not find any Japanese residents of the United States guilty of sabotage or espionage. However, courts convicted 10 Caucasians of espionage for the Empire of Japan. Velvalee Dickinson, known as the "Doll Lady," used her doll store as a front to pass information to her Japanese contacts in Argentina. She encoded U.S. ship and troop movements into routine doll repair and sales paperwork.

****

Despite America's long history of striving for homogeneity, the country has become racially and ethnically diverse. Today, the blended-food metaphor would be more like a "tossed salad" with distinct ingredients such as *frijoles*, collard greens, *napa* cabbage, and *kasaba*, united by a civility dressing. As our country becomes more culturally diverse, socioeconomic chasms continue to widen.

What can we do to bridge the gap?

By intentionally becoming more civil in our interactions with others and by altering our beliefs about people unlike ourselves, we can narrow divides. There's no telling what will happen when Millennials and their kids are in charge and make changes.

A Millennial mom explained that when her kids grow up, their melting pot would consist of blended M&M's, Reese's Pieces, and Skittles left in a hot car for too long.

3

Revisionist History

Wyoming is best known for epitomizing a standard ballad about the wide-open spaces where bison and pronghorn antelope roamed under clear blue skies. *Home on the Range* (circa 1872), a poem by Dr. Brewster Higley, became the anthem of the American West. His friend, Daniel Kelley, set the poem to music.

President Abraham Lincoln began taming the Wild West when he signed the Homestead Act in 1862, during the Civil War. The law encouraged any adult who had never fought against the United States to settle the frontier and granted them 160 acres of surveyed government land. After pioneering west from Indiana, Dr. Higley settled in Kansas on land granted to him under the Homestead Act.

In exchange for the land, the Act required pioneers like Higley to build a home and farm the homestead, which had been the traditional homeland of Native Americans. Congress amended the law in 1916 with the Stock Raising Act, increasing allotments to 640 acres to encourage ranching.

Higley's version of Wyoming's past is about all I learned in my history classes and from the movie production industry that once flourished in the state, perpetuating the *Home on the Range* view of the state.

Shane (1953), filmed in Jackson Hole, stars Alan Ladd as a dashing former gunfighter who moves to a homestead only to be called back to action when a conflict erupts after a prominent cattle rancher tries to drive other settlers off their land. The film showcases the splendor of the Grand Teton Mountains.

Gary Cooper plays *The Virginian* (1929), a ranch hand near Medicine Bow in south-central Wyoming. Owen Wister wrote his novel in a cabin across the street from the Virginian Hotel on what's now U.S. Highway 30, also known as the Lincoln Highway.

James Drury, the actor who portrayed the TV version of *The Virginian,* stayed at the Plains Hotel in Cheyenne in 2011. Larry McDonald, then the hotel manager, asked me to produce a promo video with Drury recommending the Plains during its 100th anniversary year. I had fun with that project.

"Call me anytime," Drury said after the shoot. He worked into his 80s when he passed away in 2020.

I completed a documentary, *The Arapaho Covered Wagon Redux*, in May 2024. The goal of my documentary is to counter negative Native American stereotypes by creating an original soundtrack for the silent epic *The Covered Wagon* (1923).

The story follows settlers traveling west to Oregon in a long wagon train, fending off tribal attacks, weathering blizzards, and evading a bison stampede. The Boulder Symphony and the Northern Arapaho Eagle Society drummers and singers performed the soundtrack.

Director James Kruze employed Lander rancher Ed Farlow, who hired future cowboy actor Tim McCoy to recruit several hundred tribal members, mostly Northern Arapaho, to serve as extras in Kruze's silent epic.

Before each performance, McCoy and several tribal members in full regalia delivered a prologue on Native American life. The Arapaho Redux prologue focuses on the tribe's efforts to repatriate the homeland lost after the Sand Creek Massacre and to connect their traditional ceremonies and language to the land.

"Wyoming is where the untamed spirit of the West and majestic natural beauty open your mind and invigorate your senses, awakening your inner freedom and sense of adventure." The Wyoming Travel and Tourism Office perpetuates Wyoming's romanticized vision of Western expansion.

The Laramie County School District Number One requires 4th- and 7th-graders to take Wyoming history classes. I learned about mountain men like John Colter being chased naked through the winter woods by cunning savages, and about Catholic missionaries like John DeSmet proselytizing the heathen Red Man.

****

Mrs. Knudsen at Fairview Elementary taught nothing about the Wyoming Alien Land Act, which, after World War II, prohibited Japanese people from owning real estate. I learned from my Carey Junior High teacher, Mr. Cope, that the U.S. dropped atomic bombs on Hiroshima and Nagasaki, but nothing about the Wyoming Alien Land Act, which prohibited non-citizens from purchasing land.

I lived in Lander in the 1980s, when I learned about the Heart Mountain Incarceration Camp in northwestern Wyoming, between Cody and Powell. Tall barbed-wire fences and guard towers encircled the 10 compounds scattered across the U.S. interior, where armed soldiers stood watch.

****

Each Camp published at least one paper. Heart Mountain Camp incarceree Bill Hosokawa edited *The Sentinel* newspaper and later became a well-known writer at *The Denver Post*. I think my parents befriended him through Auntie Hisako.

Hosokawa managed a staff of Heart Mountain incarcerees and published the eight-page weekly tabloid from October 1942 to July 1945. Newspapers kept incarcerees informed about WRA policies and boosted morale by covering Camp activities and human interest stories.

Before the newspaper adopted the tabloid format, its staff distributed typewritten and offset-printed handouts as early editions of *The Sentinel*. The staff named the paper after the geological Heart Mountain landmark because it watched over the Camp like a sentinel. They wanted the newspaper to serve as a guardian for the incarcerees, an irony given the armed soldiers in guard towers surrounding the Camp.

Hosokawa had dinner at my parents' house in Laramie once or twice during his book tours. I would have enjoyed meeting him, but my parents didn't invite me. I likely showed little interest in local Japanese history.

I pushed what little I knew as far back in my mind as I could, still striving to be the Model Minority. I should have paid closer attention. While researching this project, I obtained a copy of the Sentinel and am disappointed I didn't get to know Bill Hosokawa.

****

One of the great things about living in a small town like Lander is the crossover opportunities. *Wyoming State Journal* (WSJ) publisher Bill Sniffin asked me to write some stories for the paper. I eagerly accepted his unexpected offer, which gave me the chance to write again.

The WSJ pioneered the use of a network of Apple computers to publish a twice-weekly paper. I toted a Radio Shack TRS-80 Model 100, my first "laptop."

The Model 100 broke ground in the early days of personal computing. Mine had a built-in 40-by-8-character Liquid Crystal Diode (LCD) screen, eight Kilobytes (KB) of Random Access Memory (RAM) expandable to 32 KB, and 32 KB of Read-Only Memory (ROM). It is remarkable to me that we now need Giga- and Tera-Bytes of RAM and ROM.

I took my Model 100 to basketball games and wrote my stories in real time. I drove to Casper for the state high school basketball tournament and sent my stories to the office via the internal modem.

Remember the familiar "RHEEEE ... RHEEEE!" modem connection noise, audible through the phone. America Online (AOL) became the first Internet Service Provider (ISP) when the World Wide Web commercialized.

******

My Heart Mountain Camp story began in the early 1980s. I had caught a plane from Denver after a work-related trip for my day job with the City of Lander. On a commuter flight from Denver to Riverton, en route to Worland for a family funeral, I met a Japanese American woman named Mrs. May Honkawa. We chatted about her experience as a young woman at Heart Mountain.

"The Camp experience was good. I grew up fast when I got paroled to Chicago," she recalled. "I met new people and got a job, but ended up moving back to California."

Beginning in November 1942, the WRA could conditionally parole prisoners, allowing them to leave the camp and resettle if they had a sponsor and a job. This program would later cause severe headaches for the WRA.

I pulled out my TRS-80 and jotted down a few notes after our conversation ended. Her story intrigued me because, despite my general knowledge, I hadn't heard about day-to-day life in Camp.

****

Later, I drove to Park County with my WSJ colleague, Diana, to find the Heart Mountain Camp. We stopped at the Buffalo Bill Center of the West in Cody and asked the information desk for directions to the camp.

"Drive 10 or 12 miles toward Powell. You can't miss it," the attendant said. "There's a tall chimney. Look for a turnoff to your left, and after the railroad tracks, you drive up a hill."

The site had no signage. I rumbled along the uneven, dusty dirt road to explore the ruins. The Bureau of Reclamation (BoR) stored rolled-up orange plastic snow fencing in one of the abandoned barracks. Those original structures look much the same today.

The Department of the Interior (DoI) established the BoR in 1902 to build infrastructure for the newly settled lands across 17 western states, including dams, power plants, and water-delivery canal systems. These projects promoted economic expansion and encouraged homesteading on the otherwise arid Western frontier.

After the War, the WRA repurposed many Heart Mountain Camp barracks throughout western Wyoming. The new owners converted the wooden, pitched-roof structures into single-family homes.

Those are the subject of my colleague Sharon Yamato's documentary, *Moving Walls* (2017). I helped her record interviews with residents of the renovated barracks in rural Park County. Some residents moved the barracks north of Riverton, where they became the Cottonwood Cottages.

The Crow tribe named the area's physical landmark "Heart Mountain" because the limestone and dolomite geologic formation resembled a bison heart. The feature protrudes 8,123 feet above the Big Horn Basin floor and overlooks the Camp.

The weird thing about Heart Mountain is that the portion that pokes out of the top is 300 million years old, while the rock beneath it is 50 million years old, give or take a few million.

I didn't know what to make of my first visit to the remains of the Heart Mountain Camp or how I felt about being there. Looking at the vast, open terrain of the Camp area, I found it hard to believe that thousands of people had lived there. I understood it intellectually and didn't know how I felt emotionally.

I wrote about my conversation with Mrs. Honkawa in a WSJ newspaper column titled "Beyond Heart Mountain," which later became a chapter in my anthology, *Wyoming Graffiti*, my first attempt at writing a book. The manuscript had been in a notebook, gathering dust on a shelf since 1986.

I wanted to follow up with Mrs. Honkawa for this book. I looked her up on Ancestry.com, only to learn that she had passed away in 2015.

****

Local and national anti-Japanese propaganda shaped attitudes and opinions about the news that Wyoming would host a sizable Japanese population. Reactions ranged from racist to apathetic.

Practical Wyomingites believed that incarcerated people could provide agricultural and industrial labor to make up for the shortage caused by local men going to fight in the War. Regardless, Wyomingites didn't want the Japanese to remain in the state.

Despite anti-Japanese sentiment, members of the Honkawa family remained in Wyoming after their release rather than return to their homes in California.

Many local, state, and federal bureaucracies constructed, maintained, and operated the 10 incarceration and 15 assembly camps scattered throughout the United States.

The massive public works projects kick-started local economies recovering from the Great Depression. The United States stock market crashed on Black Tuesday, October 29, 1929, plunging the world into financial chaos until the onset of World War II.

The Heart Mountain Irrigation Project, overseen by the BoR as a part of the comprehensive Shoshone Project. The BoR supported the War effort by failing to complete the irrigation system. In June 1942, the BoR transferred 20,000 acres to the WRA.

Milton Eisenhower, formerly the president of three universities, became the WRA's first director when the WRA succeeded the WCCA. His brother, General Dwight Eisenhower, later won election as President of the United States and served two terms from 1953 to 1961.

Director Eisenhower initially sought to limit the internment to adult men, allowing women and children to remain free. He unsuccessfully proposed modeling the camps after the subsistence homesteads the United States had established in rural areas during the Great Depression.

In 1934, the DoI administered the Subsistence Homesteads Division. This New Deal program emphasized residents sharing resources in a community setting. The program provided safe housing for displaced urban dwellers, who moved onto plots of land where several households would cooperatively grow and sell crops to sustain themselves.

Subsistence homesteads became intentional communities ahead of their time, but marginally successful. If the DoI brought the program back today, I imagine there would be many takers, given the rise in popularity of community-supported agriculture (CSA). This system allows subscribers to share the farm's harvest.

"If you can drive a nail, you can qualify as a carpenter," read a notice in the Powell Tribune. Construction on the $5.0 million Heart Mountain Camp began soon after the BoR ceded the land. The project created local construction jobs and boosted sales for local businesses.

The Department of War, now the Department of Defense, its Army Corps of Engineers, and civilian and military labor forces built 468 barracks, 39 communal halls, utility buildings, a 150-bed hospital, schools, and a livestock farm with pigs and chickens.

Inexperienced workers hastily built flimsy structures that couldn't withstand Wyoming's harsh winter weather. Winds howled into the apartments through poorly installed doors and windows that didn't close or seal tightly.

Reatha Oakley, a writing friend from Gillette, told me that one of her relatives, Kenneth Thorpe, owned a construction company in Billings. He and his brother drove down to help build the Camp.

"Kenneth was aghast at the quality," Reatha explained. "He was disappointed in the shoddy work."

The first prisoners arrived at the Heart Mountain Camp in August 1942. Staff assigned them to quarters of varying sizes based on family size. Each room had a stove, a socket with a single bulb, and folding cots. Over time, some incarcerees improved their sparsely furnished rooms by building furniture from scrap wood.

Personal privacy became an issue. Families strung bedsheets from the ceiling, and conversations carried on through the air. Neighbors could see activity in adjacent households through the enormous gaps between wallboards that divided the barracks into apartments. Incarcerees plugged the cracks with wadded-up rags and newspaper pages.

Banks of showers and toilets, separated by gender, lacked running water. Communal utility halls included laundries with washbasins and scrubboards.

The mess hall served cafeteria-style meals featuring inexpensive, processed American foods such as pancakes, macaroni, hot dogs, and pickled vegetables. The Heart Mountain community gardens provided limited fresh produce, essential to the traditional Japanese diet.

The Camp farms contributed to the local and state economies. For example, in 1942, the WRA awarded the Big Horn Canning Company in Cowley a contract to can 12,000 pounds of surplus beans. The hog farm produced 40 animals per week and transported them to U.S. Department of Agriculture (USDA)-approved slaughter facilities.

The collective meal service led to the breakdown of nuclear-family relationships. Young children no longer relied on their parents to prepare meals. Some older kids dined with their friends rather than with their families. To get enough food, growing kids would often wander to multiple mess halls for extra meals.

Japanese people, including my family, who built lives in places like middle-of-nowhere Wyoming, posed little threat to national security. Both sets of my grandparents came to the United States as typical immigrants. They all arrived from Japan on ships that landed in the Pacific Northwest and eventually made their way to Wyoming.

My immediate family members are all native-born: Dad in Kent, Washington; Mom in Thermopolis, Wyoming, 100 miles south of Heart Mountain; and my sister and me in Cheyenne, where we grew up from the 1950s through the 1970s.

****

The Heart Mountain prison population hovered around 10,000 incarcerees. Heart Mountain High School had a first-year enrollment of 1,500 students. The WPA hired Caucasian high school administrators. It also hired Japanese and Anglo teachers and teacher aides. WRA pay grades differed by race, with Caucasians receiving higher wages.

The schools provided students with an academic routine but had to improvise with supplies. For comparison, I graduated with 450 students from my alma mater, East High School (EHS or East), one of the state's largest high schools.

I came across a 1945 Heart Mountain High School yearbook at the Wyoming State Archives, which features photos of the band and sports teams that competed against public schools.

The Heart Mountain Eagles football team, composed of Japanese American students, is a testament to resilience and spirit. Despite harsh and unjust living conditions, the young athletes went undefeated in 1943, bringing a sense of normalcy and pride to the Camp's residents.

The Eagles' success provided entertainment and served as a powerful symbol of perseverance. The games drew fans from surrounding Wyoming communities, bridging the gap between the incarcerated and the outside world.

The undefeated season boosted morale throughout the Camp, highlighting the strength and unity of the Japanese American community.

I flipped through the yearbook photos, and one caught my eye. Upon closer inspection, I found a photo of my advanced biology teacher at Cheyenne East, Miss Jean Cooper. Given the preferential treatment teachers like Miss Cooper received at Heart Mountain High School, it doesn't surprise me that she didn't mention her teaching stint there.

I scanned microfilm copies of the 1990 *Wyoming Tribune Eagle* (WTE) and came across a story about an anonymous teacher recounting her experiences at Heart Mountain. I'm pretty sure Miss Cooper gave the interview. The paper included an editorial disclaimer stating that the source didn't want to disclose her name because of the sensitivity of her Heart Mountain experience.

I hear that educators and mental health professionals think kids are resilient and can cope, or otherwise outgrow, life's small and large traumas. That's probably true to a certain extent. Still, I've been trying to outgrow my issues around assimilation and imagine what I missed by not being more exposed to Japanese culture.

I adopted the Superman's American Way and navigated mainstream society reasonably well, but as a Model Minority, I could only rise to a certain level of success. Often, I found myself, and still do, as a raisin in the oatmeal.

4

Raisins in the Oatmeal

I've always been a raisin in the societal oatmeal, no matter how hard I tried to fit into mainstream society. I knew how to act, but I didn't look like I belonged. I stood at a urinal in the restroom at the Log Cabin Saloon in Jackson, Wyoming, wearing Levi's, boots, and a baseball cap.

"Where you from?" a fellow reveler asked.

"Came over from Lander," I answered. "The (Nitty Gritty) Dirt Band's worth the drive."

"Where are you from?" He followed up, using code words about my race and ethnicity.

"Cheyenne," I said.

"No, where are you really from?"

I define my "race" as Japanese and my "ethnicity" as American. This exchange exemplifies the Plight of the Perpetual Immigrant.

Even though I'm a fourth-generation American and a natural-born citizen, the comments I hear throughout a conversation assume I'm fresh off the boat. The conversation would eventually come around to their assumption that I'm from Hawaii or California.

The Pew Foundation surveyed Asians in 2022. For many Asian Americans, discrimination is not a single event. The survey found that other native-born Asian Americans reported similar experiences. When they meet random people, they're asked, "When did you come to America?" or told to "Go back to where you came from" (78 percent).

Asian American adults, including me, have experienced incidents in which people assume they are a Model Minority and believe they are obedient and good at math and science (63 percent of cases).

"I'm a city kid from Wyoming," I tell them.

People find it surprising that I speak Spanish better than I know basic Japanese salutations.

****

After arriving in the United States, my paternal grandparents, Tochi "George" and Natsu "Mary" Ohashi, brought their family to Wyoming via Monte Vista, Colorado. Grandpa helped farmers in Fife, Washington, near Tacoma, maximize crop yields and expand markets for their produce. He brought those skills to arid Colorado and applied them to a thriving lettuce-growing operation.

He regretted the move because his source had misrepresented the farm. He made the best of it by turning to his forte. He started a truck-farming business, buying vegetables from local producers to resell to restaurants. He also parked his panel van at the roadside and sold his produce to passersby, an early version of a farmers market.

My maternal grandparents, Jusaburo "Joe" Sakata and Toki Iwasaki, also arrived in Washington state and, through jobs with the Union Pacific Railroad (UP), eventually settled in Cheyenne. They later moved to Hot Springs, Natrona, and Converse counties, where Grandpa worked for the Chicago Burlington & Quincy (CB&Q) Railroad.

My parents, Frank and Sumiko (Sakata) O'Hashi, met at a picnic at Hynds Lodge west of Cheyenne and married in October 1946. They became involved in Cheyenne's Japanese American community.

Throughout the book, you'll notice the names O'Hashi, the surname of my dad and his youngest brother, Jake, and Ohashi, the name of everyone else in the family. The reason there are two spellings is a matter of family folklore.

One explanation is accidental. In anglicized Japanese, the long *ō* has a dash over it, a macron, and when handwritten, the macron, if slid over, could be mistaken for an apostrophe.

In Japanese, ō-hashi means "big bridge" or "honorable bridge," whereas *hashi* means "chopsticks."

Hashi is a Japanese homonym. Although pronounced the same, the kanji for "bridge" and "chopsticks" are different. Both characters have strokes that refer to "wood."

What's the best explanation? My father's birthday is St. Patrick's Day, and a school principal added the apostrophe in jest. I've had this Japanese-Irish thing following me around since junior high school.

People are often surprised when they see me in person for the first time if we've only communicated by phone or email.

"Your English is excellent," they say. "Are you Irish?"

The bane of the Model Minority and Perpetual Immigrant.

****

My parents attended the United Presbyterian Church (UPC). I didn't ask why they chose that denomination. My maternal grandparents converted from Buddhism to Episcopalian. Auntie Hisako held prominent roles in the Episcopalian Church in Washington, DC. Dad's family practiced Shinto Buddhism.

Mom wanted to blend in as a mainstream Protestant, and I surmised that he didn't care and went along with Mom's choice. A few of her friends from the Ex-Junior Women's Club (X-JWC) singing group, called the Dearies, attended the Presbyterian Church.

I went through the Christian intellectual motions in Sunday school, youth groups, and summer church camp, but I didn't understand the emotions associated with Christianity. I wondered if Superman went to church. He rescued people and walked and flew his talk. Maybe he'd pass some pointers on to me.

Although comic books don't provide details about Superman's religious affiliation, I have come across accounts suggesting that his adoptive parents practiced Methodism. Nonetheless, during Clark's formative years, they taught him about the Christian-focused American Way. Superman doesn't wear his faith on his sleeve but lives it.

"Do nothing out of selfish ambition or vain conceit. Rather, in humility, value others above yourselves, not looking to your own interests but each of you to the interests of the others," Paul wrote in Philippians 2:3-4 while serving time in prison for preaching the Gospel of Jesus.

I always thought Superman and Moses had similar origin stories. His parents sent infant Kal-El in a rocket from the doomed planet Krypton to Earth. His new parents taught him to be a Moses-type superhero who conceals his secret identity and stands up for crime victims.

Compare that to Jochebed, baby Moses's mother, who places him in a basket that floats down the Nile to escape Pharaoh's decree to drown Hebrew male infants. The Pharaoh's daughter rescues Moses, raises him as her own, and conceals his Hebrew identity. Moses grows up, defies his adopted grandfather, and leads the Israelites out of Egypt.

****

The UPC didn't preach Christian dogma. Instead, it favored acceptance. My parents had to walk on eggshells to avoid subtle discrimination. They spoke only Japanese with my grandparents. I couldn't understand their conversations and asked why they didn't teach us the language.

"You have to be American," Mom told me. "There's no reason for you to speak Japanese."

We blended into the background, taking the path of least resistance. Joining a Christian church embodied Superman's American Way.

Throughout my time in Wyoming, I chose to be upwardly mobile as a Presbyterian. In high school, Reverend Pattison asked me to serve as an Elder on the Session, the church's governing body. The senior pastor laid his hands on my shoulder and ordained me.

"You kids work hard and be like Alan, the Model Minority," is what my jaded self thinks. Nonetheless, Rev. Pattison looked out for my best interests. He singled me out, gave me opportunities to succeed, and set a good example.

We attended many church-related activities. I remember going to a potluck dinner where mostly Jell-O salads showed up on the table. I still like green Jell-O with canned fruit mixed in. I now make Cherry Coke Jell-O salad for special occasions.

In a sense, the Cheyenne UPC, on the "other side" of town, gave me a sense of social integration. I met kids from the other junior high feeder schools.

We went to church most Sundays. My sister and I sang in the choir. The youth choir sang as the opening act for the early-service, followed by Sunday School. My ulterior motive for attending Sunday School? Receiving Jesus trading cards at the end of class. The adult choir sang during the main event at 11:00 a.m.

The youth fellowship group met at 4:00 p.m. on Sundays and after school on Wednesdays. We had fun at those get-togethers, with little emphasis on Christian topics. We had to get home before *Batman* came on TV.

My parents volunteered for group activities such as the Women's Circle, which organized events like the fall rummage sale, and the Mariners stewardship group, composed of men, which annually asked the congregation for funds to support church operations. I'm pretty sure my mom instigated all of that. Dad tagged along for the food.

******

I went to the Skyline Summer Church Camp, the one closest to Cheyenne in the Medicine Bow National Forest. I enjoyed myself, for the most part, meeting kids from other parts of the state.

A few campers bullied me because of my size and skin color. Kids would pull on the sides of their eyes to make them slanty and to make garbled, nonsensical, Asian-sounding noises. That annoyed me, but I didn't engage.

I did have allies, but they didn't know how to confront bullies, let alone racist ones. I have since learned that bystanders enable aggressive behavior. You can learn my take on that in my book, *Aging Gratefully in Good Company:* Brewing with happiness, purpose, and connection adds life to our years and years to our lives (2025).

One kid from Rawlins teased me so badly one summer that I didn't go to the bathhouse. I didn't shower for the entire week. Instead, I plunged into the nearby ice-cold pond.

My Cheyenne UPC pastor, Bob Walkley, Rev. Pattison's son-in-law, and the Camp Director never said anything to me, but based on how my fellow campers' behavior toward me changed, he must have said something to my harassers.

I had creativity going for me. When it came to arts-and-crafts activities, I excelled, which served as a hedge against being bullied.

I don't recall any Bible study at Church Camp. Rev. Walkley blessed the food before dinner, and the camp counselors took turns leading an evening vesper service that included a discussion about life.

UPC's brand of Presbyterianism didn't emphasize the "Jesus Saves" drills: Bad = Hell, and Good = Heaven. The liturgy of church life dominated UPC thought, including my baptism and my sister's christening as a toddler.

All the 3rd graders received a Bible at a rite-of-passage ceremony. I still have mine, though I had it rebound after it wore out. I dropped it off the top bunk at Skyline Camp one too many times. High school graduates received a pocket-sized Bible, which is still in the box.

Then came the catechism lessons in 6th grade. Rev. Pattison conducted the classes. We listened to the questions and repeated the answers from the booklet. The Reverend administered a live final exam in front of the congregation. He had me memorize the answer to the question, "What is the chief end of man?"

****

Besides being a Presbyterian, Mom aspired to live the American Way with 1.5 kids, a purebred dog, two cars, and a ranch-style house in the suburbs. She settled for two kids, a re-homed dog, a house with a used sedan under the carport, and an old pickup parked out front.

My parents didn't expose me to other religions. On Memorial Day, I watched Grandma Ohashi pray and chant while we decorated graves in the segregated Japanese section of Lakeview Cemetery.

Other than the Matsukawas in Salt Lake City, none of my other Nisei relatives expressed much about their spiritual beliefs. I attribute this to their treatment during the War and the potential backlash for practicing non-Christian beliefs.

My family stood out like a raisin in the Presbyterian oatmeal. Later, Bob, Larry Walters, and their mom started attending. Mrs. Walters married a serviceman in Japan and gave birth to her *hapa* (half-Japanese) sons in Cheyenne.

My mother's upwardly mobile middle-class rise departed from her childhood. She and her family grew up in a clapboard Orpha Section house in rural Converse County, Wyoming, two miles from Fort Fetterman.

Fort Fetterman, located a few miles north of Douglas, is now a Wyoming State Historic Site. The U.S. Army established the fort in 1867 to protect settlers traveling along the Bozeman Trail to Montana.

The U.S. Army named the fort after Captain William J. Fetterman. Arapaho, Cheyenne, and Lakota warriors, led by Red Cloud and Crazy Horse, outmaneuvered the U.S. Cavalry in a battle that killed Fetterman and 80 other soldiers.

We visited Orpha a time or two. Joe and Lucy Shinmori, Mom's childhood friends, lived across the road. They all attended the one-room schoolhouse in Orpha.

My mom befriended the children of immigrant *traqueros* (railroad section workers) from Northern Mexico. Her *Mexicana* friends taught her to make flour tortillas. I surmised they immigrated from Northern Mexico because flour tortillas are more common in states like Sonora and Chihuahua.

Mexican laborers worked for the Union Pacific as the Transcontinental Railroad extended westward from Nebraska. *Traqueros* transitioned into railroad maintenance and other industries across the United States. They faced racism from the dominant culture, unlike Chinese workers, who faced deportation.

Instead, Mexico fostered positive relations with the United States when, in 1881, Governor Luis Terrazas of Chihuahua drove a silver spike to complete a line that facilitated trade with and emigration to the United States.

The recipe is simple: Mix flour, water, salt to taste, and lard. Knead the dough, then flatten and cook it in a skillet or on a griddle. I later learned from a Border Patrol agent that lard is the key ingredient. Mom stopped making flour tortillas by hand when prepackaged ones in plastic bags hit the grocery store shelves. They're the world's worst culinary innovation.

We only ate flour *tortillas* and Wonder Bread as our staples. I preferred *tortillas*. Mom made a dish called *fideo* from *vermicelli* (thin wheat noodles) mixed with tomato sauce, ground beef, chopped onion, and spiced with *cumino* (cumin). Then we rolled up the *fideo* in a flour *tortilla.* One of these days, I'll cook up a batch of *fideo*, one of my childhood favorite meals.

****

Talk about Asian raisins in the oatmeal. I met a multi-talented guy, Aaron Linsdau, from Jackson, at the 2024 Wyoming Writers, Inc. (WWI) conference. He owns Sastrugi Publishing, a small traditional press, and has published books on mountaineering, the outdoors, and general-interest commercial topics. I pitched a story about a murder in a Japanese incarceration camp, which piqued his interest because he's part Japanese.

The WRA transported his family from the Riverside, California, area to the Poston Camp in Arizona on May 19, 1942. Later, the WRA paroled them to Excelsior Springs, Missouri, where Harold Yager, who owned the Elms Hotel, sponsored Roy's work release and hired him as a dishwasher.

Roy worked his way up to become the hotel's comptroller. He married Joanne Bryant while in Missouri. Yager offered Roy a similar position at his property in Jackson, Wyoming, the now world-famous Wort Hotel. The couple moved to Jackson in 1963.

Yager, always running late, had planned to meet Roy and Joanne at the Jackson Airport. A man who identified himself as "Cliff" offered to drive them to town in his truck. When they arrived at the Wort, Yager apologized and introduced the Takedas to Cliff Hansen, the Wyoming Governor.

"It was tough for them being the only Japanese in Jackson," Aaron said, pulling his eyes sideways as people did back then to make their eyes look more squinty in a derogatory way. "Working at the Wort gave him credibility. There's a photo in the back hallway of prominent people associated with the Wort. The Asian guy is my grandfather."

I knew nothing about other parts of Wyoming, including Jackson. My dad borrowed Auntie Elsie's new Buick for a road trip to Yellowstone National Park. This would be my first time traveling west of Casper. We made a quick stop in Jackson to browse the T-shirt shops. I can't remember whether that side trip happened before or after a black bear crawled onto the car and scratched the roof and the engine hood.

On our way back to Cheyenne, we stopped in Thermopolis, Mom's hometown, for dinner. I ordered spaghetti. The meal looked good but tasted odd because the cook had spiced the sauce with cumin. I expected fennel, so I suspected the server had set a plate of *fideo* in front of me.

****

The Cheyenne Japanese community members also became raisins in the Wyoming oatmeal. Local Japanese and returning veterans formed the Skyline Nisei Club in response to the racist backlash during and after World War II. The Club elected my recently married mom as its first secretary in 1950 because she could type.

As a youngster, unaware of the self-imposed isolation, I spent quite a bit of time in the West 17th Street neighborhood. I took hanging around there for granted.

My dad worked as the production manager at the local Coca-Cola Bottling Company, owned by Cheyenne Beverage. He let me tag along on weekends and join his crew for breakfast at Jim's Café on East Lincolnway.

After the server cleared our plates, we took separate routes to restock Coke products around town. We gassed up at Buffington's Sinclair station, across the block from Jim's. The Buffington family lived up the street from us on Windmill Road.

We stopped at the Buford Trading Post, midway between Cheyenne and Laramie, off the Interstate 80 (I-80) exit for the Bureau of Land Management (BLM) Veedauwoo (Vee-Duh-Voo) Recreation Area.

I read that the Arapaho named the area of rounded, crystalline rock outcroppings *bito'o'wu* (earth-born). The 1.4-billion-year-old Sherman Granite site includes a day-use picnic area, an overnight campground, and several popular technical rock-climbing areas.

Dad let my classmates and me build our EHS senior-class homecoming float in a garage at the Coke plant. Some pals of mine liberated a water pump from a Vedauwoo campground, which added the final touch to our 1971 parade float. The Mighty, Mighty T-Birds played the Sheridan Broncos that year.

The class chose the title of the movie *They Shoot Horses, Don't They?* (1969) as the homecoming theme. The movie features a cast of popular actors, including Jane Fonda and Bruce Dern. The title references a childhood memory in which a character dreams of a horse that breaks its leg and is shot to put it out of its misery.

Float builders placed the pump next to a horse-watering tank. My mom sewed together a pretty good south end of a northbound Bronco, which we stuffed with crumpled newspapers, spray-painted yellow, and attached a blue tail that hung from the tank.

****

During my graduate student days at the University of Wyoming (UW) in Laramie, I took a rock-climbing class offered by Rocky Mountaineering, a downtown outdoor equipment store owned by a guy named Scott.

At Vedauwoo, I learned to set up a belay, tie knots, rappel down a rock face, and coil ropes. Rocky Mountaineering has stayed in business over the years and is now Atmosphere Mountainworks.

The sharp nubbins provide excellent friction for climbing. The chimneys between faces also offer challenging off-width crack climbs. Those basic skills proved helpful when I moved to Gillette, Wyoming, for my first job. I made six ascents of Devil's Tower.

I recovered from a 2013 deathbed illness and, in 2016, attempted my seventh climb with Charlie Anderson, but I couldn't make it up the leaning column on the first pitch of the Durrance route.

The last time I tried climbing in 2021 at Vedauwoo, I fantasized about ascending the Grand Teton with a crew led by a *plein air* artist from Laramie named Joe Arnold. In the mid-19th century, impressionist artists painted outdoors, a practice known as *plein air* in French, to take advantage of natural light. Joe's unique views from mountain summits are the subjects of his work.

I'm a filmmaker and videographer, among other things, and I wanted to make a movie about the ascent. I wanted to see whether I would be a help or a hindrance. Joe, his son Jason, and I tried to climb a short crack at Veedauwoo.

After a few steps up the route, I realized I still hadn't regained enough lower-body strength after my death-defying illness, even after seven years.

My role on that project didn't work out. Joe and Jason finished the short movie about that climb without me. I go to the Boulder Recreation Center a few times a week to regain my strength, and I'll check out the less intimidating indoor climbing wall.

****

South of I-80, opposite Vedauwoo, is Buford, originally a UP Section house. Section lengths range from several hundred feet to several miles of track and include maintenance equipment storage areas. Workers lived in Section houses near the railroad line. During the Transcontinental Railroad's construction in the 1860s, Buford boomed, reaching a population of 2,000. In 1905, the railroad converted a house into a one-room school.

When I began frequenting Buford with my dad, one of the section buildings became the Buford Trading Post, a quaint neighborhood bar and the area's post office. The interior, paneled with varnished knotty pine boards, glistened in the morning sunlight.

The drive from Cheyenne to Buford in my dad's noisy Ford pickup truck took about 30 minutes. He loaded yellow wooden cases of 6.5-ounce Coke bottles onto a two-wheeled hand truck. Dad handed me some quarters, let me play the arcade bowling game, and let me munch on Slim Jim beef jerky sticks, even before lunch.

A big jar of pickled eggs sat on the counter. The slightly discolored ovoids reminded me of a mysterious container I saw in a creepy *Alfred Hitchcock Presents* episode titled "The Jar" (1964), based on a short story by Ray Bradbury. It is a "must-see" TV show.

A farmer buys a jar filled with strange contents at a carnival. It frightens his wife. The man refuses to get rid of his novelty because he is now locally famous for the sideshow attention he draws. Curious people come from miles away to ponder what's in the jar. His wife gets creeped out, opens it, and removes the contents.

The enraged farmer kills his wife and refills the jar so everyone can see the same thing. You can probably guess whose head the farmer would reveal.

That story freaked me out, and it still does. I think about the TV show whenever I see a big jar on a counter filled with pickles, pigs' feet, or eggs.

I didn't dare try one of those ovoids until I reached legal age and, as a Hastings College student in Nebraska, knew better. Instead of drinking Coke and aiming stainless-steel pucks at arcade bowling pins at the Buford Trading Post, I drank beer and slid pucks down the sawdusted shuffleboard at the Wagon Wheel Bar.

****

In April 2012, Buford's owner, Don Sammons, served as its mayor, police chief, public works director, and dogcatcher. He bought Buford in 1992, decided to retire, and listed his hamlet for sale. Sammons advertised the "Buford: Population 1" auction, which instantly made him the subject of international news coverage.

Erika Dobrin, the casting director for a California-based reality TV show, contacted me to ask whether I had time to help document Buford's auction.

"I know Buford. I went there with my dad on Saturday mornings," I explained to Erika. "The Buford store has changed drastically since then."

I met my TV crew in Cheyenne for a production meeting. The following day, we formed a caravan to Buford. We arrived on location early, scouted and set up the master shot, then I picked up some B-roll at the convenience store.

Travelers, unaware of the impending auction, pulled up to the gas pumps. Tourists and the curious browsed the nearly empty shelves and the souvenir clothing rack, admiring T-shirts emblazoned with Sammon's mugshot.

Soon, a steady stream of cars carrying auction bidders, news media trucks, and the curious pulled into the gravel parking lot.

The bidding began at noon. Organizers didn't allow me to record the auction, so I set up a GoPro for a wide shot. Qualified bidders had to provide proof of ready access to at least $100,000. The bidding opened quickly. The rapid escalation left many who had traveled to Wyoming hoping to buy the unique hole in the road behind.

A Vietnamese business executive named Nguyen Dinh Pham placed the winning $900,000 bid, making him the proud owner of a house, a store, and a gas station on 10 acres of land. Rozetta Weston of Al-Roz Auction and Realty in Cheyenne represented him.

Roz is married to Alan Weston, a high school classmate of mine. We first met while playing Little League Baseball for the AAA Red Sox around 1965. He later worked as a pressman for my uncle Jake at Pioneer Printing on West 19th Street. His mom, Dot, played softball with Auntie Elsie.

Legend has it that after buying Buford, Pham proudly strutted his newfound cowboy swagger, wearing a Stetson western hat on the streets of his native Ho Chi Minh City (formerly Saigon). When I heard that, I couldn't help but picture myself as the "Kimono Kowboy" at Cheyenne Frontier Days (CFD) of yore.

Ho Chi Minh founded the Indochina Communist Party and served as President of North Vietnam from 1945 until his death in 1969.

Pham rebranded Buford as PhinDeli Town and sold Vietnamese coffee to Americans. Vietnam is one of the world's largest coffee-exporting countries.

Over the years, I'd stop for a cup at the PhinDeli whenever I found myself between Cheyenne and Laramie. The coffee tasted good, but it's tough for a business to make a go of it in the middle of nowhere, two bucks at a time.

The point-of-sale displays didn't exactly catch your eye like those at a Starbucks. Impulse snackers could choose Lay's potato chips and

Hostess Twinkies. The deli offered unique Vietnamese drip coffee makers as the highest-value products on the shelves.

Erika couldn't interview Pham, but it didn't matter because the reality TV producers hoped one of the American families would be the winning bidder. They wanted an interesting story about a family moving to Wyoming from out East and all that goes with it. If you ask me, a Vietnamese raisin-in-the-oatmeal would have made for a pretty good story.

After the auction, I visited with Sammons, who served in Vietnam with the U.S. Army from 1968 to 1970. He told me that he and Pham, a member of the Army of the Republic of Vietnam (ARVN), served there at the same time during "Vietnamization."

As the Vietnam War became increasingly unpopular across America, President Nixon, following his reelection in 1972, began a gradual withdrawal strategy that reduced American involvement in Vietnam by transferring military responsibilities to the ARVN.

I think that if Pham had brought his family members from Vietnam to set up shop in Buford, they would have made for a great reality TV show, with unintended negative consequences, as Pham fumbled and bumbled his way through Wyoming, trying to fit into an unfamiliar culture.

Sammons pocketed his money and moved to Windsor, Colorado. Pham realized the inefficiencies of managing a property from 8,300 miles away. Sammons returned and regained his mayoral status. The two hired a property manager who couldn't keep the doors open, leaving the windows covered with plywood and the gas pumps removed.

****

Given his brief military background, I doubt Pham ever imagined, during his basic training, that he'd own a place named after Civil War hero Major General John Buford. Buford participated in the Gettysburg Campaign, which signaled the end of the Civil War in the United States.

Buford is Wyoming's link to the Battle of Gettysburg, which took place July 1–3, 1863. The Confederate army, commanded by General Robert E. Lee, invaded Pennsylvania. Buford's defensive troop positions on the high ground south of Gettysburg enabled additional troops to support and control the field of battle.

The Union won a decisive victory at Gettysburg, and both sides suffered heavy casualties. Buford continued to pursue the Confederates in Virginia until General Lee abandoned Richmond, the Confederate capital. Unable to reunite his forces, Lee and his 28,000 troops surrendered on April 9, 1865.

John Buford knew the American West well. He attended school in the North and graduated from West Point before being deployed to the rugged West. The army stationed him on the western frontier in the 1860s. He and his fellow soldiers heard talk of the South's secession and the possibility of war. The Pony Express delivered news of the bombing of Fort Sumter on April 12, 1861.

Confederate troops in South Carolina opened fire on the Union-held stronghold in Charleston Harbor. After 34 hours of bombardment, Major Robert Anderson surrendered.

The attack prompted President Abraham Lincoln to call for 75,000 volunteers to suppress the rebellion, which led to the Civil War.

Like many West Pointers, Buford faced a hard choice between siding with the North or the South. He had cultural reasons for joining the Confederacy, as a native Kentuckian and the son of a slave-owning father. Still, he remained loyal to his U.S. Army West Point roots. Several family members, including his wife, joined the Southern cause.

Whenever I drive by Buford, I recall fond memories of being allowed to goof around the bar and store as a kid. At 8,000 feet, Buford is the highest point on I-80. Because of the 2,000-foot drop in elevation, I looked forward to the faster, uneventful drive back to Cheyenne in my dad's pickup truck, shifting into high gear.

Most recently, I drove past Buford on my way back from a screening of my documentary, *The Arapaho Covered Wagon Redux,* in Lander. Patrons filled up their tanks and carried coffee cups out of the store.

****

When Dad and I returned to the Japanese community, we stopped at my grandfather's pool hall at 516 W. 17th St. to restock the Coke machine.

I had to wait at the door, but I remember the stale smell of tobacco in the room, dimly lit by bluish fluorescent lights that glowed above each green felt-covered table, and the clatter of billiard balls.

We drove to Boyd's Cigar Store at 308 W. 17th St. I couldn't go in there either, but an old sepia-toned cardboard "Call for Philip Morris" advertisement sign featuring Johnny, the bellhop, hung on a post near the store entrance. I still wonder what happened to that poster. It would be a real find today.

Uncle Mooch, cousin Mathew's dad, from Salt Lake City, took me to other strange places. He collected various things, including shelves of old Kodak box cameras neatly lined up beside each other.

Mooch and his family regularly visited Cheyenne during the summer for family activities. He had all the junk stores scoped out, including the Salvation Army store on the east edge of the Japanese community at the corner of Pioneer Avenue and West 17th Street. I started collecting affordable junk, like green and pink Great Depression-era glass, blue glass canning jars, paper stuff like posters, and baseball cards.

As a kid, I saw old glassware on the shelves at the secondhand store. I knew little about it, except that it would be valuable later. During the Great Depression, inexpensive pieces came as premiums in soap and cereal boxes.

Heirs salvaged leftover junk from their family estate sales and hauled it to secondhand stores, which resold it for a dime or a quarter, making it affordable for a kid like me. I know Grandma Sakata used her green ice cream cups as regular tableware.

Fast-forward to the 1980s, when green and pink glassware suddenly became collectible. The most valuable pieces are Vaseline glass made with small amounts of uranium, which gives it a yellowish, iridescent look, reminiscent of radioactive Vaseline.

I still have a box filled with Depression glass plates and serving dishes. Their value has increased by 300 percent. Unfortunately, collectors have glutted the market. It will take me a long time to sell my collection piece by piece. I'll likely donate it back to a second-hand store so others can enjoy my stuff.

My parents supported my glass-collecting hobby and encouraged me to save baseball cards because they took up less space. Most of my original trading card collection, dating back to 1962, consisted of baseball cards. I collected and compiled complete sets, but that became tedious and lost its appeal. In the end, only the star players appealed to me.

I shifted my focus to rookie cards and autographs of Yankees from specific World Championship teams: 1927 (Babe Ruth hit 60 homers), 1932 (Babe Ruth's famous "called shot"), 1953 (my birth year), 1960–1964 (My first exposure to the Yankees), 1977 and 1978 (Back to Back Championships), and 2001 (The Series I attended).

Trading cards interested me before I became a baseball fan. I went to Sunday School for the swag: Bible verse #2, leaded pencils, cookies, and Jesus cards. My teacher required us to pay attention to the lesson, then she passed out the loot.

I coveted my 1965 Topps baseball card of Jesus (heh-zoos) Alou. He and his two brothers, Matty and Felipe, all played for the San Francisco Giants. Baseball factoid: The trio played together in the same outfield in three games in 1963.

I held onto my cards as an investment. Then, high winds and extremely dry conditions near the town of Marshall, south of Boulder, sparked the December 30, 2021, suburban Marshall Fire.

Fueled by wind gusts up to 100 mph, the fire quickly spread through neighborhoods in Superior and Louisville. It burned more than 6,000 acres and destroyed more than 1,000 homes and businesses.

The fire spread rapidly, forcing residents to evacuate without time to gather their belongings. The Marshall Fire caused an estimated $513 million in damage and resulted in two confirmed fatalities.

"Will I be able to load all the boxes of autographed baseballs into my car if need be?" I wondered. After that, I sold my card collection in 2022 to lighten my load and minimize the brain damage caused by worrying about how to store and move my collectibles in case of a catastrophe. I also realized that my heirs would have absolutely no idea where to sell a 1951 Bowman Mickey Mantle rookie card.

I'll trade you my Mickey for your Jesus.

By the way, man's chief end is to glorify God and enjoy him forever.

5

Mid-Century Modern

Optimism and anxiety defined the mid-20th century, shaped by the dual forces of Cold War tensions and rapid technological advances. Mid-Century Modern became the era's popular design aesthetic, blending futuristic aspirations with an existential urgency fueled by the nuclear threat.

Superman's stories intertwine with the contemporary cultural and political landscape of the Mid-Century Modern era. "Superman Under the Red Sun," in *Action Comics* #300 (May 1963), is a story about a mad scientist named Ral-Kar, who lures Superman to a planet whose sun has expanded into a red dwarf, stripping him of his powers and leaving him struggling to survive.

Superman discovers that Ral-Kar plans to launch a bomb to destroy the planet. The story reflects contemporary fears of nuclear annihilation and the long-term consequences of rebuilding society from scratch.

****

The Cold War spanned from the end of World War II, when the U.S. dropped atomic bombs on Japan in 1945, to the fall of the Berlin Wall in 1991. During the Cold War, the U.S. military expanded the national nuclear arsenal in Wyoming, fueling Cheyenne's economy. The U.S. Department of Defense is updating its missile program, which will bring another economic boom, beginning in 2024 and operational by 2030.

The Sentinel Ground-Based Strategic Deterrent (GBSD) will replace the aging Minuteman III intercontinental ballistic missiles (ICBMs) at an estimated cost of $95 billion. The 90th Missile Wing at Fort Warren oversees 150 missiles currently deployed in silos across Wyoming, Colorado, and Nebraska. The GBSD program is a key part of the U.S. Air Force's modernization of land-based nuclear deterrence.

The construction of Mid-Century Modern suburban homes with basements that could double as fallout shelters helped my parents maintain a sense of normalcy during times of uncertainty, given their paranoia following the atomic bombings of Hiroshima and Nagasaki, which ended World War II.

After an atomic attack, "fallout" is radioactive dust that lingers in the atmosphere and eventually settles to the ground. Homeowners built shelters primarily for peace of mind, but they also provided limited protection against the atomic flash, the thermal radiation emitted by the weapon as visible, infrared, and ultraviolet light.

The flash can cause first- to third-degree burns. First-degree burns can feel like a severe sunburn and can appear up to seven miles from the explosion. Second-degree burns cause blisters and scars when the blast occurs up to 6 miles away. Third-degree burns destroy skin tissue and occur up to five miles from the explosion.

In addition to the flash, nuclear wind from an atomic blast can reach speeds over 600 miles per hour, destroying buildings.

My dad hired Bill Fisher to help build our family's bomb shelter, which would theoretically provide a few rudimentary creature comforts during a nuclear war. Bill worked for my dad at the Coke plant. He had a little practical knowledge about everything, and I found that inspiring.

During our bomb shelter project, he taught me practical skills such as mixing mortar, leveling, and laying concrete blocks. Bill and I arranged concrete blocks on top of the shelter. The roof consisted of one-inch plywood sheets.

He and I painted the exterior white to reflect some of the radiation. We added Mid-Century Modern accents by painting individual blocks green, pink, and yellow.

Bill designed our shelter in the northeast corner of the basement, at the bottom of the stairs, for easy access. Bill welded two steel pipes at a right angle to form an air shaft that ran from the inside and vented to the backyard through a window well, which I then filled with sand.

My dad set up U.S. Army surplus bunk beds and a pantry for storing canned goods, water, plates, and tableware.

We had a Sterno camping stove that could heat a can of soup in a small space. By this time, we had roughed in a downstairs bathroom that would be accessible during a period of isolation, but in the shelter, a galvanized-steel water tank with a sealed cover would be our toilet.

After helping with the bomb shelter project, Bill worked with my dad to finish the basement, which included two large recreation rooms, my new bedroom, and a full bathroom. Bill also taught me how to solder a sweat joint to join two pieces of copper tubing.

My out-of-town cousins visited Cheyenne, mostly to see their grandparents in the summer. When my family hosted activities, the constant 70-degree Fahrenheit (F) temperature made the fallout shelter the most popular place to play.

****

Dad and I spent hours browsing the Salvation Army, Goodwill, and war surplus stores. We looked for items to stock our bomb shelter, including extra can openers, water containers, tableware, and other sundries to make life as normal as possible in a 10-by-10-foot concrete room with no windows.

"Don't fuck with the Americans," my Vietnam War veteran housemate, Tom, used to say. The United States became the first and, to date, the only country to deploy nuclear weapons when B-52 bombers dropped Little Boy and Fat Man over Hiroshima and Nagasaki on August 6 and 9, 1945.

World War II ended with massive destruction. My distant relatives in Japan lived outside the blast zone but still experienced fallout. The horrific destruction had an enormous effect on my parents. I'm pretty sure Dad supported Barry Goldwater, the Republican nominee for President in 1964, who didn't rule out using nuclear weapons to end the Vietnam War, the impetus for our bomb shelter.

The Mid-Century Modern era brought technological advances, leading to an undeclared war between the United States and the Union of Soviet Socialist Republics (USSR or Soviets). The two superpowers clashed on ideological battlefields, beginning with a contest to see which country could amass the most atomic weapons.

Planes flew long distances to deliver bombs, which didn't make much sense. The U.S. military began researching more efficient ways to deploy nuclear ordnance on missiles and developed the much lighter and more powerful hydrogen bomb in November 1962. The less bulky payload meant missiles weighed less. Accuracy became less important because of more powerful warheads. Close only counts in horseshoes and nuclear blasts.

Twelve years after Hiroshima and Nagasaki, the Air Force oversaw ICBM deployments, with the Atlas program managed at Fort Warren in Cheyenne and Titan operations staged at Lowry Air Force Base in Denver.

America's nuclear weapons cache sparked the Cold War, creating tension between two superpowers that persists today. The U.S. led the Western World, and the USSR led the Eastern European Communist countries until 1991.

The Allied nations, including the USSR, led to the defeat of the Axis powers, Germany, Japan, and Italy, during World War II. The Allies neither approved of nor trusted Joseph Stalin's cold-blooded and violent leadership.

A race to conquer outer space began in 1957, when the Soviets launched Sputnik, the first satellite to leave Earth's atmosphere. That achievement lit a fire under the U.S. space program.

The technological battle intensified in 1961 when Soviet cosmonaut Yuri Gagarin became the first person to orbit the Earth. Later that year, astronaut Alan Shepard Jr. became the first American in space, followed by John Glenn, who orbited the Earth in 1962.

The U.S. government feared that the USSR had an intellectual and physical edge over the American public and implemented the National Defense Education Act (NDEA) of 1958. The Act provided funding for science, technology, engineering, and mathematics (STEM) programs and foreign language education from elementary through graduate school, including teacher training.

The NDEA offered scholarships and student loans to encourage more students to pursue higher education, particularly in STEM fields, and provided grants to universities and research institutions to promote scientific research and technological innovation.

The Cold War competition extended beyond intellectual capabilities to physical fitness, reflecting broader concerns about the nation's preparedness and the health of its citizens. In the 1950s, awareness grew of the lack of physical fitness among American youth compared with their Soviet counterparts.

In 1956, President Dwight D. Eisenhower established the President's Council on Youth Fitness to encourage schools to improve their Physical Education (PE) programs and to provide physical fitness guidelines.

The Council launched public awareness campaigns and fitness programs to promote physical activity. These national security initiatives aimed to improve the population's overall health and readiness.

President John F. Kennedy (JFK) continued and expanded these efforts. His administration launched the "President's Challenge" program, which included fitness tests for schoolchildren and promoted a culture of regular physical exercise.

"Superman's Mission for President Kennedy," *in Superman #170* (1964), recounts JFK's request for Superman to promote physical fitness among America's young people, reflecting the Kennedy administration's real-life national fitness initiatives.

Educational and physical fitness reforms ensured the U.S. could compete effectively and maintain its national security despite Soviet advancements. Russia invaded Ukraine on February 22, 2022, straining relations with the U.S. and the North Atlantic Treaty Organization (NATO) member countries.

Now would be a good time to revive JFK's Physical Challenge, given that childhood obesity rates in the United States have risen sharply since the 1960s. In the early 1970s, the rate hovered around five percent. By 2023, it had reached 20 percent.

****

The USSR and the U.S. engaged in proxy wars, with each superpower backing opposing sides, for example, in the undeclared wars in Korea and later in Vietnam. The Cold War ended in 1989, symbolized by the fall of the Berlin Wall, and the USSR dissolved in 1991. Russia continues to be at odds with the United States.

Poland changed regimes in 1989 and became the first country to break away from the USSR. The Solidarity trade union won an overwhelming victory in a partially free election in Poland, which led to the fall of Communism there. Soon, citizens overthrew Communist governments in Hungary, Bulgaria, Czechoslovakia, Romania, and East Germany.

Russia and the U.S. continue to proliferate nuclear weapons, pitting their best firepower against each other in a battle of Mutually Assured Destruction (MAD), with the idea that stockpiled weapons would deter each side from ever initiating an attack on the other.

Cheyenne became a primary target during the Cold War because of the high concentration of ICBM sites around the city. I understood the likelihood of a nuclear attack, and my parents believed one could happen.

The U.S. Air Force deployed the first 24 Atlas missiles in 1960, boosting the Cheyenne, where a military presence has been constant for parts of three centuries.

By 1963, Fort Warren controlled nearly 200 Minuteman-1b missile silos, scattered across ranches and farmland in Southeast Wyoming, Western Nebraska, and Northeast Colorado.

The atomic arsenal around Cheyenne normalized the Cold War. My Fairview Elementary Cub Scout Den took a field trip to a missile silo north of Cheyenne. We climbed into our Den Mother's station wagon and drove to an isolated farmhouse.

The building's exterior looked like a farmhouse, but it concealed the entrance to the missile silo control room. An Air Force security guard met us and accounted for everyone. I had to verify my identity with my Social Security number for the first time. I can't remember whether we descended in an elevator or climbed down a ladder, but the guards led our tour to an underground vestibule.

A thick, beveled, round, heavy metal door swung open, and we entered the command room. Two Airmen explained that a missile couldn't be launched by accident because each Airman had to turn a key at the same time. I had the impression that the missile sat in an underground silo some distance from the control center.

A friend who restores old train cars bought an abandoned missile site east of Cheyenne. Missiles lay horizontally in an above-ground structure, and operators raised them upright through a retractable roof.

The U.S. Air Force phased out Atlas missiles between 1963 and 1965, replacing them with Minuteman-I. The Air Force didn't deploy the Minuteman-II program in Wyoming. Minuteman-III became operational between 1972 and 1975. The Air Force placed 50 Peacekeeper missiles on alert in 1988 and lowered them into modified Minuteman-III silos. The U.S. and Russian nuclear stockpiles continue to be governed irrationally by MAD.

I made a second silo tour when my East High School physics class visited in 1971.

"We should be able to withstand a direct hit," an airman said. "But it's never been tested."

****

October 1962 marked a period of heightened international tension, culminating in the Cuban Missile Crisis between JFK and Soviet Premier Nikita Khrushchev.

I remember reading in the *Weekly Reader* about the standoff that began when the U.S. placed nuclear missiles in Turkey, near the USSR border. In response, Soviet Premier Nikita Khrushchev placed nuclear missiles in Cuba, 90 miles from the U.S. coast, to restore the balance of power and deter a potential American invasion of Cuba.

On October 14, 1962, an American U-2 spy plane captured photographs revealing Soviet missile bases under construction in Cuba. These bases could launch nuclear missiles capable of reaching much of the continental United States.

JFK's advisors informed him of the situation on October 16, 1962. After days of intense deliberation, he decided to impose a naval blockade on Cuba to prevent additional Soviet missiles from arriving. He announced the blockade to the public on October 22, 1962.

Over the next several days, the world watched anxiously as the U.S. and the USSR came to the brink of nuclear war. The U.S. demanded the removal of missiles from Cuba, while the Soviets insisted on the removal of U.S. missiles from Turkey and a pledge not to invade Cuba.

After intense negotiations, the two adversaries reached a deal. On October 28, 1962, Khrushchev agreed to dismantle the missile sites in Cuba in exchange for a U.S. public declaration and a commitment not to invade Cuba. The U.S. also agreed to remove its missiles from Turkey within six months.

I don't know whether schools still subscribe to the four-page tabloid *Weekly Reader*, which featured age-appropriate news for elementary students.

The *Weekly Reader* as required reading would have changed the way I learned. My 1st-grade teacher, Mrs. Stogsdill, sorted kids into reading groups based on skill level. The teacher assigned the top readers to the Eagles and the slower readers to the Sparrows. The classification system demeaned students, including me.

"Do you remember me?" asked Mrs. Stogsdill, who attended my 10th East High School class reunion.

"Yes. You taught me how to read," I responded. I think my teacher appreciated hearing that.

I read the *Weekly Reader* cover to cover. Dad bought a set of encyclopedias, and Santa brought me a world almanac every December. The Friends and Neighbors storylines, with no character arcs for Dick, Jane, Sally, Puff, and Spot, felt unrelatable. To this day, I'm not much of a reader. It turned out I'm an auditory and kinetic learner.

We read about and experienced the Cold War. The prospect of a nuclear attack prompted periodic air-raid drills at Fairview Elementary.

We learned what to do by watching Civil Defense filmstrips and movies that told us to duck under our desks and "Do not look at the fireball." We practiced leaving the classroom and walking to the bomb shelter in the boiler room, ably operated by Mr. Costello, the custodian.

During recess, we boys would cover our heads with the tails of our coats and chase the girls around the playground, yelling, "Duck and cover!" The drills gave us a false sense of security because the Soviets' nuclear missiles aimed at Cheyenne would vaporize everything within a five-mile radius.

When I'm in Cheyenne, I often drive by my old house on Windmill Road. One of these days, I'm going to get up the nerve, ring the doorbell, and ask if I can look around to see if the bomb shelter is still there.

I still roam around secondhand stores and flea markets. The big collectibles now are Mid-Century Modern artifacts my family used every day during my Baby Boomer childhood. I scrounged up an old Cold War-era cardboard sign I had framed. It reads, "Nuclear Fallout Can Reach Your Community."

I toted around a set of Mid-Century Modern nested mixing bowls made of milky Pyrex glass, painted brown, with stalks of wheat silk-screened on the sides. My parents bought that set at Gambles and gave it to me when I set up my household in Gillette.

I hauled those bowls around for years. They took up too much cabinet space, so I donated them to my Silver Sage Village cohousing community kitchen. I know I can use the big brown Pyrex bowl whenever I want to make a batch of my famous potato salad.

Hey, wait a second. I'm Mid-Century Modern!

****

Ral-Kar forces Superman to confront his vulnerabilities. Despite being powerless, he relies on his intellect and resourcefulness to overcome obstacles. Superman meets a being named Jhorl. The two don't judge each other for their differences. Jhorl helps Superman, and together they repair an old spaceship.

Superman and Jhorl fly the ship close to a nearby yellow sun, which restores Superman's powers. Like Superman, we have to become more collaborative and reimagine our American Way as times change and the country's complexion evolves.

6

A Life of Intentional Communities

Civility includes mundane actions, as well as arch-enemies deciding to get along. Donating my brown mixing bowl set, though an insignificant gesture, exemplifies living in harmony with others.

I could have kept my Pyrex bowls, but I gave them up for the good of the group. What you give up to reimagine Superman's American Way means living less as an individual and more as a collaborator who shares.

In "The Battle of the Atlantic," *Superman* #34 (May-June 1945), The Daily Planet sends Clark Kent on a follow-up assignment to cover a story aboard the United States Ship (USS) Davey Jones, a destroyer. He had previously written about three former Metropolis College football players who enlisted in the military.

Shep Shepard is aboard the Davey Jones; Al Wade pilots a Navy PBY reconnaissance plane; and Dan Ryan is a submarine crew member. The story flashes back to their college days, when Superman teaches the boys a hard lesson. Three classmates learn that teamwork is a better way to complete a task than dominating individually and taking credit for the accomplishment.

****

Civility is about cooperation. My family's open-door social environment in Cheyenne and Laramie prepared me for future living situations, including college dorm life, my first co-op home in Gillette, mixed-use urban living in Lander, and a Boulder cohousing community.

Dad had 13 brothers and sisters. One sister, Mae, died in Washington, and the remaining 12 grew up in a boarding house in Downtown Cheyenne, first across from the UP Depot on West 15th Street and later at 620 W. 18th St.

My grandparents later moved from the Westside to 714 E. 8th St. on the Southside, which became the family headquarters. Uncle Rich, a native-born citizen, purchased it in his name.

I spent quite a bit of time with Dad's Cheyenne family. Elsie, Rich, George, and Roy didn't have children. Many single adults influenced me at an early age. I remember one group activity at 714 during the polio epidemic.

Superman played a significant role in the national effort to eradicate polio from the 1940s through the 1960s. The March of Dimes (MoD) used Superman's image in promotional materials to support polio eradication and encourage vaccinations.

In the early 1950s, polio rates in the United States exceeded 25,000 cases annually. In 1952, a domestic outbreak occurred, with 58,000 cases and 3,200 deaths. A few kids at my school had polio in the early 1960s. One neighbor, Tim, wore leg supports and a hearing aid. Nobody thought much of the bullying he faced.

According to historical accounts, polio has existed since ancient Egyptian times. A hieroglyph dating back to the 14th century Before the Common Era (BCE) appears to depict a polio-stricken man with a withered foot.

American urbanization and higher population densities during the 19th-century Industrial Revolution facilitated the spread of the virus. In crowded cities, close contact among individuals made it easier for the virus to spread from person to person.

Ironically, improvements in sanitation in the early 20th century contributed to the spread of polio. In previous generations, exposure to the polio virus, particularly when maternal antibodies presented themselves at a very young age, led to mild or asymptomatic infections. As sanitation improved, children encountered the virus later in life, when they no longer had natural immunity, resulting in more severe cases.

In 1953, Jonas Salk developed an inactivated-virus vaccine. Two years later, public health officials made the vaccine available to prevent paralysis. Doctors found it easy to distribute and administer, making it ideal for mass immunization campaigns. I received the Salk vaccine by injection.

The MoD shifted its focus to promoting the newly developed, easy-to-administer, and more effective oral polio vaccine. To encourage mass participation in polio vaccination programs, the MoD organized National Vaccination Days to distribute Albert Sabin's attenuated vaccine.

In 1962, we had a big Ohashi family gathering at my grandparents' house. We all walked down to the neighborhood fire station, where we stood in a long line. A volunteer passed around trays of small paper cups containing a sugar cube laced with the pink Sabin vaccine, which encouraged antibody formation.

At school, teachers handed out cardboard coin holders. Every week, the MoD asked kids to donate a dime. Slipping a dime into the sleeve gave me a sense of pride and sacrifice, considering my dad gave me a 25-cent allowance.

****

The fight against polio earned me a badge of honor. It felt like taking my first communion, when I savored a few drops of grape juice from one of those micro-chalices and washed down a crouton-sized cube of Wonder Bread. I demonstrated my patriotism by taking my sugar cube, participating in civil defense drills at school, and helping Dad stock the fallout shelter.

I inspected Grandma Ohashi's musty cellar, which had a solid concrete foundation, and thought it would serve as a bomb shelter in case of nuclear war if we didn't have time to get home. I don't know how long anyone could stay down there. She stored jars of dill pickles and spicy radishes (*takuwan*). We would be good for a while.

Over the years, Uncle Rich built an addition to the back of the house without encroaching on my grandmother's garden. She had a green thumb. The family gathered to pluck string beans from the vines that wound their way up the laths that Grandma had poked into the fertile earth.

After the harvest, I popped off the stems and plinked the pods into a pan. My grandmother rewarded the family harvesters with *yasai wo itameru* (stir-fried) beans and bacon, served with rice. When in season, the *okazu* (side dish) featured the coveted *matsutake* mushrooms.

A revolving door of uncles and aunts stopped by daily, not to mention frequent formal and informal family gatherings: holidays, birthday parties, random dinners, and watching sports on TV.

When I left the house for college, my parents experienced "empty nest" syndrome. I didn't realize until later that I mourned the loss of my vast extended family, who had been my community. It took time, but I eventually got used to not having my grandparents, uncles, and aunts around.

****

My dad often dropped me off to visit Grandpa Ohashi. I liked going over to his house and flipping through Ring magazine to find the latest heavyweight rankings. His living room felt like a clubhouse. Uncle George subscribed to magazines from salespeople who came to the Café.

My grandfather stacked outdated magazines on one of his end tables. I ended up with a beat-up Sgt. Fury and the Howling Commandos' first-appearance comic book, which I sold for $300. Had I known it would one day be valuable, I would have taken better care. My magazine could have fetched $2,000.

I enjoyed watching professional heavyweight boxing with my grandfather. Because of his diabetes, he couldn't see very well, but he could still make out the contrasting black-and-white trunks on the B&W Zenith TV in a blonde Mid-century Modern Asian cabinet.

"*Kuronbo*," he said, using the Japanese word to describe African American boxers. I laughed because it sounded funny.

One night at the dinner table, I asked my dad what *kuronbo* meant. I had heard Grandpa, Uncle George, and Uncle Rich say it. My mother quickly chimed in, forbidding me from using the African American racial slur. I thought it meant "boxer" in Japanese.

I became a fan of the flamboyant Cassius Clay, who won the gold medal at the 1960 Olympics in Rome.

I remember huddling around my parents' clock radio in their bedroom in 1964, listening to the bout between Clay and Sonny Liston in Miami. Even though gamblers had pegged Clay as the underdog, he knocked out the Denver boxer in six rounds.

A year later, Liston and Clay booked a rematch in Lewiston, Maine. My dad, my sister Lorinda, and I lay on my parents' bed and settled in for a night of boxing.

By then, Clay had converted to Islam and changed his name to Muhammad Ali. Ali knocking out the Big Bear in the first round disappointed me. Hard-core boxing fans have questioned the win. Sports pundits think the "fix was in" and that Liston took a dive.

"I ain't got no quarrel with them, Viet Cong . . . Why should they ask me to put on a uniform and go 10,000 miles from home and drop bombs and bullets on brown people in Vietnam while so-called Negro people in Louisville are treated like dogs and denied simple human rights?" Ali mused.

Muhammad Ali refused to be drafted into the U.S. military, citing his Muslim faith and opposition to the Vietnam War. The U.S. Federal Court for the Southern District of Manhattan convicted Ali of draft evasion, sentenced him to five years in prison, fined him $10,000, and banned him from boxing for three years. He remained free while appealing his conviction.

The New York State Athletic Commission and other boxing organizations stripped him of his titles. Ali couldn't compete from 1967 to 1970. During that period, he emerged as a prominent civil rights activist, speaking out against the Vietnam War and advocating racial justice.

I've always admired Ali for challenging the dominant culture. In 1971, the U.S. Supreme Court (SCOTUS) overturned Ali's draft-evasion conviction because the FBI failed to adequately explain why agents denied Ali's conscientious objector status.

****

Uncle Rich kept *Field and Stream* in the stacks with the boxing magazines and comic books, which reinforced my interest in the summer fishing season. When my cousin Matthew and I had finished our CFD parade pop selling preparations, he and I helped Rich collect night-crawling earthworms from the backyard after dark.

The worms wiggled their way out into the grass on cool evenings. Matthew spotted by scanning the moist lawn with a flashlight. I grabbed the slimy creatures before they retreated into their hole.

The Westside and Southside kids had a niche selling worms around town, but I realized I didn't want to be responsible for any product with a shelf life.

The summer between my kindergarten and 1st-grade years, Dad bought identical bait-cast fishing reels from the Gambles store at the Cole Shopping Center for my sister and me. That's the same Gambles where my mom bought the set of nested mixing bowls.

We still lived on East 10th Street. Mom labeled each rod with our names using red fingernail polish, well before felt-tipped Magic Markers entered the market.

A bait-cast reel mounted on a pole is the purest form of fishing. Fishers attach bait to the hook at the end of the line, then lower it into the water or make a light cast.

We would take family outings to the lake near the Cheyenne Country Club. We came across some pretty good holes near the concrete rip-rap made from busted-up street curbing and old sidewalks. We would stop by to see Uncle Rich and pick up a few worms on the way out.

My dad helped bait the hooks. Bloody worms didn't bother me as I threaded the hook through the wriggling critter. Mom spent her time untangling the fishing line. It was my first time fishing. I caught and cleaned a small perch, which Mom pan-fried for our dinner that night. She coated it with flour, dipped it in egg, then in cornmeal, and pan-fried it.

Uncle Rich avidly hunted and competed in fishing tournaments. Rich and Hank Omoto entered fishing contests on some of the state's largest lakes. Hank repaired cars at Halladay Motors. The Skyline Nisei Club elected him its first president. Rich took two enormous trout to the taxidermist, who mounted them for display above the archway separating his living room from the dining area.

The Club organized fun summer picnics at nearby lakes around Cheyenne. Uncle Rich invited cousin Leonard and me to fish with him. We climbed into his pickup and drove to Crystal Lake and Granite Reservoir. Even though I didn't do much fishing, I enjoyed hanging out with Rich and Leonard.

I spent my time staring at the ground for round, flat stones to skip across the lake's surface so Uncle Rich could use my pole as an extra. Leonard became a more focused fisher, taking to the deep waters near San Francisco.

The picnics and outings brought my immediate and extended family together. We had disagreements, but we always resolved them. I remember, as a kindergartener, having to give up my bedroom when my grandfather moved in with us for a while. I complained, but I understood the importance of my parents' role as caretakers because they owned a private home.

My grandfather had diabetes, and Grandma couldn't care for him. After he moved in, it didn't occur to me to complain about sleeping on a cot in my parents' room or on the couch. Being displaced from my usual sleep schedule from time to time taught me to sleep anywhere and in any position.

His large insulin syringe, with a glass barrel, a stainless-steel plunger, and a needle, fascinated me. One morning, he showed me how to give himself his medication by jabbing the syringe into his thigh muscle. Maybe that's why I'm okay with being poked by 50 acupuncture needles at once.

Both sets of grandparents lived in Cheyenne and hosted multiple holiday celebrations: two Thanksgivings and two Christmases. My dad always invited Bill Fisher over for Thanksgiving.

Mom let Bill know he had us as his holiday family. After our Christmas festivities, on the way to visit the grandparents, we always stopped by Bill's place to drop off baked goods and a present.

More about Bill. He lived a hermit's life in the basement of a never-completed house foundation across the street from the Coke plant. Bill built rooms by digging tunnels, which he reinforced with timbers, like a gold mine.

Post-Traumatic Stress Disorder (PTSD) from service in the U.S. Navy during World War II and in Korea may have influenced his lifestyle, but he knew about science. Bill worked around the plant, sorting bottles and helping on the production line, though he mainly worked on the vending machine refrigeration systems.

On Saturdays, when I went to work with my dad, I goofed around, rode a Coke crate around the conveyor system, and sorted a few bottles before eventually making my way over to Bill's.

He subscribed to "Things of Science," an educational program launched by the nonprofit news syndicate Science Service in November 1940. Subscribers received a monthly series of science kits by mail.

The Science Service packed each kit in a small blue cardboard box about the size of a portable hard drive, with a yellow address label. Each kit contained a simple science project. I remember one being a crystal radio set and another being the assembly of a small motor powered by electromagnetic current.

Although quiet, Bill had an enormous influence on me. One Christmas, he bought me a year's subscription for five bucks. In high school, I set aside my artistic talent to focus on the hard sciences he had first nurtured in me.

Bill and I preferred to keep to ourselves, but we always welcomed opportunities to be around others. Over the years, I've learned the importance of staying optimistic around anyone. I never know when I'll have a constructive influence on someone.

****

Clark Kent shaped his character and came to better understand his superpowers throughout high school. I've read that Clark attended Metropolis College, where he studied journalism before Daily Planet editor Perry White hired him as a reporter. At least he learned something relevant to a job.

My parents didn't offer me academic guidance or discuss upward mobility. Dad had reached his potential in middle management, and Mom stayed home. Neither of them went to college, and neither had career paths based on college curricula. They let me follow my interests rather than pursue studies that might have led to employment.

If anyone had pushed me in one direction or another, I would have majored in something more practical than political systems analysis and ecological sciences. Nonetheless, my circuitous academic path brought me back to the Hitching Post Inn, where I took my first job at age 12.

I identified with a TV show called *The Many Loves of Dobie Gillis* (1959–1963), starring Dwayne Hickman, about a high school kid who always had some crisis with the women he dated. Maynard G. Krebs, Dobie's beatnik sidekick, pounded on bongo drums and collected tin foil.

Like Maynard, I didn't think much about the future other than attending college after high school. Nobody offered me any suggestions about potential job opportunities. There are so many more jobs available than the guidance counselors told me about, like making movies and writing books.

I enjoyed telling stories through my art, first as the cartoonist for my school papers from junior high through college. I became more committed to biology after a student exchange trip to St. Louis Park, Minnesota, in April 1971.

Each exchange tripper had to raise funds to pay their way. That became a family effort that began in 1970 and gave me a chance to get to know Uncle Roy better. A growing middle class fled to the suburbs, taking their mass consumerism with them. Aluminum cans became an externality of the "throwaway society."

Uncle Roy worked night-owl hours as the janitor at Town & Country Liquor on the Southside. He suggested I save aluminum cans from the bar and sell them at the scrap yard.

"Free money," he said. "I'm getting paid to bag them up. I can put them in the dumpster or give them to you. You'll need to get them ready to sell back."

Throughout the year, I picked up bags of cans from the bed of his pickup next to a very cool trailer house in a mobile home park behind the Highway Café, which had changed little since my days in elementary school.

When I visited the Café, I always walked over to his place and pounded on the door with a porthole window near the front of the two-toned silver-and-blue aluminum outer skin. I hadn't been up close to an airplane, but I thought that's what one would look like.

A smoldering briar pipe dangled from his mouth as he swung the door open. He always chuckled and waved me in, like the gatekeeper of the Land of Oz. Cherry-flavored Sir Walter Raleigh tobacco smoke wafted out of his dimly lit digs. I considered it a pleasant aroma.

Uncle Roy never married and had little food to share because he ate at the Café or at his mom's place, but he offered his menagerie of birds and fish for me to admire. He took care of colorful parakeets and little finches in cages.

The *tweet*, *tweet*, *tweet* from the warbling birdies and the gurgling bubbles from the submerged fish tank aerators filled his front room and kitchen.

He stocked aquariums with smallish exotic fish: sunfish, Dory clownfish, guppies, and goldfish. I liked watching the suckerfish clean the inside of the glass and vacuum up the fish poop the others dropped on the bottom of the tank. I realized that a self-contained bowl held my life, like a bottom feeder.

He loaned out his parakeets. My parents allowed me to keep only one at a time if I learned to care for it. I'm not over-nurturing, but I enjoyed replacing the newspaper at the bottom of the cage and picking out food at the Petland store on the east edge of town.

By the time summer rolled around, I had outgrown the part-time job at the Hitching Post I held through junior high school. Dad hired me during my high school summers. I earned double the wages at Coca-Cola compared to what the Hitch paid me for clearing tables, and I didn't have to wear a uniform. I also learned about mass production and efficient workflow. My dad took pride in his work, adding value to water, sugar, and flavoring.

Working for my dad gave me enjoyable and valuable experiences. I learned to drive a forklift, and for a 17-year-old, unloading a truck and balancing a pallet of bottles so they wouldn't topple over became practical life skills.

In the early 1970s, Coke adapted to industrial progress to boost profits. Our little bottling plant joined the throwaway society to cut costs.

We stopped filling returnable glass bottles, which made my job easier. I no longer had to fish cigarette butts out of the bottles with a hooked wire before loading them into the soaker and the washing machine. The Coke crew spent hours smashing glass bottles in the dumpster to make room for the endless supply of disposable ones.

Corrugated cardboard boxes containing thin-walled bottles arrived on pallets, shrink-wrapped in plastic. One day, the delivery truck didn't park on the crown of the street but on the downslope. After inserting the forks and lifting the pallet, I maneuvered the forklift to a flatter grade, but the top-heavy load slowly collapsed onto the pavement. Lucky for me, few bottles broke.

Around that time, we stopped sweetening our soft drinks with granulated sugar and switched to high-fructose corn syrup. Sugar was sugar. Who knew one would be healthier than the other?

That change also eliminated one of my jobs. Before each bottling run, I lifted 50-pound bags of sugar, poured them into a stainless-steel vat, added a measured amount of Cheyenne tap water, and stirred the mixture with a large stainless-steel paddle.

Instead, I opened a large valve, releasing the premixed sweetener into the stainless-steel vat, where it blended with the top-secret Coca-Cola flavoring. The mixture was gravity-fed to the bottling line, then filled with carbonated water. A machine crimped a cap on each bottle. Afterward, I grabbed four bottles at a time and placed 24 of them in a cardboard box.

I hadn't seen my dad around other men except for neighbors and relatives. He could cuss and talk trash with the best of them. Still, the guys liked and respected him. He brought doughnuts for coffee breaks and let them off to see their kids or run errands during the workday.

Dad saw himself as a team player and a community builder. He managed the crew so that nobody stood around doing nothing. He also filled in for any job in case of illness or an emergency. He managed horizontally. As one of the middle kids among 12 surviving brothers and sisters, he developed herd-management skills as part of his upbringing.

In my past "real job" life, and to this day, I've learned everyone's jobs and made it a point to help everyone understand one another's roles.

****

Roy salvaged $450 worth of cans. That, plus the money I earned working for my dad, covered the costs of the springtime exchange trip, including my first jet ride on Western Airlines from Cheyenne to Minneapolis and a stay in the wealthy St. Louis Park suburb in 1970.

A casual guitarist named Bret Gardner and his family hosted me. There, I learned to take morning showers, while working-class people like my family took baths at night.

St. Louis Park High School administrators dismissed the school on April 22nd. Attending Earth Day for the first time in a progressive community sparked my late-blooming interest in biology and politics.

I ended up taking more science classes and, despite being terrible at math, did well in my courses, including advanced biology taught by Miss Cooper, the science teacher at Heart Mountain High School. I became a science major in college.

I wrestled from junior high through high school. Terry Williams, one of my coaches, took me on a recruiting trip to Colorado State University (CSU) in Fort Collins.

As I write this, I realize Coach Williams took an interest in me. I should have been more appreciative.

"I'm done with sports, Coach," I insisted.

"At least take a look. You're good enough to get a scholarship."

"My role would be the other guy."

"Yeah, but you're coachable and not a jerk."

Great. Just what I needed: another four years of cutting weight so the first-stringer could toss me around the mat in the overly hot practice room. Besides, how could a Wyoming fan become a student at CSU, the Cowboys' archrival?

****

I had a knack for helping people do their best and be team players. That's a throwback to a Fairview Elementary basketball game. My small size overshadowed my skills. Back then, the school district required students to attend neighborhood schools. I went to Fairview with the same kids, including star athletes Bobby McMurray and Husty Twitchell.

Fairview had scheduled an away game at Eastridge Elementary School, across the street from the Grand Central store, which sold 10-cent French fries. Coach Goff selected me to join the traveling team.

Maybe everyone got to go, but it didn't matter. Seeing my name on the roster posted on the corkboard outside the gym made me feel proud. We loaded up onto a school bus, my first time riding one because I had always walked or ridden my bike to school.

We disembarked and entered the dark gym. Our footsteps echoed across the linoleum floor, reminiscent of the Oscar-winning movie *Hoosiers* (1986). The awestruck underdog basketball players of Hickory High School entered the gigantic arena, where a washed-up coach, Norman Dale (Gene Hackman), inspired them to win the state championship against the heavily favored big-city team from Indianapolis.

The two stars on the Fairview team, Bobby and Husty, didn't have their best games. Coach Goff subbed me in for one of them. I finally got to play. I stole the ball twice and scored four points on easy layups.

"That O'Hashi had a pretty good game yesterday," Coach Goff said the next day at practice. His comment boosted my self-esteem. Ever since then, I've always given people a chance. I've hired workers based on their word and have had no disappointments with my random vetting process.

Out of the hundreds of kids who went through Mr. Goff's basketball program, I doubt he knew what a positive influence his words had on me. I recognized then how important it is to always be on top of my game.

****

A bunch of my Presbyterian Church pals from East and Central decided to attend Hastings College in Nebraska. I knew about Hastings from the back of my 1965 Jesus Alou baseball card, which notes that he began his career in 1959 with the Hastings Giants, who played in the short-season Class D Nebraska State League. The Hastings College Broncos baseball team also played at Duncan Field, built in 1940 as a WPA project.

The Presbyterian Church has affiliated with Hastings, as it has with Sheldon Jackson College in Sitka, Alaska. In 1970, I spent the summer of my junior year in high school doing community service. I joined a bunch of Wyoming kids, including my future Hastings College roommate, who drove to Alaska's Inside Passage for a community service project at Sheldon Jackson. I happened to meet my great-uncle Buck at his drugstore in Ketchikan on that trip.

I didn't have a fallback school, not even UW. I wanted to get out of Wyoming. Moving to faraway Nebraska, with a few familiar faces around, made me feel comfortable. Plus, I wanted to attend a smaller school. Although I learned during my collegiate travels about other compatible colleges if I had looked around.

After being on campus for a semester, I found the weekly schedule liturgical. An optional chapel service happened every Wednesday. Excellent speakers such as Barbara Jordan and Dick Gregory headlined many of the events.

The national Jesus Revolution, an evangelical Christian movement, drew a following at Hastings College in the late 1960s and early 1970s. The counterculture movements and social turmoil of the time prompted an age-appropriate Christian response.

The Jesus Revolution (2023) is a historical fiction film set in the 1970s. It follows the unlikely partnership between a young, spiritually lost Greg Laurie (Joel Courtney) and two men who would shape his life: traditional Pastor Chuck Smith (Kelsey Grammer) and a charismatic hippie preacher, Lonnie Frisbee (Jonathan Roumie).

Laurie seeks meaning in the Southern California counterculture. Smith opens his church and partners with Frisbee to teach the Gospel to disillusioned youth. What begins as a small gathering of hippies soon becomes a nationwide spiritual revival.

I went through the motions of Christianity but didn't experience the religious side of campus life as much as some of my Evangelical and Jesus Freak classmates did.

Nobody wanted to dress up and organize six classmates for a family-style dinner on Wednesday night, but the fancy meals on the menu enticed us to attend.

The school's higher-ups imposed social engineering.

The rules prohibited first-year women from leaving campus for a few months at the start of the first semester. All women had to return to the dorms by 1:00 a.m.

The women looked forward to Daylight Saving Time because springing ahead added an hour. In the fall, the clock would "fall back," and women would lose an extra hour of freedom.

There aren't women's hours these days, but the school is still white bread, which fits the middle-of-the-grain-belt culture, which is okay.

Nebraska, like Wyoming, had a predominantly Caucasian population. As a raisin in the Go Big Red oatmeal, I got to know very few minorities: a Latino, two African Americans on the football and track teams, a Chinese guy, and me. The Black guys noticed the racial differences more than I did and kept to themselves.

If I had to make the choice again, I would still choose Hastings.

****

After living through my extended family experience, I joined my next intentional community in Altman Hall, the coed dorm on campus. Coed in the sense that one side housed men and the other housed women. A basement with a TV room, washers, and dryers connected the two wings.

Every semester, the other dorms reported numerous infractions involving opposite-gender students in the dorms after hours and failure to return before curfew. Students routinely turned in their classmates.

Altman Hall rarely had rule violations. The Dean of Women suspected collusion, called the dorm leadership into her office, and accused us of a cover-up. The Altman Angels had a code of honor and didn't patrol the halls looking for trouble.

Hastings College didn't have a wrestling program. I missed organized, competitive activities, so I joined the Hastings debate team. I took a speech class as an elective in my senior year at East. The major benefit? I didn't have to monitor my wrestling weight week to week.

I competed in debate with a partner. I read *Newsweek* and *Time* magazines as part of my weekly routine. Impromptu and extemporaneous speaking on current events didn't require much preparation, and became my favorite individual events.

The speech jocks traveled as much as the football or basketball teams. I traveled to tournaments, sometimes two or three days a week throughout the year rather than during a specific season, and saw the world.

I had no desire to live off campus, not seeing the value in living with a couple of other classmates who may or may not be more irresponsible than me. Most of the kids at Hastings lived in Nebraska and thought that renting in an off-campus house at 20 demonstrated their maturity.

I preferred having many classmates around, sharing meals in the cafeteria, and playing pool or shooting the breeze afterward. Going off to college, a day's drive from Cheyenne, liberated me.

I blended in very well at Hastings as a Model Minority. Society stereotypes all Asians, regardless of ethnicity, as hardworking and obedient, which are good characteristics for an outsider wanting to fit in with the American Way.

****

Many of my Wyoming acquaintances believe I still live in my home state. Wyoming is one of those places where it's tough to make a clean break because there's still a lot of "street cred" in being a Wyoming native. It's the least populous state, with 580,000 people.

There are twice as many cattle roaming the Equality State as people. Cows have more rights than humans. Wyomingites describe our home state as a small town connected by long streets. There's a lot of truth to that.

When I see a random person walking around, pretty much anywhere, wearing a Wyoming-marked garment or a ball cap with the bucking horse logo, I stop and talk with them. Chances are, we'll have a person in common or, at a minimum, a story about a place or an event.

Diana and I took a cruise through the Inside Passage of Alaska. We stopped at the Red Dog Saloon in Juneau.

"Where's everyone from?" the lounge singer yelled while he tuned his guitar.

"Tensleep, Wyoming!" a guy yelled from the back.

"Do you know Jalan Crossland?" I hollered back. Jalan is a musician we know from the small town at the foot of the Big Horn Mountains. We had a good Wyoming chat with the two hunters on their way back from the bush after a successful hunt.

Since 1986, one of my destinations in New York City has been Sardi's, a bar and restaurant in the Manhattan Theater District that has been in business since 1927. Hundreds of celebrity caricatures from the showbiz world cover the walls.

Sardi's is a famous before- and after-theater gathering spot. A scene in Mel Brooks' 1967 movie *The Producers* offers a satirical look at theater-business corruption and the casting couch, starring Zero Mostel and Gene Wilder.

During the intermission of their fictional musical *Springtime for Hitler,* the enthusiastic and entertained theatergoers flow into a bar reminiscent of Sardi's.

I mentioned that I wrote for the Lander WSJ. The best benefit of being part of the working news media is press passes. I covered the UW basketball team that played in the 1986 National Invitational Tournament championship games at Madison Square Garden. The Cowboys lost the title game to Ohio State, 73-63.

A group of Pokes fans who stayed at the Marriott Marquis Hotel drank the nearby Sardi's bar out of tequila.

"I didn't know you could drink it by the shot," the bartender observed. I've been going there ever since. The bar snacks are Ritz Crackers with cheese spread mixed with port wine. I generally keep a container in the fridge for old-time's sake.

A few years later, I visited Glen Ridge, New Jersey, for a project. It's a quaint place, considering that I'd stereotyped all of Jersey as urban Newark. I based a location in *A New Dawn at Libby Flats,* my first historical fiction novel, on Glen Ridge.

Anyway, my colleague and I ended up in New York City in the late 1980s, including an obligatory stop at Sardi's. A tall, broad bouncer stopped us as we tried to enter the bar. A private post-theater event had closed the upstairs bar.

Who should walk down the stairs? U.S. Senator Al Simpson and his wife, Ann. We first met during my first year in grad school at UW, when I served as an intern at the Wyoming State Legislature, and Al represented Park County.

The Simpsons came to town for the opening of a show at the Helen Hayes Theater across the street. We shared one of those "What are you doing here?" moments. After a brief chat about the event, the bouncer stepped aside and let my colleague and me into the private party.

Another time, I met my cousin Milton from San Francisco in Laramie, and we went to the Buckhorn Bar.

"Hey, I know you," the bouncer said. He and Milton had attended Galileo High School, O. J. Simpson's alma mater.

Any Wyomingite who reads this book has a similar "all roads lead through Wyoming" story.

****

As a newcomer, I didn't feel Colorado welcomed me as warmly as Wyoming did. None of my Wyoming contacts helped much when I decided to hang my hat in Boulder. When I commuted from Lander, I did my share of sofa surfing with friends and strangers.

Eventually, I grew tired of transient living and settled into an intentional cooperative community whose higher purpose was Buddhism. Four of us had separate rooms, and we made household decisions by consensus, especially when Richard, the house organizer, invited a new member to live with us. We asked a new housemate to join us. He turned out to be a slob who didn't keep up with his assigned chores and didn't last long.

Living around and on top of other people remains my way of life in the Silver Sage Village cohousing community in North Boulder, Colorado.

My Silver Sage Village community consists of 16 privately owned condominiums, home to 28 residents who have agreed to share a common mission and set of values for living together, maintaining shared spaces like the courtyard, and providing neighborly help to one another.

Because cohousers agree on civility as a means to reimagine Superman's American Way, they can effectively bridge today's deep cultural divides.

Individual material accumulation characterizes success in America. Bigger and more is better than smaller and less. The majority controls decision-making, and the dominant culture excludes those who differ unless they conform.

There's nothing inherently wrong with material success or with individuals excelling to the best of their abilities, but what if rugged individuals achieved Superman's American Way collaboratively?

The core idea of cohousing prioritizes the group's well-being over individual desires.

Cohousing returns to a community model in which families know one another because their kids all attended the same neighborhood school. That would be my Baby Boomer socialization.

While the tenets of cohousing are noble, they are easier said than done since society pounds Superman's American Way into our heads from the moment the obstetrician clips our umbilical cord.

****

Communities come together in many forms, depending on circumstances. I had a simple transition to cohousing because I grew up in a close-knit extended family, lived in the dorms, and became a first-time homebuyer in a co-op. Getting along by giving and taking has been my way of life.

At the end of Clark Kent's assignment at sea, Japanese depth charges sink Al's submarine. Shep and Dan team up to lead the rescue mission. Superman initially helps, but the three crewmates fall back on the lesson Superman taught them about working together as college students. Their actions save countless lives.

The Japanese neighborhood on West 17th Street accidentally became a community through business owners and residents who knew one another and contributed social capital that enhanced its vibrancy.

7

Last Cupid Standing

My upbringing in Cheyenne's Japanese community couldn't have been more different from my cousins' upbringing in an urban Japantown in San Francisco, yet the way the 500 and 400 blocks of West 17th Street evolved from vibrancy to parking lots is a cautionary tale.

I had forgotten my childhood on West 17th Street. Then I saw John Dinneen give an interview on the local TV news about the Lotus Townhouse redevelopment.

John and I graduated from Cheyenne East in 1971. He and his family have deep roots in Cheyenne, dating back to the 1890s. His great-great-grandfather and great-great-uncle established the Bon Ton Livery Stable. When the horseless carriage arrived, they closed the stable and opened an automobile dealership, a business that spanned four generations.

My dad did a lot of business with the Dinneens over the years. One memorable family car, a white-over-forest-green 1963-or-so Monterey sedan, had a rear window called the "breezeway" that could roll down.

We also had a big avocado-green Mercury "family truckster" station wagon with fake wood paneling on the sides. The family truckster, of course, is the car the Griswolds drive from Chicago to

Wallyworld in the cult classic *Vacation* (1983), starring Chevy Chase and Beverly D'Angelo as Clark and Ellen.

John and his brother Jim sold their family's car business but retained the historic automotive repair garage. They repurposed and renovated the garage into an office building anchored by a steakhouse.

The Dinneens had acquired two nondescript, long-vacant buildings at 509 and 511 W. 17th St. to demolish them and consolidate the townhouse construction site. They tore down the 511 property but encountered a stumbling block.

The Cheyenne Historic Preservation Board determined that the building at 509, over 50 years old, didn't meet the criteria for architectural significance. The Board also determined that the last building standing on the 500 and 400 blocks of West 17th Street is a historic place in the heart of the once-vibrant Cheyenne Japanese community.

Mrs. Yoshio Shuto first operated a boarding house there. She arrived in Cheyenne shortly after her divorce, traveling through Nebraska and Colorado.

The Board required a public hearing and approved John's demolition request on the condition that he complete a cultural and historical survey of Japanese-operated businesses and residents. Some Board members wanted the building preserved because razing it would remove the last physical remnant of Cheyenne's Japanese community.

Souvenir scroungers salvaged building materials, including the tin ceiling tiles and the storefront's leaded-glass windows. I suggested that the Dinneens save a few red bricks and repurpose them as the base for the sign the Board required to summarize the neighborhood's history.

Most of the two-block area is now vacant. By the 1970s, the businesses that hustled and the residents who bustled around the neighborhood had moved out. Unable to keep their buildings occupied, the landlords razed them once they became empty.

Given my renewed interest in the neighborhood, John asked me to complete a survey of past residents and land uses. That survey forms the basis of this book.

A combination of a cultural identity crisis and urban sprawl, occurring concurrently and culminating in the late 1960s and 1970s, led to the demise of the Japanese neighborhood.

Because my family is part of the Japanese community, I have wondered how my assimilation contributed to the two blocks becoming a sea of parking lots.

Japanese Americans categorize themselves by generation. My grandparents are called Issei (first generation in the United States). My parents are Nisei (second generation, born in the United States). My sister and I are Sansei (third generation, born in the United States). The offspring of Sansei are called Yonsei.

When Lorinda and I grew up in Cheyenne, I didn't even self-identify with a race or notice anything about my Japanese heritage.

My dad's second-youngest sibling, Marie, left Cheyenne to attend Weber State in Ogden, where she met and married Masao "Mooch" Matsukawa. He taught me to keep an eye out for potential collectibles. She taught school and worked as a Veterans Administration social worker. They lived in the suburb of Murray and had two children, Matthew and Mauri.

My family often drove to Salt Lake City, Utah, to visit Marie during Easter break. My mom told a story about our first time attending Marie's all-Japanese Church of Christ.

"Why are we the only ones not Japanese?" I asked Mom when we sat down.

I liked going to their church because afterward we could walk to the Church of Jesus Christ of Latter-Day Saints (LDS) Temple Square, where the Mormon Tabernacle and the Mormon Temple are located on a beautiful campus.

Our visits included staying with one of Dad's older sisters, Amy. She and her husband, Ichiro "Ich" Doi, lived in Bountiful, a Salt Lake

City suburb. They ran the Deluxe and the Excellent dry cleaners. They had no children. Amy had kidney disease, which eventually took her life before dialysis became a standard treatment.

I had fun going to work with Amy and Ich at their always humid, warm storefront. Dry cleaners have a distinctive odor. Customers dropped off clothes that Ich soaked in a chemical solvent, which somehow clung to clothing crud. When the garments tumbled in the dryers, big fans vented most of the residual solvents into the outside air. Ich steam-pressed out what remained on the clothing.

Amy introduced me to live theater during a visit in the summer of 1962. I reluctantly went along to be courteous. Besides, my mom made me go. Little did I know she had bought tickets to *The Music Man*, whose theme would influence my outlook on life. James Shigeta, playing Professor Harold Hill, intrigued me as a raisin in the River City oatmeal.

****

After agreeing to help the Dinneens with their historical survey of the neighborhood, I realized that most building owners had razed their properties over the years, dispersing the Japanese neighborhood and its history. When I began the survey, I walked the 500 and 400 blocks of West 17th Street, stared at the asphalt parking lots, and reflected on my childhood in Cheyenne.

8

The 500 Block: The City Café and Tokyo Pool Hall

Across the street from her boarding house at 509, Mrs. Shuto turned her culinary skills into her most successful business venture, the City Café, which epitomized America's mishmash culture.

Flower Drum Song, a musical, opened on Broadway in 1958. The Richard Rodgers and Oscar Hammerstein II stage play explores the conflicts between older immigrants from China and their children. The story centers on the romantic entanglements and cultural conflicts among the characters. Mei Li (Miyoshi Umeki) is a traditional Chinese immigrant.

Wang Ta (James Shigeta) straddles two cultures and embodies the American Way. The exotic entertainer Linda Low (Nancy Kwan) lures Ta into questioning his traditional cultural past, making nightclub owner Sammy Fong (Jack Soo) jealous. Fong is further upset when he learns that his parents had traditionally betrothed him to Mei Li, which is why she and her father hid aboard a steamship and illegally entered San Francisco.

In 1967, the East High School theater department staged the musical. The director cast my sister, the only Asian in the cast, as one of Wang Ta's younger siblings. I tagged along to watch rehearsals.

One of the big production numbers is a song about how living in America is like chop suey. The Americanized Chinese food dish serves as a metaphor contrasting cultural symbols, ranging from Hula Hoops to nuclear war, Dr. Salk of polio vaccine fame, and the sexy Hungarian-born screen siren Zsa Zsa Gabor. The music director updated the original lyrics to reference President LBJ and his Veep, Hubert Humphrey.

The Tony Award-winning musical ends on a happy, chop-suey note. The story acknowledges the diversity of immigrant experiences. Not all immigrants assimilate in the same way, and not all reject their heritage entirely. The contrast between the traditional Mei Li and the modern Linda highlights the spectrum of immigrant experiences.

Wang Ta reconciles with his heritage by choosing Mei Li, while Linda embraces contemporary American life with Sammy. This dual resolution highlights the complementary nature of traditional and modern values, showing that both paths are valid and can coexist within the community. That's the story of the City Café.

****

The Tokio Café and rooming house opened at 514 in 1926. Several restaurateurs operated the business until 1934, when Mrs. Shuto acquired and ran the place with Seiyo "Johnny" Saiki (aka Saiki San). She renamed it the City Café.

The City Café provided segregation in reverse. Non-white patrons sat in the front, while Caucasian customers walked through the kitchen and sat at large tables in the back, like the mob bosses who wander through an Italian restaurant's back door on *The Sopranos*.

The place became known for its Americanized pan-Asian short orders with a Japanese twist. Customers loved the *teriyaki* steak, egg foo young, chop suey, and chop mein with crunchy noodles. The Café also offered American staples such as pot roast, hot beef sandwiches, and burgers.

When we ate out, my family chose the City Café. I always ordered the same thing: the pork noodle bowl made with bone broth, thick *udon* noodles, a slice of pork, napa cabbage, maybe thinly sliced carrot for color, and, when available, sliced kamaboko (fish sausage, for lack of a better descriptor) and a sliced hard-boiled egg.

Pork noodles are my preferred choice, even though fancy *ramen* is now trendy. *Ramen* noodles made from wheat flour originated in China. Whenever I order beef noodles at a Chinese restaurant, the noodles are *ramen*.

Thinking back, most other downtown restaurants, like the Plains Hotel, offered upscale American fare. The City Café had a socially integrated customer base. Locals considered the Westside the rough part of Cheyenne.

The Café had a big takeout business for those who thought the area too seedy. Regardless, patrons came from all over for the cooking of Mrs. Shuto, Saiki San, Haruyo Tani, and my Grandma Ohashi.

From the 1940s through the 1960s, the City Café stayed open after hours. It became a safe gathering place for the Skyline Nisei Club's indoor Japanese community events for the Issei generation.

A high level of camaraderie among Japanese community members developed as they recoiled from the racism experienced during and after the War and as Nisei soldiers returned from Europe.

The Club later rented a separate community hall in the 400 block of West 17th Street, near the California Fish Market and Baker's Place, for events such as a dinner honoring Japanese judges who visited Cheyenne in November 1950. Thirty-nine Issei and Nisei attended the dinner.

Cheyenne attorney George Guy, best known for defending Japanese war criminal General Tomoyuki Yamashita, invited the judges to Wyoming, where he gave them a tour of the justice system in Cheyenne.

A U.S. military commission tried Yamashita for alleged war crimes committed by his troops during the Japanese defense of the Philippines in 1944. The tribunal found the general guilty of wartime atrocities, even though prosecutors presented little evidence that he had approved or even been aware of them.

It came out at trial that troops not under his command committed many of the crimes. The court sentenced and executed Yamashita by hanging in 1946.

****

The City Café became a Friday-night destination. On Skyline Nisei Club nights, Mrs. Shuto opened the jukebox so teenagers could play rock 'n roll for free. Dad joined the other men in the back to play cards. My sister and I stayed with my mom, our babysitter for the night, to watch samurai movies.

I liked the silent films about the Japanese warrior class that thrived in Pre-Modern Japan between the 17th and 19th centuries. The 16-mm movies had no soundtrack except for the sound of the projector ratcheting the film onto the takeup reel.

One of my favorites is *Yojimbo* (1961), directed by Akira Kurosawa. It stars Toshiro Mifune as an unattached samurai *ronin* who arrives in a town where two rival gangsters want to hire him as their bodyguard. MGM and director Sergio Leone remade the plot as a western, Fist Full of Dollars (1964), starring Clint Eastwood.

Mrs. Shuto reserved the back of the Café for men to drink scotch whiskey and play rousing hands of *Hanafuda* (flower), a card game similar to gin rummy, with pictures of flowers on thick cardboard tiles that clattered when slammed on the table.

In 1958, Mrs. Shuto invited her nephew, Tadayoshi "Tommy" Takeda (Shuto), from Japan to help run the Café. Tommy overstayed his visa and on the verge of deportation. An act of Congress sponsored by U.S. Senator Gale McGee (D-WYOMING) permitted Mrs. Shuto to adopt her nephew. Mrs. Shuto returned to Japan in 1964, where she became ill and could not return to Cheyenne. She eventually died in Japan.

During the heyday of the City Café, the Skyline Nisei Club traditionally prepared mochi during a New Year's ceremony called *Os-*

hogatsu, which translates to the first three days of the New Year. It's a big group activity called *mochitsuki*.

The chef places hot rice into the *usu*, a mortar carved from a hollowed-out section of a large-diameter tree trunk. Rice pounders take turns mashing the rice into mochi paste with a giant two-fisted *kine*, or pestle. The City Café kitchen crew loaded the rice into a hand-cranked sausage-grinding machine to make the paste.

The women in my family didn't pound rice, but as a team sport, they smooshed hot rice in a *suribachi* (ceramic mortar) and kneaded it with a *surikoji* (wooden pestle).

The closure of the City Café and the Tani family's rooming house marked the last hurrah for the West 17th Street Japanese community. Besides the Tanis, residents included Kanji Nagata and Mrs. Shuto. The Tani family moved to West 27th Street.

Tommy and his family built a new building on a parcel of land owned by Johnny Baker at West 19th Street and O'Neil Avenue. It still stands as a pan-Asian restaurant.

The City Café would become the allegory for my life. Chop suey, a staple on the menu, became a staple and my connection to Japanese culture.

****

My parents moved away from our East 10th Street home when the boundaries of Fairview Elementary School changed after my kindergarten year. Had we stayed, I would have attended Alta Vista Elementary School, which had a diverse student body of Latinos and Southsiders and, in my mom's view, would have been too rough for me.

They invested in land on the east edge of Cheyenne, later sold the property, and kept their East 10th Street house as a rental. We bought a house in the Cole Addition at 1115 Windmill Rd. to remain within the Fairview School boundary.

I had the best of both my bicultural worlds. Most of the time, I lived a steady life in the Cole Addition, and on weekends and holidays, I got to hang out in the Japanese neighborhood and with my relatives.

We dined at the City Café, where Grandma had a steady job, and later at the Highway Café. My entrepreneurial Grandpa bought the pool hall at 516 from the Kubota family.

Several businesses operated there before it became a pool hall. Taigo and Nao Suzuki ran a store selling Japanese goods in 1922 and lived in the apartment above. The Suzukis sold their market to Kazuma and Ume Mikawa. Kazuma initially worked for the UP Railroad.

Ume, recently widowed, married Kazuma in 1924. Two years later, they bought the grocery and *tofu* factory next to the David Cantor Meat Shop, which sold kosher food to the local Jewish community, also prominent in Downtown Cheyenne. The Mikawas closed the store when they moved to Colorado in 1932.

Masaka Hosokawa originally came to Cheyenne in 1930, when the UP hired him as a machinist. He roomed with Takematsu Matsushima in Matsushima's barbershop apartment at 408. In 1939, Masaka converted the meat shop at 516 into a pool hall and, three years later, sold it to Gontaro and Kiyo Kubota. After selling out, Masaka worked odd jobs and lived above the City Café.

Gontaro Kubota came to the United States in 1906. He moved to Wyoming in 1915 and worked for the UP as the Sherman Hill Section Supervisor east of Laramie. In 1921, he returned to Japan, where he married Kiyo.

The two returned to Wyoming and spent their first night at Mrs. Shuto's rooming house at 509. The UP rehired Gontaro, and they returned to the Sherman Hill Section, where the couple started a family. They later moved with the railroad to the Buford Section between Cheyenne and Laramie.

The railroad fired Gontaro after Pearl Harbor. He moved his family to Cheyenne and bought the Hosokawa Pool Hall. The Kubotas sold it to Grandpa Ohashi in 1957. According to the Cheyenne City Directory, he owned the business as the Tokyo Pool Hall.

My parents didn't let me enter his den of iniquity. While on the weekend Coke route with my dad, I had to wait outside. I posted on Facebook asking for any recollections of the West 17th Street business district.

Henry Pacheco responded. He worked for my grandfather, who paid him 50 cents per table to remove the covers and brush the green felt. He racked the 15 balls for tips. Henry befriended a "Fat Anglo," the bouncer who took side bets for all the tables.

Grandpa Ohashi owned the pool hall until he died in 1966. I inherited one of his old Brunswick tables. The heavy oak rails and pedestal supporting two flat-slate table pieces weighed a ton. When my dad and I assembled it in the basement next to my new bedroom in our home on Windmill Road, I had plenty of time to set up shots and developed a pretty good eye.

I hauled it to Lander and later donated it to the Northern Arapaho Senior Citizen Center in Ethete on the Wind River Reservation. I kept the 9-ball and many memories of that table.

I spent a lot of time shooting pool while working the late shift at the Bellevue House student center at Hastings College. I didn't play much 8-ball, but learned to play snooker on a larger table with small pockets.

I joined the One Shot Lounge Valley 8-Ball team in Lander. The games moved quickly because of the small tables with large pockets. Given my grandfather's legacy, I passed my rite of passage by winning two trophies and playing countless 9-ball games.

****

Grandpa Ohashi would be happy to know I kept up his pool-hustling tradition. He came to the United States in 1898, worked in agriculture in Fife, Washington, and then moved to Ketchikan, Alaska.

In 1970, the Wyoming Presbytery organized a group of high school students to join a summer work crew at Sheldon Jackson College, a two-year school also affiliated with the Presbyterian Church. Our group drove to Prince Rupert, British Columbia, then took a ferry through the Inside Passage to Sitka. My future Hastings College roommate, Sam Allen, and I made a side trip to Ketchikan. We walked along the boardwalk where I saw a wooden sign that read, "OHASHI Candy and Tobacco."

We went in and learned that my grandfather's brother, George, owned the store. I have relatives who live in the Pacific Northwest. In a past life, I attended a Habitat for Humanity conference in Seattle and ran into a distant cousin.

In 2022, Diana and I took an Alaskan cruise through the Inside Passage and made a pilgrimage to my family's store in Ketchikan. The local historical society had set up a display featuring old photos of my family. I joined a Ketchikan Facebook group, and a long-lost relative informed me that my great-grandparents emigrated from Japan to Alaska. They are buried in the Ketchikan cemetery.

As a teenager, Grandpa cooked at an Alaskan mining camp and learned the ways of the world by hustling pool. He learned to say all the best curse words in English.

He returned to Japan in 1911 and married Natsu Yonago. While in Washington, they had eight children. Their other five became native-born Coloradoans.

In 1925, my Grandpa got a lead from a friend about a productive lettuce farm in Monte Vista, Colorado. He regretted the move because the land didn't produce as his friend had led him to believe.

He made the best of the decision and ended up in Brighton via Denver and Ft. Lupton, where he opened a produce store selling vegetables from local farmers. He expanded his business to Cheyenne, where he and his family eventually settled in 1934. According to Auntie Elsie, the family originally lived in a boarding house across from the UP railyard, near Grandpa's vegetable exchange storefront.

****

Tsunesaboro "Tsune" Ogasawara owned a cigar store at 515 across the street and opposite the pool hall. He operated the business from 1920 to 1936, died in 1937, and is now buried in the Cheyenne Lakeview Cemetery.

Arlene Ogasawara, a well-known member of the Cheyenne Ogasawara family, is distantly related to Tsune. In 1922, her father, Shiro, immigrated to Reliance in Sweetwater County, where he ran a boarding house for miners. He married Chizo Futa, a Cheyenne native. The couple eventually returned to Chizu's hometown.

Arlene and her family lived in Stockton, California. When Japan attacked Pearl Harbor, the WCCA sent them to the Rowher Incarceration Camp in Arkansas. After the War, Chizu and Shiro moved to the Southside, where they live today.

The WRA built Rohwer, the easternmost camp, and nearby Jerome Camp in the Jim Crow South. Jim Crow refers to legal segregation and discrimination, particularly in the South.

Jim Crow isn't an actual Southerner. A Caucasian actor named Thomas Dartmouth Rice, based in New York City, began performing in blackface, wearing shabby clothing and emulating the stereotypical slow-moving demeanor of a lazy enslaved man he claimed to have observed. He titled his racist song-and-dance act "Jump, Jim Crow."

New Yorkers loved his act. Blackface minstrel shows became a common form of musical theater. Jim Crow became associated with legalized racial segregation.

Arkansas Governor Homer Adkins opposed the Rowher Camp in his state. He agreed after being assured that Caucasian soldiers would hold the incarcerees under armed guard and that the WRA would transport the Japanese out of Arkansas after the War.

Rohwer is in Desha County, 12 miles northeast of McGehee and 110 miles southeast of Little Rock. It's in a forested lowland within the Mississippi River floodplain, with Jerome Camp 27 miles away.

During the Great Depression, the newly established Farm Security Administration (FSA) purchased unproductive farmland from struggling farmers and resettled them on more productive group farms. The WRA purchased the 10,000 acres from the FSA in 1942, and the Army Corps of Engineers built the Camp. The FSA preceded what is now the Farmers Home Administration within the USDA.

Rowher had a large population of school-age children, similar to the other camps. Nearly 90 instructors taught more than 2,000 students from kindergarten through high school. WRA wanted to hire Caucasian teachers from the local community.

The federal teachers earned more than twice the average salary of Arkansas teachers. To avoid luring too many local teachers to Rowher, the WRA agreed to a quota system that limited hiring to one or two teachers per school district.

Spectator sports such as softball, baseball, basketball, and football entertained Rowher incarcerees. The Camp's softball teams drew up to 2,000 fans per game.

The Issei Recreation Department produced popular variety shows that drew audiences of 5,000. The traveling revue visited different blocks over several days.

The Camp's entertainment included audience participation in the Obon Festival's *bon odori* folk dancing. The Japanese American version evolved from o*dori* nembutsu, a popular Buddhist chant and dance dating back to the 8th century.

The timing of the Japanese *Bon* Festival is based on the lunar cycle and, later, on the Western solar calendar. Japan celebrates the *Bon* Festival from early to mid-August. During this time, families reunite, honor their ancestors, visit cemeteries, and clean gravesites.

Bon odori is a circle dance in which participants of all ages move to the music and the rhythmic beat of *daiko* (drums). Daiko come in various sizes. Players use bachi (sticks) of different sizes to play the *daiko*. A *yagura* stand is the perch for the ō *daiko* (big drum).

Rohwer Camp incarcerees created unique *kobu* (natural-wood sculptures). Artists scoured Rohwer's swampy terrain for hardwood limbs from oak, hickory, elm, and cypress. Artisans crafted hand-polished pieces for display.

****

Toward the end of the block, a business owner named Mr. M.S. Jow opened the Continental Supply Company at 517 W. 17th St., across from the pool hall. He specialized in imported food and sundries from Japan. He and Mr. T.S. Okana owned the Bon Ton Café, a block south at 531 W. 16th St. The Okanas adopted the name Bon Ton, the name of a well-known department store.

Wortham Machine eventually took over the buildings at 515 and 517. The Dinneens purchased the lots, which are now part of their Nishigawa Neighborhood Lotus townhouse development.

At the end of the block, Tetsu Takahashi, the Kubota family, and Fred Futa rented apartments near 520. Fred, the son of Chizu Futa and Shiro Ogasawara, played baseball for the Cheyenne Nisei team.

All that remains at the end of the 500 block, where the City Café once stood, is a parking lot. The Cheyenne Historic Preservation Board required the Dinneens to erect an information sign about the Japanese community that once thrived there.

9

The 400 Block: The California Fish Market and Bake

The California Fish Market and Baker's Place anchored the vibrant 400 block of West 17th Street. Beginning in 1920, Itsuo and Kamo Hashimoto owned the California Fish Market at 402, on the east end. I knew about some Japanese-run businesses but don't remember setting foot in the California Fish Market.

Itsuo immigrated to the United States in 1905 and worked in the gold mines of California, Nevada, and Arizona. He moved to Cheyenne, where he worked for the UP Railroad in 1913 and married his "picture bride," Kamo.

In the early 20th century, immigrant workers in the United States, mainly from Asian countries, would choose a bride through a matchmaker in their home country. The matchmaker paired the bride and groom using photographs and family suggestions to find the best marriage combinations.

Japanese matchmaking is the subject of the 1995 movie *Picture Bride*, about a young Japanese woman who travels to Hawaii to meet her future husband at a pineapple plantation. His "dating" profile didn't quite match his current persona, and his bride couldn't afford to return to Japan.

Kamo operated the Fish Market while Itsuo worked for the railroad. Their two sons, Harry and Kaye, worked in downtown Cheyenne. Harry cooked at the UP Depot and the Plains Hotel. Laramieites knew him as the food services manager at UW. Because I lived in both Laramie and Cheyenne, and since "all Asians look alike," people often mistook me for a Hashimoto.

Kaye took pictures and became a prominent portrait photographer in Cheyenne. He opened his first studio downtown at 2300 Carey Ave. He took my high school graduation photo at his studio on East Pershing Boulevard.

Their sister, Grace, befriended my Auntie Rose. They both ended up in San Francisco. The two couples lived in adjacent apartments on Webster Street near Japantown. Grace married Toshiaki "Gump" Kubota. Rose married Haruo "Vince" Ichiyasu and raised my California cousins, Carolynn, Milton, Teresa, Leonard, and Walter.

****

Grace and Gump had two sons, Warren and Russell. Warren wrote an award-winning play about his Vietnam War-era childhood, *The Webster Street Blues*, set in 1972. Given Warren's background, the play's narrative is an introspective autobiography based on the Kubota and Ichiyasu families.

The story follows four Sansei friends hanging out in San Francisco's Japantown as they grapple with the angst of living in their Japanese world while existing within the dominant culture. The story ends with the characters, as adults, giving in to mainstream society without forgetting their roots.

California theater critics failed to grasp the story's familial subtexts and panned the play. Warren died shortly before the August 1987 San Francisco premiere. His brother, Russell, gave me permission to produce it. He sent a draft of the stage play, which I edited and produced at the Mercury Café in Denver.

Unfamiliar with Denver's theater production community, I had a tough time recruiting four actors to portray Japanese teenagers. The cast ultimately consisted of four pan-Asian 20-somethings with little or no acting experience: Keith Lin, Seraphina Lin (no relation), Casey China, and Andy Uehara. I found the four to be highly coachable and to rise to the occasion. The project raised disaster-relief funds following the 2011 earthquake in Japan.

The Hashimoto family sold the Market to Masuji and Yoshi Matsuyama in 1931. The Matsuyamas abandoned their farming near Fort Lupton, Colorado, and then moved to Cheyenne.

The Hashimotos reinvested the proceeds from the Fish Market sale and opened the Mikado Cleaners nearby at 1617 Pioneer Ave., north of the Dinneen Garage, between 16th and 17th. They operated the business until 1946, when they sold it to Tatsu and Marie Takahashi, who renamed it Miracle Cleaners. During the War, the Japanese community hall rented space on the second floor above the Mikado Cleaners and later near the California Fish Market.

Masuji worked as a railroad machinist at the UP roundhouse, where crews serviced and repaired locomotives. Yoshi tended the store. The UP fired Masuji in 1942.

The Matsuyama's oldest son, Bill, took over the business in 1932, shortly after he graduated from Cheyenne High School, now Central High. At the beginning of the War, Bill and his wife, Mary Arima, moved the business to 422 W. 17th St.

The couple lived in the upstairs apartment with their two sons, Brian and Jim, who are much older than me. I didn't know them, although Brian provided information and old photos for this story and my PBS documentary, *Beyond Heart Mountain*.

Mary ended up in Cheyenne via Worland in Wyoming's Big Horn Basin after her internment at the Tule Lake Camp in California, one of the first to open in May 1942. Tule Lake became the largest and most notorious of the 10, with a peak population of nearly 19,000 internees.

****

In February 1943, the Tule Lake Camp became the most infamous. In response to public and institutional outcry, the WRA and the U.S. Army distributed and required completion of the Statement of U.S. Citizenship of Japanese American Ancestry application form.

The WRA intended the Statement to serve as a symbolic declaration of loyalty to the United States. Camp prisoners, particularly U.S.-born Nisei, asserted their allegiance to the United States and distinguished themselves from those perceived as disloyal, even though the Statement conferred no legal status.

Initially, no formal parole process existed. Japanese Americans forcibly moved and imprisoned had no mechanism for release.

Over time, some internees could request parole or early release for specific reasons, such as poor health, the need to care for dependents outside the camps, or for educational purposes. However, the WRA closely scrutinized these requests and limited the number of approvals granted.

The WRA implemented work-release programs beginning in 1942. These programs allowed internees to leave the camps temporarily to work in agriculture, at local businesses, or as domestic laborers, often in regions facing labor shortages because of the War.

As the war progressed and the immediate threat of a Japanese invasion of the U.S. mainland diminished, the government reconsidered the necessity of incarcerating all Japanese Americans. However, the government wanted to ensure that any paroled prisoners could demonstrate loyalty to the United States.

Politicians faced criticism for the mass internment of Americans, from both within the government and from the public. The government recognized that few Japanese Americans posed a threat.

As more internees applied for work release, the WRA required internees 17 years of age or older, regardless of gender, to complete the Loyalty Questionnaire (formally known as the Application for Leave Clearance (Form 304A) and the Statement of Citizenship.

The authors conceived their questionnaire with little forethought, resulting in disharmony. Internee reactions ranged from refusing to complete the form to outright violence. The ensuing political and bureaucratic nightmares jolted the WRA into a reactionary mode.

Two questions designed to separate the "loyal" from the "disloyal" internees sparked the most controversy when respondents answered "no" to both. Those classified as disloyal became known as "No-No" boys. Conversely, the WRA classified those who answered "yes" to both questions as "loyal" and nicknamed them "Yes-Yes" boys.

Question #27. Are you willing to serve in the armed forces of the United States on combat duty wherever ordered?

Issei men, far older than the age allowed, couldn't serve in the military, and authorities construed a "no" answer as "disloyal." This question caused a split. Some draft-age Nisei men demonstrated their loyalty and enlisted, while others, most infamously the Heart Mountain Camp Fair Play Committee, resisted and ended up in prison.

Question #28. Will you swear unqualified allegiance to the United States of America, faithfully defend the United States from any attack by foreign or domestic forces, and forswear any form of allegiance or obedience to the Japanese emperor or any other foreign government, power, or organization?

The Issei also found this question problematic because federal law denied them U.S. citizenship and required them to renounce allegiance to the only country that recognized them as citizens. The Nisei hesitated to complete the Questionnaire because answering "yes" to both questions would contradict their parents' responses and appear disrespectful.

****

The Tule Lake Camp had the most internees who gave clear No-No responses. Those who responded with qualified yes answers and comments such as "when our family civil rights are restored" also received a disloyal designation.

The WRA classified 30 percent of the nearly 11,000 responses to Question #27 about military service as qualified "Yes" responses and deemed them disloyal. Another 16 percent responded to Question #28 about disavowing loyalty to Japan with qualified "Yes" answers. The WRA categorized them as "disloyal."

Authorities could fine violators $10,000, sentence them to 20 years in prison, or both. Authorities incarcerated the Tule Lake No-No boys in the county jails in Klamath Falls and Alturas.

Several months later, thousands of men, women, and children gathered for an impromptu meeting at the Tule Lake WRA administrative headquarters. The crowd came to support their elected representatives, the *daihyo sha kai* (negotiating group), who protested food shortages, poor working conditions, and the medical staff's bedside lack of manners.

A story circulated through the crowd about the death of an infant girl who fell into scalding water at the medical clinic. The attending physician refused to transfer the girl to a fully equipped hospital. The crowd received a report that a pack of young men entered the hospital and severely beat the doctor.

In response, the U.S. Army occupied Tule Lake, with tanks rolling through the barracks. Soldiers fired tear gas and aimed .50-caliber machine guns at bystanders. The Camp came under maximum-security martial law from November 1943 to January 1944. Camp workers added barbed-wire to a 16-foot-high fence.

News of the Tule Lake "riot" spread quickly, further fueling already high levels of anti-Japanese sentiment in the American public.

The WRA increased the number of guard towers to 28 by constructing six additional towers and deployed a battalion of an estimated 1,000 military police officers (MP) who brought armored cars and tanks. They pawed through private quarters in search of contraband and searched the entire Camp, hunting down the negotiating group leaders.

In 1943, the WRA converted Tule Lake into a Segregation Camp. Two-thirds of the transfers came from the other Camps. Administrators offered fewer daily recreational activities and imposed a curfew.

A loyal third of the Tule Lake population did not want to be reassigned, though the WRA dispersed some of them to other Camps for their safety.

The activist prison reminded me of Stalag Luft III in Germany, the German POW camp that imprisoned Allied military officers, fictionalized in *The Great Escape* (1963), a movie starring Steve McQueen about how the cunning POWs planned the most daring escape during the War in Europe.

Toward the end of the War in 1945, Tule Lake developed manufacturing businesses, including a *tofu* factory, a bakery, a furniture factory, a hog farm, and a slaughterhouse. It also had a shoe repair shop, a beauty shop, a fish market, a funeral home, and co-op stores that provided goods and services. The Camp had eight Buddhist churches, three Christian churches, and four dojos where internees practiced judo (the gentle way). *Judo* is a martial art that uses an opponent's force against them rather than brute strength.

A *dojo* is a formal training space for Japanese martial arts. The term derives from the Chinese Dao, meaning "the way" in the context of a path or course.

****

While he owned the Fish Market, Bill Matsuyama became a trusted leader in the Cheyenne Japanese community during the War. The community named him the liaison to federal and local law enforcement, which helped prevent any confrontations or uprisings in Cheyenne.

In 1951, the Matsuyamas sold the Market to my coattail uncle and aunt. Kaneichi "Carl" Kishiyama emigrated from Oredo, Japan, and settled near Scottsbluff, Nebraska. Lucy Shiyomura grew up in Lucerne, Colorado, and worked in Denver to earn extra income to support her family.

Their parents served as matchmakers, arranging for Carl and Lucy to meet. Two days later, they married. The newlyweds later farmed near Meridan in eastern Laramie County before moving to

Cheyenne. The family lived above the Fish Market with their children, Carol Lou, Jeanne, and Lucy, and their brother, Larry.

I didn't know Larry very well because several years separated us. One time, though, I stopped at the Summit Rest Area and Visitor Center between Cheyenne and Laramie. I recognized Larry climbing off of his motorcycle through my Eurovan windshield as he walked toward the parking area and waved him over.

"I'm in Boulder now," Larry said during our random meet-up by the 12-foot-tall Abraham Lincoln bust atop a 30-foot-high granite pedestal monument.

Robert Russin, an art professor at UW, sculpted and erected Honest Abe's bust in 1959 near Sherman Hill, overlooking the old U.S. Highway 30. After the Department of Transportation completed I-80, the Wyoming Highway Department moved the monument to its current location.

Russin gained his initial notoriety as a New Deal artist. He has two sculptures at the U.S. Post Office in Evanston, Illinois. I produced a PBS documentary, New Deal Artist Public Art Legacy (2018), that featured Russin and his work and aired on the Wyoming Public Broadcasting System (PBS).

Larry and I agreed to meet in Boulder. We traded services, with me digitizing some of his martial arts video recordings in exchange for carpentry work. Larry passed away before he could build the flower box.

His sister Jeanne married Uncle Jake, who owned Pioneer Printing at 514 W. 19th St. The company also carried other paper products. Jeanne and her sister Carol Lou delivered paperware, such as napkins and cups, to area restaurants.

Jake and his partners sold out around the time digital printing took off. The newly configured business moved out of downtown but failed to gain traction. After 148 years in business, Pioneer Printing closed in 2018.

Jake and Jeanne had two daughters, my cousins Alison and Leslie. They are the only O'Hashi/Ohashi and Sakata family members living in Cheyenne. Jake and my dad are the two siblings who use the O'Hashi spelling.

Alison is a psychologist, and Leslie operates a Pilates business and the nonprofit Body Lines Dance Studio, for which Wyoming Governor Matt Mead presented her with an art award in 2017 in recognition of her work in adaptive dance for youth with mental and physical disabilities.

My dad's youngest brother, Jake, gave an interview to the local newspaper in 1990. He recalls the Federal Bureau of Investigation (FBI) searching their home. According to the article, agents confiscated the hunting rifles and checked the radio to see whether it had shortwave capabilities.

Jake's taste in music rubbed off on me. Radios in all the family homes played easy-listening music on KFBC instead of pop tunes on KRAE.

He listened to Burt Bacharach, a prolific pop composer in the 1960s. He collaborated with lyricist Hal David, and together they wrote several hits for Dionne Warwick, including "This Guy's in Love with You," which topped the charts in 1968.

My taste in music differed from that of my peers. I attribute that to my being "planned." Mom and Dad had been married for seven years before I came along. My peers had parents much younger than mine and listened to rock-and-roll, whereas my folks liked Big Band-era music.

While all my friends listened to the Beatles' record albums, I chose Herb Alpert, Frank Sinatra, and Andy Williams. When I'm in the car by myself, which is most of the time, my Bacharach mix is the most played, truth be told.

After the Kishiyamas left the seafood business in 1955, the location became Ace Billiards, Dunbar's Recreation, and Geeche's Pawn Shop before being vacant in 1961.

Carl Kishiyama stayed downtown and worked as a custodian at Stockgrowers Bank. Lucy became a well-known florist for most of her career.

****

John A. "Johnny" Baker, a former Cheyenne police officer, owned a bar and boarding house at 416 and 418 W. 17th St. As early as 1922, Aikichi Kake, Sami Yoshimura, Kambe, and Yoshio Nomura occupied the boarding house above 416, which had previously housed the Walter Davis Barber Shop.

According to Brian Matsuyama, after his family moved out of the California Fish Market apartment, they lived next door to Baker, near the West 17th Street Japanese community.

"He was a good neighbor," Brian recalled. "I was young and didn't know him very well. I remember he had this bushy hair."

All I've found out about Baker is that his family keeps a nice headstone in Lakeview Cemetery, where he, his wife, and his mother lie buried.

The Cheyenne City Directory first mentions Baker in 1926. Baker's Bar reportedly integrated in response to more Americans owning automobiles and becoming more mobile. *The Negro Motorist Green Book* (The Green Book) travel guide listed restaurants, bars, lodging, and services where traveling African Americans and other non-Whites, including Japanese Americans, could safely eat, drink, stay, and receive services during the era of racial segregation.

Victor Hugo Green, a New York City letter carrier, authored *The Green Book,* published annually from 1936 to 1966 and eventually expanded its coverage from New York City to continental North America.

Advertisements and subscriptions supported *The Green Book.* According to a note at the front of the publication, the editors compiled many of the listings by word of mouth, and no one told the book about Baker's Place.

Miyamoto family members say that African American enlisted men from Fort Warren, including Private First Class (PFC) Sammy Davis, Jr., regularly patronized the Bar during the War.

Typical of the time, Davis Jr. experienced high levels of racial prejudice while in the service. African Americans considered Baker's Place safe. In various TV talk-show interviews, Davis Jr. has fond recollections of one of his sergeants who helped him become a better reader, a skill that later proved important as he built a career as an A-list entertainer.

The 1950s and 1960s *editions of the Green Book* listed a few Westside businesses as safe places: The Barbeque Inn at 622 W. 20th St. and the Minnehaha Motel (now the Firebird) on East Lincolnway at Logan Avenue.

The Green Book listed two Cheyenne tourist homes. A tourist home functioned like a bed-and-breakfast. Mrs. L. Randall at 612 and Mrs. M. Hermann at 621 W. 18th St. offered spare rooms or apartments in their private homes for travelers. My father's childhood home occupied the same block at 620 W. 18th St., and it is now a vacant lot.

If you want to get a feel for the world of segregation, watch the Oscar-winning movie *The Green Book* (2018). It's about an African American concert pianist, Dr. Don Shirley (Mahershala Ali), and his racist Caucasian driver, Tony Lip (Viggo Mortensen), as they navigate a concert tour through the segregated South. Through their association, both men learn more about themselves and become more accepting of one another.

The 18th Amendment to the U.S. Constitution prohibited "intoxicating liquors." Wyoming eventually ratified it in 1919, becoming the last state in the Rocky Mountain West to go "dry" in 1920. By then, the Bar's name no longer referenced alcohol. Baker changed the name to John Baker Billiards in 1932, John Baker Soft Drinks in 1934, and John Baker Beer Parlor in 1938. In 1950, he called the bar Baker's Place.

Tomizo "Bill" Miyamoto moved from Denver to Cheyenne around 1939 to begin a partnership with Johnny. He moved his family into the apartment at 418, where he and his wife, Hatsuye, raised their three boys, Ted, Bill (Doc), and Tom, the eldest, who graduated from Manual High School in Denver. He excelled in wrestling and baseball at UW.

Interested teams chose not to risk drafting a Japanese player. World War II squelched Tom's chances of playing professional baseball. He joined the Wyoming Nisei All-Star baseball team, which played throughout Wyoming, Nebraska, and northern Colorado.

Instead of pursuing a sports career, Tom joined his brothers and worked with their father and Johnny Baker to manage the bar. The three brothers bought out Baker and operated the business as Tomi's Bar and Lounge.

Tom eventually married Californian Connie Yashiro. The Yashiros owned a grocery store, which they abruptly closed when the WCCA sent her family to the Pomona Assembly Camp.

In May 1942, the Pomona Camp cost more to construct than the other 14 Assembly Camps, at a little over $1.0 million, because few buildings existed on the Los Angeles County Fairgrounds, about 30 miles east of downtown Los Angeles, and the only camp that had a perimeter fence topped with barbed-wire.

That summer, the Pomona population peaked at around 5,400. The detainees originated mainly from Los Angeles, San Francisco, and Santa Clara counties.

Despite operating for only three months, construction workers built 309 housing barracks across eight buildings. These included combined bathroom, shower, and laundry facilities. Each building also included mess halls and kitchens.

The Pomona Camp provided 36 communal shower and latrine buildings. Detainees wore *geta* (Japanese clogs) to keep their feet off the concrete floors and avoid exposure to the fungus that causes athlete's foot. Soon, a small *geta*-making industry thrived.

The U.S. Army imposed a curfew requiring detainees to remain indoors from 10:30 p.m. to 6:00 a.m., later tightened to 9:30 p.m. The WCCA prohibited and confiscated Japanese-language publications. Internees submitted notices written in Japanese, accompanied by an English translation, to the Camp Director for approval before posting them.

A detainee could request a pass to visit in a fenced-off zone at the Camp's far west end between 3:00 p.m. and 5:00 p.m. Other camps adopted Pomona's efficient visitor pass system.

As with all short-term assembly camps, a full recreation program included sports leagues and games, such as bridge tournaments. The detainees organized the activities.

They organized and taught classes in ikebana (flower arranging), woodworking, sewing, and band and orchestra. The American Friends Service Committee (Quakers) donated 1,700 books to the Pomona Camp library.

Detainees demonstrated their patriotism and supported the War effort by collecting money from others to purchase defense stamps and war bonds. On Veterans Day, they raised additional funds by selling small artificial poppies.

Unlike other assembly camps, Pomona did not have a comprehensive school program. However, a temporary school in two recreation halls held classes after regular hours. Administrators enrolled children ages four to 10 on a voluntary basis.

The Camp Director had to approve the use of the Japanese language in church services held in two barracks, with Catholic, Protestant, and Buddhist services each week. The required space doubled by June to accommodate 2,700 detainees. The Camp opened a small store that sold sundries, including candy, cigarettes, soft drinks, and toiletries.

Camp administrators assigned 1,600 detainees jobs across the compound. Some detainees worked in postal operations, saving the WCCA money.

Connie worked in paperwork processing before being assigned to the Heart Mountain Camp. She applied for parole and eventually moved to Denver, as did Mrs. Honkawa, who left Heart Mountain to work in Chicago.

Connie met Tom in Denver after the WRA approved her work release in 1944. They married and had three sons, Glenn and twins Ron and Marty. I met Glenn and Ron for the first time at a recent Miyamoto family gathering. Marty, a popular schoolteacher in Rawlins and later in Parker, Colorado, died in 2008.

Brother Bill "Doc" Miyamoto completed his optometry degree after returning from combat. He married Margaret "Marge" Makino while in school in Chicago. They had a daughter, Linda, who moved to Colorado, where she served a term as the Boulder County Clerk and Recorder. She recently passed away.

The WRA sent Marge to the Tule Lake Camp and later relocated her to Camp Amache in southeastern Colorado after Tule Lake became a militarized, high-security Segregation Camp for dissident internees.

The third Miyamoto brother, Ted, and his wife, Yoshi Ogata, had two children, Terie and Steve, who are older than me. Terie and I became better acquainted when I interviewed her for my *Beyond Heart Mountain* documentary. She worked for the phone company through its various name changes and retired in the Denver area.

The WRA reassigned Yoshi to the Minidoka Incarceration Camp in Idaho around the time a parole board approved her release. She later moved to Minneapolis, where she met Ted.

The Minidoka Camp comprised 44 residential blocks and more than 600 buildings, housing a peak population of over 7,300. Located 16 miles east of Eden, Idaho, in Jerome County on the Snake River Plain of south-central Idaho, and 20 miles northeast of Twin Falls, the camp housed incarcerees from Oregon, Washington, and Alaska who arrived in August 1942.

The WRA approved the Minidoka Camp site on BoR property, where the Miller-Gooding and Northside canal systems supplied irrigation water to the arid agricultural lands. The camp's configuration differed from the other camps, with building layouts that followed the bends of the North Side Canal rather than a perpendicular grid.

The BoR assumed internees would provide an inexpensive labor force to build irrigation canals and laterals. Instead, most worked in local fields because of labor shortages caused by the war effort. Some local farmers set aside their prejudice and hired internees to help with the harvest.

Camp tensions ran high at Minidoka when the WRA required internees to complete the loyalty questionnaire. In 1944, law enforcement arrested 38 men for draft evasion.

To ensure their safety, the WRA transferred nearly 2,000 Yes-Yes Japanese from the turbulent Tule Lake Camp to live among the highly compliant Minidoka internees.

****

A few other Asian-owned businesses thrived on the 400 block of West 17th Street. In 1922, Takamatsu Matsushima, born in Kumamoto, Japan, in 1887, opened a barbershop at 408.

Although records are missing, Takematsu returned to Japan after the start of World War II and died there in 1944. His wife, Kikuyo Matsushima, kept the barbershop open until 1939. She also died in 1944. The family lived across the street at 415 W. 17th St.

Henry and Harry Wahl owned Wahl's Bicycle and Key Shop, which opened at 408 in 1942. Wahl's had the local Schwinn dealership. The store became a central gathering point for kids from all over town. I enjoyed going into Wahl's when my dad needed to copy keys. I browsed around at the bikes.

My parents couldn't afford a Schwinn. Santa brought me my first bicycle, a blue one that girls rode. It didn't have the top tube. Danny Shipley, our across-the-alley neighbor who worked for my dad at the Coke plant, restored the bike.

Unsurprisingly, my friends ridiculed me for riding a girl's bike. After being socially ridiculed, I wanted a more masculine Stingray modeled after chopper-style motorcycles.

Baby Boomer biker movies gained popularity, beginning with *The Wild One* (1953), starring Marlon Brando, who leads one of two rival gangs that terrorize a small town. In *The Wild Angels* (1966), a Hell's Angel member, Bruce Dern, has his chopper stolen, and Peter Fonda and Nancy Sinatra help track down the thieves.

I didn't know or care much about motorcycles, but Danny and his friend Verlin liked fast cars and Harleys. They built me a red Stingray, the customized foot-pedaled version of a bad-boy motorcycle with a banana seat, high handlebars, and a knobby back tire.

That bike served me well around the neighborhood until I had to ride it to junior high school. I later rode a full-size Montgomery Ward Hawthorne three-speed, which made more sense for longer trips. Although I rode a Cushman scooter in Lander, I didn't get into motorcycles. I rode an Aprilia Mojito scooter that I recently traded in for an electric scooter in Boulder. I sold that and am now researching electric bicycles.

Several businesses preceded Wahl's 408, including the Shamrock Café, Niven's Café, Webb's Café, and Wheel of Fortune. Recently, several retail stores have moved into 408. The storefront currently sells antiques and furniture. At press time, yet another business may be occupying the space.

Continuing west, the Mikado Restaurant occupied 420 W. 17th St. from 1910 to 1920. The restaurant later became the Lee Wung, presumably serving Chinese food, and through 1938 operated as the Manila Café, likely Filipino. A restaurant in the 100 block, called the Shanghai and across from the Mayflower Café and Tavern, later became the Valencia.

I produced a short film titled *On the Trail: Jack Kerouac in Cheyenne* (2010) and speculated that Sal Paradise met a Latina food server at the Valencia during Wild West Days (aka Cheyenne Frontier Days) when he stopped in Cheyenne one night.

My latest book, *What the Morning Brings* (2026), is an adaptation of Ernest Hemingway's *The Sun Also Rises*, which entered the public domain in 2022. I shifted the setting from post-World War I Paris to Boulder. Instead of traveling to Pamplona, Spain, and a bullring, my characters head to Cheyenne for the Wild Prairie Stampede, where they take part in a deadly bull ride.

The immigrant workforce from Japan, China, and Mexico maintained the railroads, thereby accelerating westward settlement. Japanese families lived on West 17th Street to be near their downtown jobs.

Workers in the Japanese neighborhood could walk to the UP and CB&Q railroad yards. Jitsuzu Tani came to the United States in 1916. His soon-to-be wife, Haruyo Tsukichi, arrived two years later with her mother. The two married in Colorado and farmed until 1926, when they moved to Cheyenne.

Jitsuzu went to work at UP, and Haruyo managed the City Café rooming house. When the War broke out, the railroad laid off Jitsuzu. They both worked odd jobs until retiring in 1960.

10

Walking to the Railroad

The railroad is important to my story because maintaining the transportation infrastructure became a livelihood for Asians in Wyoming, including Grandpa Sakata.

Approximately 12,000 Chinese laborers, primarily employed by the Central Pacific Railroad, helped build the Transcontinental Railroad's western segment across the challenging Sierra Nevada Mountains. Without Asian labor, the UP wouldn't have been able to complete the monumental project in 1869.

Chinese laborers faced significant discrimination after the Transcontinental Railroad's completion. The Chinese Exclusion Act of 1882 led to their deportation or unemployment.

None of my relatives helped build the railroad, but they joined the crews that maintained it. Grandpa Sakata transferred around Wyoming, retired in Douglas after 43 years, and then moved to Cheyenne.

He lived to be 103 and attributed his longevity to a shot of Old Grand Dad and a Coors beer with dinner. He lived quite a life, witnessing the Wright Brothers' first airplane flight and humans setting foot on the moon.

The Transcontinental Railroad made mass transportation easier for settlers seeking their fortunes on the western frontier as the United States population rapidly expanded across tribal lands.

I doubt my grandfather gave much thought to the Native Americans killed or displaced by westward expansion. Another revised historical tidbit: the dominant culture justified tribal genocide as necessary to promote the American Way.

It's still amazing to me that individuals and families risked trekking thousands of miles on foot, by horse and wagon, from points east to Wyoming, seeking different lives.

****

My maternal grandparents emigrated from Japan as typical immigrants who arrived by steamship in the Pacific Northwest. My grandfather, Jusaburo "Joe" Sakata, born in 1879, had a close relationship with his father. At age six, he lost his mother.

As a young adult, he and three friends chopped and gathered firewood. They had deep conversations about the merits of moving to the United States. They had heard about the good quality of life and steady jobs.

It would be a new start. In January 1900, he left the stability of his family behind and stepped onto American soil in Seattle, Washington. He traveled to Nashua, Montana, and worked for the Great Northern Railroad before working for the UP and the Southern Pacific in Washington, California, and Nevada.

Grandpa found a better, more prosperous life in the United States. Eastward and northward expansion from Asia and Latin America aren't typically associated with "Manifest Destiny." I've wondered what the United States would be like today if West Coast growth had been more prevalent.

The *New York Democratic Review* newspaper editor John O'Sullivan first used the phrase "Manifest Destiny" in 1845. A rift grew among Americans following the annexation of Texas. Texas not only provided vast territory for more settlers to live in but also meant that more non-Whites would become United States citizens.

O'Sullivan urged the country to unite as it expanded westward to accommodate an ever-growing population. Between 1800 and 1860, the U.S. population grew from 5.0 million to 30 million. Immigration and high birth rates fueled this growth.

Early American colonists, including President Thomas Jefferson, believed that God had intended White people to take over the entire continent from coast to coast. The Jefferson administration's 1803 purchase of Louisiana from France nearly doubled America's size.

President Andrew Jackson legalized the displacement of Native Americans when he signed the Indian Removal Act of 1830, which displaced tribal members from the southern United States to federal lands in the newly acquired territories west of the Mississippi River in exchange for their fertile ancestral lands.

The forced exile became known as the "Trail of Tears" and included members of the *tsalagi* (Cherokee), *mvskoke* (Muscogee), *oconee* (Seminole), *chikashsha* (Chickasaw), and *chahta* (Choctaw) nations.

President Abraham Lincoln accelerated the U.S. government's expansionist philosophy when he signed the Pacific Railway Act on July 1, 1862. The 1862 Act created and subsidized the UP and Central Pacific railroads, granting one Section of land on each side of the track for every mile of track laid, totaling 6.6 million acres in the Wyoming Territory.

A railroad Section measured one-half mile wide. The land grant created a checkerboard pattern of odd-numbered rectangular Sections on each side of the line. The railroad companies could then sell the land to help finance the construction of the railroad.

The 1864 Pacific Railroad Act retroactively doubled the land grant to two Sections per mile, adding 3.3 million more acres in the Wyoming Territory alone. The land grant also included mineral rights beneath these lands.

The U.S. Congress also loaned the railroads $27 million, amortized over 30 years at six percent interest. That amount covered half the cost of construction.

The UP and New York financiers sold $11 million in stocks and $30 million in bonds to East Coast and European investors, including merchants who made their fortunes trading in China, Civil War-era investors, and European nobility.

The U.S. government viewed the wars against the indigenous tribes in the 1860s as consequences of Manifest Destiny. The conflicts pitted Native Americans, a new enemy reclaiming their conquered homelands and defending what remained, against migrating settlers seeking new places to live. The railroads enabled easier westward expansion, and the U.S. military protected settlers and railroads while fending off Native Americans.

Native American tribes entered into many treaties with the U.S. government, including the Treaty of Fort Laramie, Wyoming, approved in 1851 among the United States and several Plains and Northern Rocky Mountain tribes. The treaty allowed roads and military troops stationed along the Oregon Trail to protect migrating settlers.

Construction funds ran short as the rails extended into Utah in early 1869. Unexpected obstacles included blowing out additional road cuts, feeding mules that graded rights-of-way across rugged terrain, and extra costs for loggers chopping trees for track ties.

Hacks cut railway ties from trees and laid them perpendicular to the tracks to keep the rails the same width along the route. More workers had to be hired to spike the rails across the high plains of southern Wyoming, increasing labor costs.

Despite the multi-million-dollar investment, underfunding of the railroad project delayed the ceremony by a few days. The train carrying UP Vice President Thomas Durant and his entourage pulled into the tiny Wyoming town of Piedmont, near the Utah border. Piedmont had a stop with a roundhouse for train maintenance, a water tank to replenish steam engines, a telegraph office, and a few businesses serving the railroad crews.

Over 400 laid-off tie hacks had waited three months for their back pay and hijacked the Durant Special on May 6, 1869. The mob greeted Durant and switched his car onto a sidetrack, where they chained his luxurious train car to the tracks. He finally relented after a futile attempt to regain his freedom. The men's pay soon arrived from UP headquarters in New York.

The UP route linked the United States from coast to coast at Promontory, Utah. Stanford University founder Leland Stanford drove the final Golden Spike into the track on May 10, 1869, to celebrate the completion of the Transcontinental Railroad. Photographs of the event excluded Chinese workers.

Little remains of Piedmont today, but the town bustled 10 miles southwest of Evanston during the railroad boom. In 1868, Mormon pioneer Moses Byrne built five beehive-shaped kilns to produce charcoal for Utah steel smelters. Charcoal is nearly pure carbon and, when heated, produces the high temperatures needed to smelt iron ore.

A timber supply from nearby Uinta Mountains pine forests made Piedmont an ideal location for charcoal production. Workers loaded the kilns with wood, fired them up, and sealed them so the fire smoldered slowly for several days until only charcoal remained. The Piedmont charcoal kilns are now part of the Wyoming State Parks and Historic Sites (Wyoming State Parks) system.

****

By 1908, my grandfather had left California for Wyoming. For the next nine years, he worked for the UP in Hanna, Dana, and other sections across Nebraska and Iowa.

He appreciated the stability of 1917 Wyoming and began working for the CB&Q Railroad in Cheyenne. He joined a maintenance crew and later became the Powder River Section Supervisor.

Grandpa took leave and returned to Japan to marry my grandmother, Toki Iwasaki. After a year away, he and his bride returned to Hot Springs County, Wyoming, where he started his family. They had three children: my mother, Sumiko; her middle brother, Tokinori (George), born in Thermopolis, where he supervised the railroad section; and their oldest sister, Hisako, in Bishop, Wyoming.

My grandfather always had a job, even during the Great Depression. Unlike other railroads that fired their Japanese employees after Pearl Harbor, the CB&Q kept my grandfather on the job.

His supervisors viewed him as a reliable boss in the interior of Wyoming and respected by his Mexican *traquero* gang. Finding a replacement would be more trouble than risking cultural backlash.

By then, my grandparents had settled in the Orpha Section, across the road from Fort Fetterman in Converse County, Wyoming. Their three children graduated from Converse County High School in Douglas.

Mom's sister, Hisako, graduated from college, the first in the family to do so. She later moved to Washington, DC, where she worked at the U.S. Department of Health, Education, and Welfare (HEW), now the Department of Health and Human Services and the Department of Education. She retired from her civil service career as an Environmental Protection Agency (EPA) Budget Analyst. After retiring, she returned to Cheyenne and became her parents' caretaker.

Brother George upheld his family's tradition and worked for the CB&Q in Alliance, Nebraska. He raised his family there in a converted train boxcar, equipped with the amenities of a mobile home. I didn't visit them, but I saw pictures.

The CB&Q, the Spokane, Portland, and Seattle Railway, the Great Northern Railway, and the Northern Pacific Railway merged in 1970 to form the Burlington Northern (BN). When Grandpa Sakata turned 99, a PR representative from BN attended the birthday party and presented him with a commemorative pin. While living in

Gillette, I ran into a college friend, Steve Plummer, who worked for BN and lived in a converted boxcar.

BN acquired the Atchison, Topeka, and Santa Fe Railway in 1996 and formed the Burlington Northern and Santa Fe Railway, which is still in operation as the BNSF, owned by Warren Buffett's Berkshire Hathaway, a multinational holding company.

Uncle George had undiagnosed PTSD. My mom described him as "shell-shocked." He chain-smoked menthol cigarettes. Black soldiers in the 92nd Infantry Division showed him how to open the bottom of the pack to keep the filter tips clean.

After returning from the War, he refused to sleep on the ground again. He transported a fully equipped camper, complete with fishing tackle, in the bed of his pickup.

George married his Caucasian wife, Perry, in Kansas. They had two daughters, Tracy Ann and Tami Jo, and a son, Robert. We keep in touch on Facebook.

When Grandpa Sakata retired in Cheyenne, he and Grandma lived in a quiet neighborhood a few blocks from the state capitol building. They lived within walking distance of Brannen's grocery store. As long as I knew them, they didn't drive. My mom or dad drove them around.

Mayor Bill Nation lived across the street with his large family. Grandpa landscaped his manicured yard with bonsai-style trees. A block away, he did some paid gardening for retired Judge Bloom.

My grandmother's alteration business in their spare bedroom led her to return to Japan, where she became a master Japanese *ningyo* (doll maker). She designed and sewed her beautiful, to-scale doll clothing. My sister ended up with all the dolls. They are museum/art gallery-quality.

Wyoming Secretary of State Thyra Thomson became one of her regular customers. She worked two blocks away in the Capitol. Over the years, she became a family friend. She and her sons lived a few blocks to the east and south, on East 22nd Street and Warren Avenue.

Thyra and her husband, Keith, had become highly popular in Wyoming. Keith, a three-term Congressman, died of a heart attack a month after taking office as a U.S. Senator in 1960. Governor J.J. Hickey appointed himself to complete the remainder of Thomson's term. In 1962, Wyoming elected Thyra to her first of six terms as Wyoming Secretary of State.

After her sons left home, Thyra moved to the Cole Addition and lived a block from us on Windmill Road. I reconnected with her son, Bruce, through our mutual connections in the Wyoming arts and culture community.

Grandma also studied *ikebana* and, in a class by herself, won ribbons for her flower arrangements at the Laramie County and Wyoming State fairs.

As a junior high school student, I learned a few basics of flower arranging from my grandmother. We designed arrangements together when the Laramie County Fair came around. The fair had a men's category. I had the distinction of being the defending men's blue-ribbon winner until we moved to Laramie in 1973.

We gathered at their house during CFD near Downtown Cheyenne. We took a shortcut up the back steps, through the rotunda, and down the front steps to the head of the parade in front of the state capitol.

My grandparents didn't ride the train after Grandpa retired, but he kept me interested in his railroad life. I inherited two of his railroad lanterns: one battery-operated and the other kerosene-fueled. Working for the railroad never crossed my mind, even though I knew it would have been steady, well-paying work. I'm surprised Grandpa didn't offer more encouragement when he gave me his "work hard" speech when I went off to college.

The UP continued to provide passenger service through Wyoming during my childhood. My family took the train to Salt Lake City. My parents allowed my sister and me to ride the train by ourselves. My parents entrusted me with a wad of money for the first time, much larger than my weekly allowance.

The dining car provided full service to all passengers. I surprised myself by being able to read the menu and order food. I'd had better hamburgers before, but a steward in a white jacket and bow tie delivered the meal to the table.

We stopped in Rock Springs to stretch our legs. I turned around, and my sister had vanished. She eventually ended up at the ticketing area, where the railroad attendant reunited us. I don't recall whether I got in trouble, but it freaked me out.

Passenger rail service boomed, with 98 percent of intercity travelers using trains in 1916. Before World War II, amid increased competition from airlines, commercial buses, and automobiles, the railroad's market share fell to 67 percent. That share surged during the War, but in the 1950s, train travel fell to 34 percent.

By 1971, all but five of the 25 railroads had transferred their passenger service to the National Railroad Passenger Corporation, branded as "America's Track" and shortened to Amtrak.

Wyoming has always been a "pass-through" state, marked by the Transcontinental Railroad bringing business and settlers west, by beaten paths along which livestock companies drove their cattle herds and flocks of sheep to the north, and by the subsequent need for the protection provided by the U.S. Army.

11

The U.S. Army and the Pass-Through State

Why my immediate family stayed in Wyoming as long as they did remains a mystery to me, given that Wyoming has always been a pass-through state. My parents worked alongside all-Caucasian employees. After Pearl Harbor, Mom and Dad stuck it out, resentful of how people, from friends to strangers, treated them. They found solace in their families and the Japanese community on West 17th Street.

We could have moved from familiar Wyoming. Breaking into a new town elsewhere would have been difficult. We would still have been Japanese, no matter where we moved. My family often took quick day trips around Cheyenne to visit passing attractions.

The Lone Tree is a stop on westbound I-80 near Buford, en route to Laramie. I learned in my 4th-grade Wyoming history class that a pine cone became trapped in a crack in an enormous boulder, sprouted into a sapling, and has been growing since the 1870s. Over the years, railroad workers would pour day-old coffee onto the pine. The tree's growth eventually split the rock, which the Wyoming State Parks secured with a cable.

We took drives to Fort Laramie National Historic Site in eastern Wyoming, near Nebraska, where the U.S. government and Native American tribes signed the 1851 and 1868 treaties.

When we visited Mom's childhood home in Orpha, my family stopped at Fort Fetterman, the site of the Fetterman Massacre. Back then, nothing remained except a sign and the imagined scenes of Chief Red Cloud overrunning the Fort.

As my sister and I got older, our family took vacations across southern Wyoming to visit my relatives in Salt Lake City, Utah. We stopped at the sites of Army forts, now rest stops.

The UP stayed north and plotted its primary route through Cheyenne rather than Denver. That decision transformed Cheyenne from a dusty prairie town into a booming 19th-century center of commerce. The UP later paid to build a railroad line to Cheyenne.

As more settlers arrived, businesses sprang up to serve the growing population, necessitating U.S. Army protection.

****

Beginning at the eastern Wyoming border, the U.S. Army established Camp O.O. Howard, near Pine Bluffs, in 1885, as a temporary military encampment to protect the railway and its maintenance workers.

General Oliver Otis Howard won the Congressional Medal of Honor during the Civil War. The U.S. Army later deployed him to the West, where he became a decorated soldier who fought against Native Americans. Howard integrated freedmen (formerly enslaved people) into American society after the Civil War.

In 1867, the U.S. Army designated the Post on Crow Creek, a tributary of the South Platte River and the present-day location of Cheyenne, as the base for the 2nd U.S. Volunteer Cavalry, which included soldiers from Crook, Weston, and Sheridan counties in northeastern Wyoming.

When World War II ended, Grandma Ohashi opened the Highway Café on U.S. Highway 85, also known as the South Greeley

Highway, on the banks of Crow Creek, where my dad and I hiked around the sandstone cliffs above.

The U.S. Army renamed the post Fort David Allen Russell, honoring the Civil War general, killed in 1864 during the Battle of Opequon in the Shenandoah Valley of Pennsylvania. After his death on the battlefield, President Andrew Johnson nominated Russell for the rank of Major General retroactively in 1867.

Fort Russell protected the railroad settlement in the Dakota Territory, which the U.S. Army called "Cheyenne" after the Cheyenne tribe, closely allied with the Arapaho.

Brigadier General Grenville Dodge, who served in the Union Army during the Civil War, put Cheyenne on the map as an important railroad town in March 1868. He surveyed the 1,200-mile Transcontinental Railroad route from the Missouri River to Utah.

Dodge selected the Cheyenne location for the UP roundhouse maintenance yard for locomotive repair and later established a central passenger train depot, now listed on the National Historic Register.

Transient workers nicknamed Cheyenne "The Magic City of the Plains" because of its rapid growth to a population of 4,000. Local businesses provided the railroad with materials and supplies and entertainment for the workers, who had money but nowhere to spend it. By 1868, Cheyenne boasted brothels, gambling parlors, live theaters, and 70 bars.

A big tent called "Hell on Wheels" followed the boom and set up at the end of the tracks in Cheyenne, where patrons could down a shot of whiskey, try their luck at poker, and hire a prostitute.

Off-duty railroaders ordered *Sarsaparilla*, a Spanish word meaning "prickly vine (*Smilex ornata*) with little grapes," a patent medicine anecdotally credited with curing syphilis, which explains why the bars made the patent medicine available during the boom.

Over the years, root beer flavored with sassafras, an aromatic deciduous tree that grows mainly in the eastern United States, replaced *sarsaparilla.*

During CFD in the 1960s, the local Junior Chamber of Commerce Club (Jaycees) set up a large Hell on Wheels canvas tent along Crow Creek and later in Holliday Park. The Jaycees is a community service and leadership development organization for men and women ages 18 to 40.

Danny, my across-the-alley neighbor who built my red Stingray bike, joined the Jaycees. I worked at the Coke plant in the summer, helping my dad mix batches of sarsaparilla soda. The seasonal drink sold well at Hell on Wheels. I'm pretty sure Dad had no idea *sarsaparilla* would sell so well.

Despite unchecked rowdiness, the westward expansion of the railroad brought more settlers, which created a need for a stronger military presence in Cheyenne. The U.S. Army renamed Fort Russell as Fort Francis E. Warren (Fort Warren) in 1930.

During the Civil War, Francis E. Warren became a hero at the Battle of Port Hudson in Louisiana on May 27, 1863. John Wilkes Booth assassinated Lincoln in 1865. After Reconstruction, President Benjamin Harrison awarded Warren the Medal of Honor on January 30, 1891.

Warren served as Wyoming's first territorial governor in 1885 and as the state's first governor in 1890. He resigned after Wyoming elected him to the U.S. Senate. The Air Force assumed control of Fort Warren in 1948.

In 1866, the U.S. Army built Fort John Buford south of Laramie and east of the Laramie River to protect railroad workers and settlers traveling west along the Overland Trail. The Army later renamed it Fort Sanders in honor of General William P. Sanders, who died during the Civil War's Siege of Knoxville. The site is now home to the Cavalryman restaurant.

The ruins of a stone guardhouse and magazine remain. The Daughters of the American Revolution erected a commemorative monument in 1914. Frontierswoman Martha "Calamity Jane" Cannary stationed herself there in 1872 as a scout during the Indian Wars.

Cheyenne lost population to fast-growing Laramie by the winter of 1868 as the end of the tracks moved west, staying true to the boom-and-bust cycle. Crews laid rails to Laramie, but not before extending them over Sherman Hill in the Laramie Range at an elevation of 8,200 feet above sea level. Upon its completion a year later, in 1869, the line became the highest railroad point in the world.

Crews constructed a 125-foot-high, 1,400-foot-long bridge spanning Dale Creek west of Sherman Hill. The trestle became the highest along the UP route west of the Missouri River.

Fort Fred Steele, built in 1868, 90 miles west of Laramie, protected the railroad and settlers heading north to Montana along the Bozeman Trail. The Fort Steele settlement protected the railroad bridge across the North Platte, a shipping point for lumber and railroad ties cut from timber in Medicine Bow National Forest and floated down the North Platte to the railroad loading dock.

Major General Frederick Steele served in the U.S. Army during the Civil War, and historians credit him with capturing Little Rock and returning Arkansas to the Union.

The U.S. Army abandoned Fort Steele in 1886 as more businesses opened and settlers took up residence. The State of Wyoming restored the outpost, which is now part of Seminoe State Park.

Fort Rawlins, initially established in 1868 north of the current city of Rawlins, protected railroad workers. Civil War General John Aaron Rawlins, a longtime advisor to President Ulysses S. Grant, gave his name to the Fort and city.

In 1870, the U.S. Army moved the Fort to the north bank of the Timpanogos River, two miles east of Provo, Utah, to suppress growing Mormon insurrections.

President Grant appointed Rawlins Secretary of War. In 1869, Grant sent Rawlins to the Utah Territory, believing the dry climate would benefit Rawlins's tuberculosis, which took his life a few months later.

Grant ordered him to observe Mormon life, focusing on monitoring men who married multiple women. Rawlins returned to Washington, DC, and convinced Grant to adopt a hardline policy against the Mormons, particularly their polygamy doctrine.

Fort Bridger, established in 1843 by Jim Bridger and Louis Vasquez on the western edge of Wyoming, served as a trading post for the Pony Express, the Transcontinental Railroad in the 19th century, and the Lincoln Highway in the 20th century. Native American tribes also traded there.

Jim Bridger, a well-known scout, migrated west from Virginia and led many excursions across the western frontier. Bridger earned a reputation for mediating conflicts between Native Americans and settlers. *The Covered Wagon* (1923), about wagon trains heading from Missouri to Oregon, portrays Bridger (Tully Marshall) as a hard-living mountain man.

When the silent epic entered the public domain, I hired the Northern Arapaho Eagle Drum and the Boulder Symphony to compose and perform a contemporary soundtrack that tells the story from a tribal perspective. COVID-19 stalled the project in 2020. *The Arapaho Covered Wagon Redux* screened four years later.

Luis Vasquez, based in St. Louis and descended from a Spanish father and a French-Canadian mother, became a successful guide in his own right before partnering with Bridger.

Fort Bridger consisted of two log cabins, each about 40 feet long, with a fence for tying up horses. It became a military outpost in the late 1850s and is now a Wyoming State Park.

All the forts that protected the railroads and settlers across Wyoming have become state parks or historic sites and remain enduring reminders of the state's role during early westward expansion as a pass-through state.

During World War II, the U.S. government did not send federal, state, and local law enforcement to protect Japanese people passing through Wyoming, but rather to contain them.

12

Civil Disobedience

EO 9066 authorized the Secretary of War, Harry Stimson, and any military commander he designated to exclude any or all persons from prescribed military areas. The containment responsibilities also extended to local law enforcement agencies.

The Cheyenne Japanese community may have seemed normal and peaceful. However, federal authorities imposed travel restrictions on at least some Japanese because the military considered Fort Warren, west of Cheyenne, a strategic target.

I didn't know whether my parents or relatives had to report their whereabouts. On the other hand, maybe my parents didn't want me to know the FBI had them under house arrest. Carol Lou Kishiyama Hough, my coattail cousin, showed me a fistful of letters.

Her family had to notify the U.S. Attorney in Cheyenne about their travel more than 20 miles from home. They had family in Colorado. I knew my dad had filled out one of the forms because I recognized his handwriting. Any law enforcement officer could arrest a Japanese person if travel occurred without approved transit papers.

After Pearl Harbor, members of the Japanese community in Cheyenne came together, confident their patriotism would go unquestioned. Although I never discussed this with her, Auntie Hisako likely led the community organizers. She later became active in the JACL.

Her interest in national politics nurtured my campaign button hobby when she gifted me political memorabilia from one of her friends in DC, U.S. Congressional Representative Bob Kastenmeier (D-WI).

He served on the House Judiciary Committee, which began formal hearings for the impeachment inquiry into President Richard Nixon on May 9, 1974. The hearings culminated on July 27–30, 1974, when the Committee approved three articles of impeachment.

I added them to my Watergate political button collection and found them interesting because I had attended Nixon's inaugural ceremonies in January 1973.

In 1929, several established Nisei organizations merged in response to the Immigration Act of 1924. The JACL comprised the American Loyalty League in Fresno, the Seattle Progressive Citizens League, and the New American Citizens League, and the three groups joined forces in San Francisco.

The JACL held its first national conference in Seattle in 1930, where it began efforts to expand citizenship rights for Japanese and other Asian Americans otherwise ineligible for citizenship.

Several Cheyenne Japanese, including my aunt, worked with local leaders, such as Mayor Ed Warren, Governor Nels Smith, news media owners, and law enforcement officials. They published a resolution, signed by several Cheyenne Japanese, affirming their loyalty in the Wyoming Eagle and the *Wyoming State Tribune.* The two newspapers later merged into the WTE.

****

While civility prevailed among the local Japanese, U.S. Federal District Court Judge T. Blake Kennedy in Downtown Cheyenne presided over a high-profile case involving draft resisters from the Heart Mountain Camp.

In February 1944, a group of draft-eligible men formed the Heart Mountain Fair Play Committee, which drew 63 draft resisters to evening meetings in mess halls. The Committee did not wish to be perceived as disloyal to the United States or as pacifists. It set membership criteria: a man had to be a U.S. citizen, loyal to the United States, and willing to serve in the U.S. Army if the WRA reinstated his legal rights.

Meeting attendance grew as more men received orders to report for pre-induction. The resisters who refused to report for their physicals went about their lives behind the barbed-wire. The WRA prohibited organized meetings. U.S. Marshals stormed the Camp, arrested offenders, charged them with draft evasion, and eventually imprisoned them in the City of Cheyenne and Laramie County jails.

The Federal District Court in Cheyenne tried the 63 men and sentenced them to three years in prison. The younger men served their sentences at the McNeil Island Federal Penitentiary near Tacoma, Washington, while the older Issei men served theirs at the Leavenworth Federal Penitentiary in Kansas.

The U.S. 10th Circuit Court in Denver affirmed the defendants' convictions and sentences on appeal. The defendants served their jail terms and didn't return home until after the War in 1946.

The draft-evasion prosecution didn't include the elder Committee leaders. The Issei men didn't receive draft notices because of their ages. The U.S. Attorney charged the men with conspiracy to aid others in evading the draft. A federal district court jury convicted them in October 1944. A few months later, the federal court of appeals in Denver overturned their convictions on a technicality.

The military draft resistance efforts at the Heart Mountain Camp created a divide between the patriotic Japanese and those who supported civil disobedience.

President Harry Truman pardoned the 63 draft resisters after the War and recognized the injustice of the WRA and the unjust treatment of Japanese Americans.

The buck didn't stop with Truman.

****

In 1988, President Ronald Reagan signed the Civil Liberties Act. U.S. Representative Norm Mineta (D-CA), who interned at Heart Mountain Camp as a child, and U.S. Senator Alan Simpson (R-WY) sponsored the bill.

Simpson's Boy Scout troop from Cody visited the Camp, and the two met. They remained friends until Mineta's death in 2022.

Simpson and Mineta's legislation had its roots in a 1979 class-action lawsuit brought by the National Council for Japanese American Redress against the federal government on behalf of former camp incarcerees.

In 1980, U.S. Senator Daniel Inouye (D-HI), Representatives Robert Matsui (D-CA) and Spark Matsunaga (D-HI), and Mineta successfully urged Congress to establish the Commission on Wartime Relocation and Internment of Civilians to study the effects of incarceration and recommend reparations.

The Commission heard testimony from more than 700 former Japanese incarcerees, who recounted their experiences in incarceration camps and the subsequent discrimination after the War.

In 1983, the Commission reported its findings in a publication titled Personal Justice Denied, stating that the wartime displacement of Japanese Americans resulted from "race prejudice, war hysteria, and a failure of political leadership" and recommending monetary reparations for former incarcerees.

The 1988 report estimated that about 60,000 people were affected, mostly children who had grown up and survived their time in incarceration. Although President Ronald Reagan and Senate Republicans opposed increased federal spending, Reagan signed the bill into law in August 1988. The legislation included a formal apology and allocated $20,000 in reparations to each Camp survivor.

Despite the apology and reparations, American society still hasn't caught up to five centuries of exclusionary history.

13

Uncivil Unions

Poet Emma Lazarus wrote a sonnet in 1883, which she donated to an art and literary auction to raise funds to build the pedestal for the Statue of Liberty on Ellis Island. The last stanza reads:

"Keep, ancient lands, your storied pomp!" cries she
With silent lips. "Give me your tired, your poor,
Your huddled masses yearning to breathe free,
The wretched refuse of your teeming shore.
Send these, people experiencing homelessness,
Tempest-tost to me,
I lift my lamp beside the golden door!"

The New Colossus, by Emma Lazarus (1883)

Her sonnet rang true for European immigrants who agreed to hop into the melting pot of white cheese and didn't plan to marry outside their race. After the Transcontinental Railroad's completion, President Chester Arthur signed the Chinese Exclusion Act of 1882 into law, denying visas to Chinese immigrants for 10 years.

An anti-Chinese movement arose among the Caucasian workers because the UP redeployed its Chinese labor force to work for lower pay in the company's mines along the railway rights-of-way.

Labor-related racial tensions peaked in September 1885, when the Rock Springs Massacre in Wyoming killed 28 Chinese miners and destroyed 78 Chinese miners' homes.

****

The 1882 Exclusion Act made Japan another source of inexpensive labor. The U.S. Congress enacted the first widely restrictive Immigration Act of 1917 (1917 Act) in the name of national security during World War I. The 1917 Act required immigrants over 16 to demonstrate basic reading comprehension in their native language.

The 1917 Act excluded anyone born in a defined "Asiatic Barred Zone," except for Japanese and Filipinos, because the Japanese government had voluntarily limited emigration to the United States. The U.S. classified residents of its Philippine colony as U.S. citizens.

The West 17th Street neighborhood attracted many Japanese residents before 1917. Both sets of my grandparents immigrated to the United States, but their immigration contributed to the perception that immigration official had let too many Asians enter the country.

****

In 1924, Congress debated reauthorizing the 1917 Act, including the deeply ingrained quota system. While some wanted to increase the number of immigrants allowed, the agreed-upon plan lowered the quota from three to two percent of new foreign-born residents, based on the 1890 rather than the 1910 census, to further restrict immigration.

President Calvin Coolidge signed the Immigration Act of 1924 (1924 Act) into law. The subtext preserved the dominant cultural, racial, and ethnic homogeneity of the United States and suppressed the entry of a labor force willing to work for lower wages, eliminating competition with existing American workers.

The 1924 Act excluded Asian immigrants. The new provision contradicted Japan's voluntary emigration limits, which officials had informally observed since 1917. That change created tension between the U.S. government and Japan for the next 20 years.

Japan viewed the 1924 Act as an insult. As a rising world power, Japan had sought to improve relations with the U.S., but the law bred resentment.

In the late 1930s and early 1940s, as Japan expanded its empire in Asia, the United States, Great Britain, and the Netherlands imposed economic sanctions. These measures included embargoes on oil, steel, and other essential materials Japan needed for its war efforts in China and its imperial ambitions. The U.S. oil embargo in 1941 severely threatened Japan's ability to sustain its military operations.

Faced with economic oppression and diplomatic isolation, Japan felt cornered and believed it had limited options. American xenophobia, coupled with U.S. demands that Japan withdraw from China and other occupied territories, led to failed negotiations.

Japan believed that expanding its control in Southeast Asia, including the oil-rich Dutch East Indies (Indonesia), would be its best chance to secure the resources it needed, a prospect that concerned the Netherlands. Japanese military leaders believed this would provoke the U.S. Japan launched a surprise attack on December 7, 1941, to preemptively neutralize the U.S. Pacific Fleet based at Pearl Harbor.

The Immigration Act of 1924 significantly strained U.S.-Japan relations.

The U.S. Congress determined that rather than maintain good relations with Japan, it approved systemic oppression of Asians and the preservation of racial homogeneity in the United States.

The legislation criminalized Asian self-identity while continuing to favor immigrants from Northern and Western Europe. Would-be American citizens paid higher immigration taxes upon arrival. The 1924 Act gave immigration officials greater discretion to decide who to admit or exclude.

Further westward expansion, coupled with a more diverse citizenry from Southern and Eastern Europe, the Middle East, Latin America, and freed enslaved people, would mean that new citizens would dilute the dominant culture through their rights to representation in state and territorial legislatures and in the U.S. Congress.

****

Near the end of the 1943 session, the Wyoming State Legislature passed Senate File 24, the Wyoming Alien Land Act (Land Act). Governor Nels Smith signed the legislation, which prohibited land ownership by "aliens ineligible to citizenship." Two state senators representing Park and Washakie counties near the Heart Mountain Camp sponsored the Land Act.

Republican George Burke of Powell and Democrat J.A. Farlein of Worland sought to prevent Japanese relocated from the West Coast to the Camp from acquiring real estate in Wyoming. The bill excluded the Chinese from the law's provisions because China, a U.S. ally, fought its own battles against Japan. Penalties included a $5,000 fine, five years in prison, or both.

Ironically, early that week, lawmakers approved Senate Joint Resolution Number 1, which declared, "The people of the great State of Wyoming to join in a program of unity, to the end that all differences be laid aside in a spirit of mutual coordination of our efforts toward the one thing we all seek at this time: victory in the present War."

The 1924 Act and the Land Act explain why Japanese people owned no property on West 17th Street. The 1943 law remained on the books until February 2001, when State Representative Keith Goodenough of Casper introduced legislation to repeal the Land Act during Governor James Geringer's administration.

The Immigration and Nationality Act of 1965 (1965 Act), signed into law by President LBJ, abolished the national origin formula, shifting immigrant demographics to include more migration from Mexico, Africa, and Asia.

Subsequent immigration laws have focused on criteria other than quotas based on national origins, such as family reunification, employment skills, and refugee status.

The Immigration Act of 1990 increased the overall number of immigrants allowed into the U.S. and established the Diversity Visa Program, which provides visas to individuals from countries with historically low rates of immigration to the U.S.

The Illegal Immigration Reform and Immigrant Responsibility Act of 1996 introduced stricter enforcement measures, including enhanced border security and penalties for illegal immigration, but it did not reinstate national-origin quotas.

The Patriot Act (2001) and the Homeland Security Act (2002) addressed national security concerns after the September 11, 2001, attacks. They strengthened enforcement mechanisms but did not alter the fundamental immigration system established by the 1965 Act.

****

A longstanding state law in Wyoming prohibited interracial marriages, which forced Auntie Joan and Uncle Tom Lee to marry in Greeley, Colorado, in 1955.

I didn't know Joan, my dad's youngest sister, or her boyfriend, Tom, very well growing up, mostly because they had moved to Colorado. At first glance, Tom reminded me of James Dean in *Rebel Without a Cause* (1955), a film about a troublemaker who moves to a new town and learns that no matter where you go, there you are.

Joan wore an upper-body cast to stabilize her broken back following a serious car crash. I don't think she ever fully recovered from the accident.

I knew Tom as a stock car racer. He parked his car in the garage at my grandfather's ranchette house south of Cheyenne, near the racetrack. I'm unsure how or why Grandpa purchased the split-level home built into the side of a hill. I think Tom and Joan stayed there off and on. Grandpa sparsely furnished the place with Western-style oak chairs and tables. He raised a few pigs and chickens out back.

Grandma Ohashi and my parents took my sister and me there to tend the chickens, which I later saw as a rite of passage. I won't go into the gory details, but I watched a chicken run around with its head chopped off for the first time. It should have dawned on me then that animals have no chance against humans.

My dad took my sister and me to the dirt track in the summer to watch Uncle Tom race his stock car. We parked at my grandfather's place, walked down to the backstretch, and sat behind the double chain-link fence.

More than a few stock car racers had slammed into the flimsy barrier. Upon further review, we could have chosen a safer spot to watch, but my dad liked being near the flying dust and the banging of metal-on-metal, despite the risk.

Why did Tom and Joan end up in Colorado? In 1913, Wyoming became one of a dozen states to approve a law banning interracial marriage between Asian groups (Mongolians and Malays) and Caucasians.

Strong anti-Asian sentiment spread throughout other Western states. A combination of racism, economic competition, and fears of social integration reinforced support for laws written to maintain racial purity.

Wyoming had also outlawed mixed-race births. Out of the blue, a Facebook user contacted me, asking whether I'm related to Rose Ohashi. She sent me images of a birth certificate for an infant born in Denver and adopted by a family from Lusk, Wyoming.

I asked if she'd spit into an Ancestry.com tube. She and her sister joined. I discovered that the stories matched the genetics. I learned I had an extra cousin named Jerry (née Gary).

I compared notes with two friends from Lusk. One is Sue, who babysat Jerry's daughters, Kristi and Roni, my second cousins. Kristi lives in Lander. Phil Roberts, a retired UW history professor and local history buff, knew Jerry. A freakish industrial accident caused his death. Kristi, my second cousin, asked me to help unseal her father's birth certificate. The identity of his non-Japanese father remains a mystery.

Larry Kishiyama married his Caucasian wife in Colorado. Uncle George married Auntie Perry in Kansas and never returned to Wyoming.

Wyoming law allowed officials to fine interracial couples between $100 and $1,000 and to sentence them to prison for up to 10 years if found guilty of the misdemeanor. Historically, laws banning mixed-race marriage date back to 1661, when the Maryland government adopted the first law prohibiting interracial marriage.

The Wyoming State Legislature repealed the miscegenation law in 1965. Interracial marriage in the United States became legal in 1967, following the SCOTUS *Loving v. Virginia* decision.

Because interracial dating hadn't become socially acceptable, I didn't date at all during high school or college. However, my social experience coincided with a movie I directed and produced at the Heart Mountain Camp that addressed Japanese-Caucasian interpersonal relationships.

14

A Little Bit of Discipline

The Heart Mountain Wyoming Foundation, established in 1996, received National Historic Landmark status for the Heart Mountain Camp. Visitors can walk through the spruced-up grounds and view the exhibits at the interpretive learning center.

I returned to Heart Mountain in 2005 to shoot my second short film, using the Camp as the backdrop. I faced a steep learning curve while preparing for the production. I took ownership of the World War II Japanese experience for the first time.

****

When I moved to Colorado, I had a difficult transition. After being laid off twice after 9/11, I collected unemployment insurance benefits to make ends meet, supplemented my income with food stamps, and took out graduate student loans. The University of Colorado at Denver had accepted me into its Center on Domestic Violence MPA program.

In exchange for the monthly stipends, the Workforce Boulder County Office required me to seek employment, retrain for another field, or do both. I enrolled in TV production classes at the Boulder Public Access TV station and tried my hand at screenwriting.

My friend, Clay Fong, dragged me to his screenwriting class at Lighthouse Writers Workshop in Denver. A fantastic writer, Alexander Philippe, taught the class. I eventually figured out story structure after traveling to New York City to attend the renowned script doctor Robert McKee's *Story* seminar.

That class had a tremendous impact on me. I now think in a beginning-middle-and-end "three-act" structure. Brian Cox portrays gruff and cussing Robert McKee in *Adaptation* (2002), starring Nicholas Cage and Meryl Streep. It's a story about screenwriting, writer's block, and orchids. Beyond that, you'll have to look it up and watch the movie.

I volunteered with the Boulder Asian Pacific Alliance (BAPA), which sponsored an annual film festival. As part of the festival, I organized a screenplay contest with an Asian theme.

The prize? The BAPA festival would produce the winning story. A writer from Powell, Dennis Goldberg, won the 2005 contest with a screenplay titled *A Little Bit of Discipline*. I made some edits to make it more Japanese-inspired.

I had a hard time finding Japanese actors. The pan-Asian cast included Korean actor Peter Park, who played Uncle Seito, a former Issei incarceree. He remained in the rural community near the Camp and struggled with the townspeople's prejudice against Japanese people.

His Nisei nephew, Kenji (Phil Chung), and his modern ways challenge Seito to accept Diana, Kenji's Caucasian girlfriend (Robin Litt).

Aya Medrud, a Minidoka Camp incarceree as a child, played Seito's sister in the movie. I made a tribute documentary about her social justice work after the Boulder Martin Luther King Jr. Day Voices of Change committee honored her.

She worked as a librarian in occupied Japan after the War and met Nelder "Med" Medrud, a weather scientist stationed there. Aya and Med married but could move only to certain stateside locations that allowed mixed-race couples to live. They eventually came to Boulder.

"The FBI ransacked the house. I remember being a neat and tidy child and saying to the guy dumping the stuff out of my dresser drawers onto the floor, 'You're going to put it back, aren't you?' My dad didn't say anything. He put his hand on my shoulder and said in Japanese, 'Shut up,'" she said, recalling her World War II experience after EO 9066.

****

I shot the establishing scenes for *A Little Bit of Discipline* on location at the Heart Mountain Camp. A story ran in the *Powell Tribune* seeking background actors to walk around the Camp remains. I hadn't prepared for the casting call response with well over 30 would-be actors from all over Wyoming and Montana. Some brought head-shots and résumés.

I placed every extra, and I'm pretty sure there hadn't been that many people at the Heart Mountain Camp since World War II.

After the shoot, I stopped for a beer at the Union Bar in Hudson, between Lander and Riverton. A segment on Casper TV news covered my *A Little Bit of Discipline* production at Heart Mountain. There's nothing like unanticipated earned media.

When I lived in Fremont County in the 1980s and 1990s, I joined friends in Hudson, population 400, for food at two steakhouses: Svilar's, owned by the Svilar family, and Club El Toro, owned by the Vinich family. I also drank at the Union Bar, where Democrats congregated when the Vinich family owned it. The Poposia Mining Company initially incorporated Hudson as a "company town." Hudson once had as many as 10,000 miners.

The family matriarch, Mabel Vinich, served as the Mayor of Hudson for many years. I got to know her through city government circles. Her son, John Vinich, a longtime State Senator, managed the bar. I taught his sister Michelle's daughter violin lessons.

John and I became good friends. Francie Pistono and I, along with others, convinced him to run for the U.S. Senate in 1988 against two-term incumbent Malcolm Wallop. I campaigned hard for Wallop when he upset three-term Senator Gale McGee in 1976. Wallop said he'd serve only two terms and not be "out of touch" with Wyoming, as McGee had become.

John lost by 1,300 votes. I heard that Wallop operatives opened a few voting machines and helped the incumbent win. This election marked a new chapter for me. The Fremont County Republicans, for all practical purposes, kicked me out of the Party for disloyalty. I became a Democrat and a raisin in a bowl of raisins.

I didn't get to know their father, Mike, until later. He stayed in the background. At the time of his death, he and I had planned a documentary about his Navy service and his friendship with future President JFK. They served together in the U.S. Navy in the South Pacific.

****

When the War ended in 1945, the incarcerees left Heart Mountain Camp, but some, like Uncle Seito in my movie, stayed in the area.

A Little Bit of Discipline screened at the Rosebud Film Series at Northwest College in Powell in the fall of 2005. To everyone's surprise, after the pre-screening socializing, the projectionist discovered that someone had stolen the Digital Versatile Disc (DVD) from the player, disrupting the film before it began.

I learned later that a small sect of young local racists had masterminded the theft. I had another DVD in the car and played it. I received the disc back in the mail a month or so later. At least the troublemakers knew that honesty is the best policy.

I'm glad the movie got some notice, but on the other hand, I had my eyes opened, but not too surprised that some people still exhibit racist reactions to the Japanese World War II experience, even in the 21st century.

While the demographic shift to a majority-minority country by 2045 may pose challenges, it also offers opportunities for growth and enrichment.

We can reimagine Superman's American Way by proactively addressing societal concerns and fears. Fostering a culture of inclusivity and mutual respect will be crucial to shaping the future of the United States.

Most importantly, each of us must intentionally engage in dialogue about the benefits of diversity and the importance of inclusivity, which can help alleviate fears and misconceptions and make us more willing to change our ways.

Like all my work, *A Little Bit of Discipline* has a social change component. As long as I'm telling a story, it may as well serve a higher purpose.

If we are willing to adapt to an ever-increasingly multicultural world, personal change will lead to understanding and cooperation among different racial and ethnic groups.

Times are changing.

I drove through Hudson on my way from the 2024 WWI writing conference to Lander and noticed the bar had closed. Since the Vinich family passed away, Hudson's Main Street has been in transition.

15

Urban Flight

I attribute my perspective on social change to my childhood and maturation in Wyoming after World War II and during the subsequent Cold War. It's taken me a lifetime to push back against the Model Minority and Perpetual Immigrant stereotypes.

Cheyenne boomed when the railroad came through, followed by a network of U.S. Army forts to protect settlements along the railway. Pre-territorial Fort Russell, now Fort Warren, would play a role in national defense because of Wyoming's geographic isolation and sparse population.

Workers moved into town during the Cheyenne Cold War boom, which began in the 1960s, to build the country's highest concentration of Atlas nuclear missile sites. Cheyenne enjoyed a steady economy driven by national defense. By the 1970s, commercial development on the outskirts of town drew business anchors out of Downtown Cheyenne.

****

The Fairview Elementary School boundaries changed before I entered 1st grade. My parents moved to a newer neighborhood bordering "old" Cheyenne, which I call the suburbs. My sister and I would be within walking distance of each other and attend the same school.

Suburban growth exploded after the War on undeveloped land in wide-open spaces, where developers could earn more money due to desirable economies of scale. Cheyenne's Japanese community members, including my family, chose to blend in and follow the American Way, and they moved out of the urban core as the West 17th Street neighborhood declined.

The Japanese population in Wyoming has fluctuated over the years. According to the U.S. Census, between 1900 and 1910 the population rose from 303 to 1,590, surpassing the Native American population. Demographers attribute the increase to jobs available on the railroads and in agriculture.

The 1940 U.S. Census reports 643 Japanese residents in Wyoming during the War years. By 2010, the Japanese population in Wyoming had declined to 485. Suburbanization, coupled with discriminatory land-ownership laws enacted before and during World War II, contributed to the decline of the Japanese community. The population oddly rebounded to 1,495, according to the 2020 U.S. Census. I attribute the increase to a typo.

Nationally, suburban residents grew from 35 million to 84 million during the 1950s and 1960s. Americans improved their standard of living by the mid-19th century, during the Industrial Revolution. The first suburban areas developed in the early 20th century, primarily because of improvements in mass transportation and the availability of personal automobiles.

Americans no longer had to live near where they worked. This alternative to urban living gave a new middle class the chance to separate themselves from other urban-centered economic and racial groups, including our Cheyenne Japanese community.

****

My family became raisins in the mainstream oatmeal when we embraced the suburban lifestyle. Each family had a similar outward life, but each household had unique experiences.

For our birthdays, my sister and I had extended family members come from miles around to celebrate with a Japanese touch, including lots of our favorite foods, such as *maki sushi*, *teriyaki* chicken, and fresh *mochi*, which is rice pounded into a glutinous paste and shaped into sweet treats.

Then we had the neighborhood All-American version of the same birthday party for schoolmates. I remember handing out packs of 1961 Topps baseball cards as party favors on my eighth birthday. I wish I had those back. Who knew that a beat-up 1961 Mantle card would be worth $300, and that one right out of the pack would fetch $49,000 at auction? We snacked on plenty of hot dogs roasted on the charcoal grill and washed them down with Coca-Cola.

All the kids in a four-block area of the Cole Addition knew each other because we all attended Fairview Elementary. A childhood disease epidemic would sometimes spread through the school.

Parents talked among themselves about illnesses going around and planned playdays with kids who had mumps or measles so we could intentionally infect ourselves to build future immunity.

We built community through communicable disease.

Cheyenne's emerging middle class migrated from outside the state in the 1960s to join construction crews for the nuclear missile launch facility. Cookie-cutter tract developments emerged, consisting of single-family, ranch-style homes in the Buffalo Ridge, Cole, and Sun Valley additions on Cheyenne's northern and eastern outskirts.

****

In 1953, visionary Frank Cole anticipated Eastside residential growth. He plopped down the Cole Shopping Center at Pershing Blvd. and Converse Avenue on the town's edge. Over the years, the commercial oasis became surrounded by a residential neighborhood along the route to and from Carey Junior High School.

A Ben Franklin five-and-ten-cent store overflowed with kids coming home from school. The Garbers had a dry cleaning business.

The Gambles Hardware on the Southside opened a store to serve the growing Eastside market. That's where my parents bought a set of brown Pyrex bowls. The storefront later became Radio Shack.

I recall a store where shoppers could redeem Sperry & Hutchinson (S&H) Green Stamps. The company, founded in 1896, grew in popularity during the 1960s. Grocery stores and gas stations awarded customers Green Stamps for spending a set amount, similar to the "points" reward programs used by coffee shops and airlines to encourage customer loyalty.

My family assigned me to lick the glue on the backs of the stamps and place them in the books that tracked the stamp count. S&H based the trade value on the number of books.

I had fun browsing the store. We collected enough stamps to trade for knickknacks such as sets of drinking glasses, games, and toys. I don't know why this sticks in my mind, but we had two aluminum plaques featuring bas-relief pilgrims that hung on the wall.

We could make one stop at the Cole Shopping Center for multiple shops, like the Safeway, where I looked at the back of every Post cereal box for Mickey Mantle baseball cards and Roedel's Rexall Drugs for Beatles cards. I also bought red licorice whips at the Ben Franklin store. Roedel's, a West 17th Street mainstay, expanded to a second location at Cole's.

Cooksey's and the Cole Store sold apparel and competed with Fowler's. Cooksey's stocked narrow sizes, and I could consistently buy dress shoes there. Cole stocked Lee jeans for my Cheyenne Frontier Days regalia.

Moms would bring their kids to buy knock-around shoes at Dick's Bootery, which specialized in brands such as Buster Brown and Golden Goose. I bought a pair of Posture Foundation (PF) Flyers that made me "run faster and jump higher."

Thinking back, I liked PF Flyers because Boston Celtics star Bob Cousy endorsed and wore them on the Boston Garden parquet floor during the 1960s.

My dad played hoops in the city basketball league and wore natural-colored canvas Converse All-Star Chuck Taylor high-tops. I later opted for Converse black oxfords and wore them through high school because Celtics center Bill Russell wore them.

Somewhere along the way, I picked up a pair of PF Flyers that I wear when I shoot baskets, which happens on rare occasions these days.

The Carnegie Library opened a branch at the Cole Shopping Center. That meant fewer visits to the main library on Capitol Avenue, which eventually closed. Laramie County replaced it with a new structure on Warren Avenue in 1966. A bank purchased the original library property and built there in 1969.

Garvalia Music, which anchored the shopping center at one end, eventually became Blockbuster Video as the shopping center declined. Garvalia sold pianos and other band instruments. My piano teacher, Miss Hess, sent her students to buy sheet music and lesson books. She later became Mrs. Goff after marrying my Fairview Elementary basketball coach.

I classified Mr. and Mrs. Garvalia as the "older" couple, at least older than my parents, who lived two doors down from us on Windmill Road. They didn't have kids, and our careening down the hill on our skateboards freaked them out.

Remember my grandfather's ranchette on the South Greeley Highway? One of the oak end tables in the living room had broken. In my junior high wood shop class, I fashioned a skateboard from one of the table slats and mounted wheels repurposed from a pair of Uncle George Sakata's roller skates. He competed as a figure roller skater.

After gaining too much speed, we had to turn into the Garvalias' driveway or bail out onto their front yard. Sometimes a skater would make a smooth turn, but most of the time the landings lacked grace.

When one or both of the Garvalias heard the clatter of skate wheels hitting the sidewalk cracks, they pulled back their front drapes and glared at us with threatening scowls as we crashed onto their perfectly manicured lawn.

I never showed an aptitude for music, but my mom forced me to take piano lessons. I lacked confidence and didn't like performing because I feared screwing up. That's a throwback to my attempt at swimming. I reluctantly entered a freestyle race. Not only did I come in last, the pool was about to close by the time I finished. "Good job," my coach said to me. To this day, I don't like to go swimming.

I didn't feel the music. Instead, I had to memorize it. Miss Hess lived less than a block from Windmill Road, so I had no excuse for missing lessons. During the holidays, she put up a silver artificial tree, flocked with spray-on snow and decorated with the same silvery, shiny glass ornaments.

I didn't like practicing. We had an old upright piano in my sister's room. There are tales of my flogging the piano with a chain from one of the backyard swings. I also ran away from home after a frustrating practice session.

Opus 68, the *Album Für die Jugend* (Album for the Young) No. 10, "The Happy Farmer" by Robert Schumann, was the last piece of music I played when I stopped taking lessons. In 1848, Schumann composed 43 short works for his three daughters.

I quit piano in favor of baseball, which disappointed my mom. As it turned out, I didn't turn out to be great at baseball either, and later, I pursued teaching music as an avocation. As an adult, I took to the Suzuki violin and piano teaching method.

****

Meanwhile, LBJ's "Great Society" provided Urban Renewal grants to help cities eliminate "urban blight." Progress occurred at the expense of historic places.

The Cheyenne city government encouraged investment in the urban core when, during the urban renewal craze of the 1960s, developers tore down the historic Opera House at the corner of Capitol

Avenue and West 17th Street to make way for the brand-new JC Penney store and Cheyenne's first escalator.

Ironically, JC Penney at West 17th Street and Capitol Avenue started the trend, becoming one of the first businesses to leave Downtown Cheyenne when the indoor Frontier Mall opened in 1981 on the north edge of town. JC Penney first opened in Kemmerer, Wyoming, in the far western part of the state. The JCP storefront in downtown Kemmerer is now a tourist attraction.

Following suit, Fowler's department store, located in the Carey Building at the corner of Carey Avenue and West 17th Street, opened a second location at the Frontier Mall.

The Carey Building, Carey Avenue, and Carey Junior High bear the name of Joseph Carey, a Wyoming governor, U.S. senator, U.S. representative, and Cheyenne mayor who passed away in 1924.

Still, it could not compete with large chain department stores and closed its downtown and mall locations in the early 1990s. We didn't shop at the indoor mall. Instead, we shopped at the Cole Shopping Center and neighborhood strip malls.

After Fowler's closed, Z's Furniture occupied the Carey Building storefront, owned by East High classmates Dave and Kim (Stogsdill) Zwonitzer. The store eventually moved to the northeast side of town. Kim is the daughter of my 1st-grade teacher, Mrs. Stogsdill. She taught me how to read.

The Carey Building fell into disrepair under absentee ownership. The City of Cheyenne recently purchased the historic structure and razed it to construct an expanded municipal court complex.

People's Sporting Goods, a block south on West Lincolnway, sold my Cub Scout stuff. People's opened a second store there, and like Fowler's, it could not compete with larger chain stores.

A credit union recently purchased the Cole Shopping Center property and built a new campus. Like Downtown Cheyenne, the aging Cole Shopping Center could no longer compete with the Frontier Mall.

Retail economic development included a strategy to create a necklace around the outskirts of town to serve urban-sprawl communities. In Cheyenne, the Melton Shopping Center, later named Indian Hills, near Miyamoto's Two-Bar-Bowl, which held the Baker's Place liquor license, served the Northside, including the Buffalo Ridge subdivision.

Wyo Plaza opened, offering retail stores to Cole and Sun Valley residents on the Eastside. Tempo, which would now be considered a "Big Box" department store, anchored the Center. Cousin Leslie has her Pilates practice and Body Lines Dance studio in that strip mall.

I could ride my bike from my house on Windmill Road to Tempo, crossing Nationway, named after longtime Mayor Bill Nation.

My grandparents sold their Capitol Avenue home next to the First Christian Church, which had expanded, and moved closer to us on Converse Avenue and East 16th Street. A downstairs apartment eventually became quarters for Auntie Hisako, who retired from the EPA and moved from DC to Cheyenne to care for her aging parents.

Their neighbors, the Nations, also moved from town to a place on Ridge Road east of the Frontier Mall.

****

Cheyenne's Southside, on the wrong side of the tracks, had little residential development, but the Town & Country Shopping Center, where Uncle Roy worked, provided retail services for the area. That end of town now has a high concentration of discount "dollar" stores and several payday loan businesses.

Downtown activity also slowed because of infill urban sprawl, including at Grand Central Plaza, across the street from Eastridge Elementary School (now part of Carey Junior High) at the intersection of East Pershing Blvd and Concord Road.

Montgomery Ward moved from its downtown location at East 17th Street and Central Avenue. Circuit City acquired Wards and eventually went out of business. The building is now a State of Wyoming office.

Grand Central department store, the Target of the 1960s, and the only place in town that carried my mom's favorite perfume, Desert Flower, which I bought for her most Christmases.

Fairview Elementary fed Carey. Before I went home, I stopped at the Grand Central snack counter, a popular after-school hangout. I downed a bag of piping-hot French fries straight from the deep fryer for a dime. Grand Central is no longer in business. The site is now home to a fitness center.

Downtown Cheyenne has been working hard to rejuvenate itself. The Dinneen's Lotus Townhouse project has kick-started the commercial comeback by bringing in more residents, whose vibrant presence 24 hours a day and seven days a week complements the employees there during business hours.

16

Japanese Suburban Diaspora

As businesses fled Downtown Cheyenne, the Japanese dispersed due to the cultural upheaval caused by World War II and the passing of the Issei generation. The Nisei and their families no longer had to honor their mothers and fathers as heads of the family. Nisei parents taught their Sansei children to assimilate by straddling two worlds.

Superman's American Way included suburban growth and *Nihon-Jin* Crow discriminatory and exclusionary real estate practices. A *nihon jin* is a Japanese person.

The idyllic American Way, regardless of our perceived social status, stereotyped the admirable middle class as hardworking members with personal resilience.

Would the West 17th Street neighborhood have continued to exist if the broader Cheyenne citizenry had shown greater civility and collaboration with the Japanese residents and businesses after the War?

****

Even Superman had self-doubts when he confronted the Ku Klux Klan in the Fiery Kross in the graphic novel *Superman Smashes the Klan* (2019). The author set the story in 1946, when the Lees, a Chinese American family, moved from Chinatown to the Metropolis suburbs and Dr. Lee began working at the local health department.

The supremacist uniforms are nothing like the images that probably popped into your head.

The Lees encounter overt and subtle racism in their new community. The local Klan chapter targets the family by burning a cross on the Lees' lawn and firebombing their house. Tommy, the son, tries to fit in by going along with the bullying, but his sister, Roberta, struggles more visibly because she wants to preserve her cultural lifestyle.

Threats from the Klan toward the children escalate. Clark's colleagues, Jimmy Olsen, Lois Lane, and Inspector Henderson, befriend him. They offer assistance, but then the Klan targets them.

Superman steps in to help the children while grappling with self-doubt. The Klan's mesmerizing xenophobia targets anyone who is different. Its inflammatory rhetoric reminds Superman that he is an outsider on Earth and uncertain of his place in human society. Superman and Roberta confront the Klan and support her family in the fight against racism.

****

In my ideal world, the Cheyenne Nisei would have purchased the vacant storefronts on West 17th Street and opened new businesses serving the broader community. Maybe Grandma would have stayed at the City Café and eventually taken it over instead of opening the Highway Café on the Southside. The Stop 'n Shop store might still be in business, filling the retail niche left by three downtown grocery stores that closed.

The Japanese residents identified with the West 17th Street neighborhood where they lived and worked, but lost their sense of community as feelings of togetherness dissipated, with little support from the broader Cheyenne citizenry.

Urban flight affected me when both sets of my grandparents moved. My immediate family eventually did the same.

Residents with high financial risk could afford to rent or buy homes on Cheyenne's South and West sides. These underfunded "pockets of poverty" resulted from "redlining."

The National Housing Act of 1934 established the Federal Housing Administration (FHA) as part of the New Deal. FHA policies provided banks with criteria for safe lending, but they accelerated inner-city decay in areas inhabited by lower-income minority households.

During the 1960s, John McKnight, a professor at Northwestern University's School of Education and Social Policy, raised awareness of legalized discriminatory redlining practices. McKnight, known for his expertise in community organizing and protective-factor-based community development, advocated building strong, inclusive communities and empowering individuals to drive positive social change in their neighborhoods.

In 1935, through the Home Owners Loan Corporation, the Federal Home Loan Bank Board evaluated 239 cities and designated areas, mapping them on "residential security maps" to indicate real-estate investment risk levels.

* *Type A "Newer" Greenline areas in the desirable suburbs*

* *Type B "Desirable" Blueline neighborhoods*

* *Type C "Declining" Yellowline older areas*

* *Type D "Risky" Redline poor investment areas*

The Fair Housing Act of 1968 declared discriminatory the practice of charging higher interest rates to loan applicants who lived in redlined areas or requiring larger down payments based on these maps.

Racial segregation and urban decline stemmed from financial risk assumptions. Although redlining is not prevalent today, its legacy has left decaying urban areas in need of revitalization or redevelopment.

Shortly after the War ended in 1946, my parents married. With two incomes and no children, they bought their first home on East 10th Street, at the gateway to the Southside. We knew the neighbors on our side of the quiet, low-traffic street, but not as well on the other side.

As noted in the Skyline Nisei Club meeting minutes, the Club congratulated my parents on my birth in 1953. They stepped down from their community leadership roles to start a household. Mom quit her job at the Wyoming State Health Department, and Dad continued working at Coca-Cola. My sister arrived two years later. We soon outgrew the East 10th Street house.

The Fairview Elementary School boundaries changed after my kindergarten year. I walked half a mile up the street to Fairview, quite a hike for a three-foot-tall kid. My parents moved to the homogeneous Cole Addition, two blocks from the school.

We had neighborhood parties, pickup football games at the nearby Triangle Park, and half-court basketball games in the Goepferts' driveway. They had a double-car garage and the widest, flattest concrete slab in a two-block radius, compared with our narrower, more slanted one. The added rise at the free-throw line changed the trajectory of my shots at the Goepferts.

Compare that with Dad's youngest brother, Jake, who recounted his childhood in Cheyenne.

"Corlett (Elementary School) was naturally integrated since many minority families lived on the Westside," Jake said. "I grew up learning to accept others because of the diverse student body." He had the same neighborhood experiences, except with diverse classmates.

I could either move to attend Fairview or stay put and attend Altavista Elementary, a longer walk along Logan Avenue through a commercial district. Mom thought exposure to working-class Caucasian and Latino kids would detract from my upbringing as a Model Minority.

In retrospect, Altavista would have been a better fit for me. I would have had an experience similar to Uncle Jake's. I can't change the past, but I had no contact with African Americans and only a few Latinos at Fairview Elementary, a racially homogeneous feeder school for Carey Junior High.

I joined the Carey wrestling team and wrestled a Black kid named Willie Jones, who went to McCormick Junior High School. He called me "O'Haysh, O'Haysh." Wrestling opponents get pretty close. I don't know about others in the sport, but the first time I went up against Willie, his skin and hair felt different. I wondered how he experienced me.

The Westside kids seldom came to games at Carey, and we rarely ran into each other in high school. I still wonder about Willie. I asked some Central kids about his whereabouts at my 50th high school reunion. So far, no word.

I noticed a *de facto*, separate-but-equal segregation in Cheyenne. Central High School had a mix of students from wealthier families from the "Avenues" and urban kids from the South and West sides. My school, EHS, primarily comprised Caucasian, mainstream American kids.

In 1971, the SCOTUS ruled in *Swann v. Charlotte-Mecklenburg Board of Education* that school districts must achieve racial balance through busing students or redefining boundaries.

Whether forced or not, the school district integrated East High, bringing in many new students. Compared with integration in large urban areas, the Laramie County School District #1 bussed Caucasian students from rural areas on the Southside. After adding the new students, East won the state football championship, and the wrestling team did pretty well.

The EHS had a racially homogeneous student body: no Black students and only a few *Latinos* attended. A few other Japanese kids lived in the Eastside Cheyenne suburbs, not counting my sister Lorinda and me.

Classmates Bill Shiba and his sister, Marilyn, lived on the next block in the Cole Addition on Cactus Hill Road. Their brother, Bob, three years younger than me, went to school with my sister. The late Mary Tsumagari lived in the Cole Addition and later moved to the Henderson Elementary School neighborhood. Terie and Steve Miyamoto went to East, as did their cousin Linda.

****

In the early 1960s, the Miyamoto brothers moved their families from Downtown Cheyenne after transferring the Baker's Place liquor license to a location north of town and opening the 24-hour Two-Bar Bowl to accommodate the local Nisei bowlers. During World War II, the American Bowling Congress (ABC) kicked my dad and other Cheyenne Nisei out of their bowling leagues.

The ABC approved city leagues and restricted them to Caucasian men, but the ABC could also prohibit matches at any bowling alley that sponsored tournaments for mixed-gender or non-White teams and limit the number of lanes available to non-Whites.

After the War and their release from the incarceration camps, Nisei bowlers dispersed across the country, forming teams in their new communities. The JACL estimated that more than 400 Japanese American bowling teams had formed across the continental United States and Hawaii by 1947.

In March 1946, the JACL began efforts to reverse the ABC exclusion rule by picketing tournaments across the country. The protests grew into a coalition that included the National Association for the Advancement of Colored People (NAACP), the JACL, and labor organizations such as the Congress of Industrial Organizations (CIO).

Despite grassroots pressure, the ABC continued to discriminate in its selection of members. It disregarded legal actions in Illinois, Wisconsin, New York, and Ohio. ABC Secretary Elmer Baumgarten stated that the American way of life would disappear if the ABC gave up its right to select members.

In the spring of 1950, an Illinois judge found that ABC had abused its corporate franchise to do business in the state and ordered the organization to drop its discriminatory policy, pay a hefty fine, or risk having its state corporate charter revoked.

At its May 1950 annual meeting, the ABC quickly adopted a resolution by voice vote to overturn the national exclusion policy. Shortly after, the JACL issued a statement hailing the move. To secure enough votes for the change, the final ballot question proposed by the ABC included an exception allowing ABC chapters in southern Jim Crow states to use race to determine membership.

The ABC sanctioned the first integrated tournament in Minneapolis in 1951, and the league reinstated my dad. His team won the ABC Cheyenne City League tournament in 1953–1954, and I have his patch to prove it.

****

The Japanese diaspora pushed the Kubota family, who sold my grandfather their pool hall in Downtown Cheyenne, out of the city. Paul, the youngest son, became a dentist. In the mid-1960s, he moved with his parents to a house a block from ours on Windmill Road.

Paul eventually married Mary Fujikawa in 1966. They lived with Paul's folks until they passed. The only time I saw my dad with a lingering hangover was after Paul Kubota's bachelor party, when he had too much fun. Dad had a place on the floor for his lunch-hour afternoon nap, but on this after-party Sunday, he took an all-day nap.

The Kubotas provided my parents with excellent support because of their connection to West 17th Street. Paul and Mary kept in touch with some of the other Japanese families, particularly the mushroom hunters. We didn't associate with that crowd much.

The Kishiyamas last owned the California Fish Market. They moved out of downtown and bought a home with acreage south of Cheyenne, where Carl taught judo classes from a Quonset-building dojo. I took a few lessons from him, hoping it would help me adapt wrestling moves, but martial arts require a very different skill set.

The July 4th Japanese community gathered outside the city limits at the Kishiyamas. My dad had a bunch of young guys working for him at the Coke plant who made a run to Nebraska, which had legalized large firecrackers like cherry bombs and M-80s.

On the 4th of July, the neighbor kids, primarily boys, rode our bikes to the fireworks stand. The city limits ended near the Cole Addition boundary. Wyoming legally allowed 1.5-inch Zebra firecrackers.

I mounted various fireworks, such as pinwheels and giant rockets, on a piece of plywood and set off my grand finale at the Kishiyamas. My spectacular and dangerous pyrotechnic project didn't put out anyone's eyes during the festivities.

After my family moved to the Cole Addition, while not legal, we shot a few off in the backyard, mostly bottle rockets. I remember a Roman candle standoff between Mr. Murray and Mr. St. Clair, with the green, red, and white fireballs launched from the cardboard candlesticks flying across Cactus Hill Drive. The Murrays and St. Clairs lived across the street from each other.

When my dad and Bill Fisher finished our basement, short lengths of half-inch copper tubing left over from the bathroom installation ended up in the scrap pile. Bill Fisher taught me how to work with copper tubing. I dug out the tube cutter used to slice through the soft copper and buffed off the sharp edges. My friend Tad Leeper and I fashioned rocket-launcher tubes. We had wars at his uncle and aunt's home on the Preston Ranch west of Cheyenne.

I remember one of my errant rockets side-winding into Tad's cache of fireworks, triggering a series of explosions. I'm surprised we didn't shoot our eyes out.

My Cole Addition Army buddies and I unraveled firecrackers for the gunpowder and made small bombs out of Uncle George's cigar tubes. We designed Improvised Explosive Devices (IEDs) on our own, without the benefit of the internet for research.

My TV heroes, Sgt. Saunders (Vic Morrow) and Lt. Hanley (Rick Jason), starred in the TV show *Combat!* (1962–1967). I liked the program because it portrayed American soldiers not killing any Japanese. The stories focused on the lives of U.S. GIs as they fought the Germans in France. They had strong plot arcs, with World War II as the backdrop.

One of my favorite *Combat!* episodes, "Cry from the Ruins" (1965), featured a pacifist theme and aired at the height of the Vietnam War. A distraught mother searches for her baby, buried in a cellar after an air raid. The American troops encounter a German squad and open fire on each other.

The woman disrupts the skirmish and implores the two sides to lay down their weapons and help find her baby. It turns out the woman imagines her baby crying in the ruins after the bombing stops.

The story affected me as a poignant cultural cue. Germans and Americans part peacefully, realizing that killing each other is pointless.

****

Combat!, in its final 1967 season, aired in color. The previous seasons, being black and white, effectively intercut actual World War II footage with the TV story.

The Goepferts had the first color TV in the neighborhood, and their living room became a popular gathering spot for watching. The Mid-Century Modern era brought technological advances, including the availability of TV sets to the mass market. Every Cole Addition home had at least one TV.

Wars, while devastating, are ways cultures express their patriotism. We fought the Vietnam War on TV. I saw with my own eyes the devastation of Southeast Asia, rather than the edited World War II newsreel footage shown before the feature at the Paramount Theater. TV pulled back the curtain on patriotic images of heroes hoisting tattered battle flags, revealing the realities of combat.

Cole Addition on the edge of town meant we had plenty of vacant lots for war games. During the summer, day or night, we put on our *Combat!* gear, dug foxholes, and set our IEDs to blow the treads off imaginary tanks that would rumble across the fields.

"Checkmate King-2, this is White Rook, over," Sgt. Saunders barked code words into a bulky two-way radio, trying to reach his commanding officer, Lt. Hanley.

Like Sgt. Saunders, I wore a helmet covered with camouflage fabric and carried a Thompson submachine gun made by Mattel, molded from olive-drab plastic, out of continuity with the Vietnam War era.

Santa brought me another "useful" Christmas gift, a spring-loaded Remco bazooka that fired the blue plastic rockets I had seen on the shelf at Gambles.

My friends all wanted to join my squad when we played *Combat!* Bazookas are ground-to-ground anti-tank weapons with a steel tube braced on the shoulder that fire Rocket-Propelled Grenades (RPGs). An urban legend credits radio comedian Bob Burns with coining the term "bazooka," which he called an improvised musical instrument made from a length of pipe with a funnel stuck on the end.

I'm surprised I didn't shoot my eye out.

Between firecrackers, bomb explosions, and walking alone to and from school, I don't know how I made it through childhood alive.

Combat! Portrayed World War II as a drama. Compare that to *Hogan's Heroes* (1965-1971), a sitcom set during the War in a German PoW camp called Stalag 13, loosely based on the Oscar-winning movie *Stalag 17* (1953) starring William Holden. The show follows Colonel Robert Hogan (Bob Crane) and his group of Allied prisoners who secretly conduct espionage and sabotage operations against the Nazis from within. Despite being prisoners, Hogan and his team use their resourcefulness to outsmart the German officers.

Creators portrayed German characters in a comedic, exaggerated manner. Colonel Wilhelm Klink (Werner Klemperer), the bumbling, inept Commandant, is more concerned with his career and avoiding trouble than with foiling Hogan and his plots. Sgt. Hans Schultz (John Banner), the main guard, is portrayed as good-natured and oblivious, frequently turning a blind eye to the prisoners' activities, often saying his famous line, "I see nothing! I know nothing!"

McHale's Navy (1962-1966). The situation comedy, set in the Pacific Theater, follows the misadventures of the PT-73 led by Lt. Commander Quinton McHale (Ernest Borgnine). He and his ragtag crew hide their schemes and antics from their commanding officer, Captain Wally Binghamton (Joe Flynn). They bend or break military rules but always aid the War effort in unorthodox ways.

McHale's Navy portrays Japanese characters stereotypically and caricatured, reflecting the era's prevailing attitudes and American propaganda. Seaman 3rd Class Fuji Kobiashi (Yoshio Yoda) is a recurring Japanese role. He deserts the Imperial Navy, and the crew of PT-73 captures him. The show portrays Fuji as loyal, and he becomes an integral part of McHale's schemes.

The U.S. Navy transfers the PT-73 crew and their stowaway, Fuji, to Italy. They meet the all-Nisei 442nd Regimental Combat Team in Season 4, Episode 1, *War, Italian Style* (1965). McHale conceals Fuji by dressing him in a GI uniform.

"I know a Nip when I see one," Captain Binghamton says as he draws a gun on a Jeep full of 442nd soldiers, portrayed as ordinary Americans doing their jobs.

"I was born in California and graduated from UCLA," The Japanese sergeant responds. "Where did you go to college?

"I graduated from high school at the top of my dance class," Binghamton replies.

I found it much easier to make fun of Nazis than of Japanese soldiers. The JACL has worked tirelessly since the 1930s to restore civil rights for Japanese people. Home-front advocacy by groups such as the Skyline Nisei Club helped provide a safe place for Cheyenne Japanese, even though a few years earlier, Japanese people, even in Wyoming, had been required to report their whereabouts to law enforcement.

Grandfather Ohashi and his eldest son, my Uncle George, worked for themselves in the safe haven of Wyoming, but they could have picked a better time to travel to California.

17

All Asians Look Alike

Grandpa Ohashi operated a truck-farming business before the War. He won an award for his agricultural commerce innovations in Fife, Washington, near Tacoma, where he helped other farmers find new markets for their crops. He and his family arrived in Wyoming via Colorado and opened the Western Growers Exchange at 1619 Pioneer Ave., north of the Dinneen Garage. They later moved nearby to 304 W. 15th St., across from the UP and CB&Q rail yards.

Grandpa and Uncle George traveled to California's Central Valley in the summer of 1942 to source fruit and vegetables. They must have stayed there for a while, given that they had a street address in Ventura.

It didn't help that Superman had joined the fight against the Japanese in 1942. Anti-Japanese propaganda appeared everywhere, including in movie theaters with a captive audience. *Japoteurs* is one of 17 episodes in an animated Superman series produced by Fleischer Studios from 1941 to 1943. The series set a new standard for animated storytelling with advanced animation techniques and high production values.

Japoteurs opens with a Japanese spy reading a *Daily Planet* article about the completion of the world's largest bomber. The spy reveals a hidden Japanese flag in his office, then lights the newspaper with his cigarette. The scene cuts to the airplane factory. Clark Kent and Lois Lane are touring the new plane for a story. After everyone else disembarks, Lois hides aboard the aircraft.

Later, the spy and his accomplices knock out a guard during the plane's test run. Japanese spies concealed in fake bombs hijack the airplane as it takes off, then tie up the pilots. Lois discovers the hijackers, who capture her as she radios for help. The good guys dispatch fighter planes, but the hijackers drop a bomb to thwart them.

Clark Kent transforms into Superman and boards the plane. During the ensuing fight, the hijackers threaten to drop Lois out the bomb hatch. Superman saves her and defeats the hijackers. He places Lois safely on the ground as the plane spirals out of control toward the city. He then catches the plane and brings it to a safe landing on a city street.

****

Japoteurs normalized negative stereotypes about Japanese people, influenced by propaganda and the era's racial prejudices, while Grandpa and Uncle George drove their truck to buy vegetables for their customers in Wyoming and Colorado. I doubt they went to any movie theaters.

I don't know whether they voluntarily turned themselves in, but the WCCA detained them. According to family accounts, they lived at the Tulare Assembly Center for several months, halfway between Fresno and Bakersfield, California, where authorities confiscated their truck while they awaited transfer to one of the permanent Incarceration Camps in the interior of the United States.

My family said little to me about this experience. Their silence discouraged discussion of World War II. I didn't know anything about this story until my Auntie Elsie told me about it from her hospice bed at a continuous care facility in Cheyenne.

It's not that I didn't have time to visit her. I should have kept in better touch with my uncles and aunts. After Elsie's death, I became the unofficial keeper of family history and inherited a box of her old photos. I've been sorting through them and trying to identify the people as best I can. The American Heritage Center at the University of Wyoming invited me to donate these photos and more to its collection.

If you've lost touch with your aging relatives, call, write a letter, or visit them. Ask for help identifying the people in the photos.

I should have been more curious and asked about family stories. Don't make the same mistake I did. I hung around with Grandpa and Uncle George at the Café as a youth. Even if I knew about World War II, hearing about EO 9066 would have flown over my head. I might have been less oblivious if those stories had been told to me in high school.

I would have appreciated hearing about this chapter in the Ohashi family history book and the circumstances of their experience as two of 92,000 Japanese people forced into one of the 15 assembly camps established by the Western Defense Command (WDC). A third of incarcerees not sent to assembly camps went directly to one of the 10 incarceration camps.

The WDC hastily established the assembly centers to detain West Coast Japanese immediately before they traveled elsewhere in the United States or returned to Japan.

The Tulare County fairgrounds outside Tulare, California, hosted its first fair in 1915 as a livestock sales ring and later became one of California's most important county fairs.

In March 1942, the WCCA leased the fairgrounds. It renovated the site to accommodate approximately 4,800 Japanese residents living north of Los Angeles in Ventura, Santa Barbara, Guadalupe, Santa Maria, Arroyo Grande, Pasadena, Torrance, and Gardena.

The Army Corps of Engineers renovated 19 horse stalls at the Tulare County Fairgrounds, which measures about half a mile long and a quarter mile wide, and constructed barracks and communal halls for housing, food services, and sanitary facilities. The barracks measured 20 by 100 feet, with eight-foot-high plywood partitions dividing the long, narrow structures into family apartments. In April 1942, the Army Corps completed the retrofit construction project for $5,000.

Auntie Elsie told me she worked with Cheyenne law enforcement agencies, the U.S. Attorney's Office, and the WCCA. These agencies agreed to return her brother and father to Wyoming.

She played down the incident, saying everything worked out. We talked shortly before Christmas 2015. I planned to stop by again in January but missed the trip. She died in February, and I never heard the full story.

The WCCA would have transferred them to the Rivers Relocation Camp in Arizona (also known as the Gila River) if Elsie had failed to secure their parole.

The Bureau of Indian Affairs (BIA) selected the Gila River Reservation, home to the *akimel o'odham* (Pima) and the *pee-posh* (Maricopa) tribes, as an incarceration camp site. The WRA named the Camp after Jim Rivers, the first *akimel o'odham* tribal member killed in World War I.

The Gila River Camp interned more than 1,300 Japanese, mainly from California. The WRA divided Gila River into two Sub-Camps: the Canal, which had the fire station, and the Butte, which had the hospital. Both Sub-Camps had elementary and high schools.

BIA Commissioner John Collier proposed authorizing the DoI to work with the Japanese, who would provide labor for the BIA and the BoR on irrigation and agricultural projects. The BIA manages land held in trust by the U.S. government for recognized Indian tribes.

In addition to the Gila River Indian Community, the U.S. War Department placed the Poston Camp on the Colorado River Indian Community, also in Arizona, which is home to the *nüw* (Chemehuevi), the *aha makhav* (Mohave), *hisatsinom* (Hopi), and d*ine* (Navajo) tribes,

The BIA, originally formed in 1824 under the Department of War and later transferred to the DoI in 1849, administered both camps. The WRA approved the BIA's management of Gila River Camp. The WRA took over the Poston Camp after disagreements with the BIA over which lands incarcerees should farm.

The WRA gave Gila River tribal members low priority for jobs during construction and for work inside the Camp, favoring local Caucasian residents.

Incarcerees first arrived at the Canal Sub-Camp in July 1942 to complete the setup of the main Gila River Camp before others arrived from Assembly Centers or directly from restricted areas.

Initially, the 10,000 incarcerees who arrived at the Canal Sub-Camp exceeded the planned capacity by double. The first group crammed into the limited, uninsulated living quarters until the Butte Sub-Camp opened a month later.

Gila River opened during the height of Arizona's summer heat, with 48 days over 100 degrees F in July and August 1942. Some incarcerees fashioned homemade swamp coolers to lower the temperature.

The loyalty questionnaire also sparked widespread dissent in Arizona. The WRA designated about 1,300 incarcerees as disloyal No-No boys and transferred them to the newly designated Tule Lake Segregation Camp.

The WRA transferred 450 No-No incarcerees from Gila River to the Crystal City Detention Center in Texas, allowing families to remain together or reunite if members had been separated. The FBI barged into homes, split up families, and placed them in different Assembly Centers.

Former Minidoka Camp incarceree Aya Medrud told me about the time the FBI came to their home in Washington and took her father away, believing he might be a Japanese spy. She didn't learn his whereabouts for three weeks.

The Gila River Camp incarcerees learned to grow crops in central Arizona's hot, dry climate, operated a dehydration center to preserve surplus vegetables, and later established a canning operation. In 1944, Gila River shipped 4.0 million pounds of produce to the other WRA camps.

Life at Gila River featured activities similar to those at the other camps, including Boy and Girl Scouts, women's clubs, theater groups, and sports teams. Incarcerees attended Buddhist and Christian services. Students attended elementary and high schools at the Canal and Butte sub-camps.

My grandfather and uncle avoided the Incarceration Camp experience, even though living in an Assembly Center sounded similar. Their parole to Wyoming must have been smoother than the return of 125,000 incarcerees to their points of origin.

The remote location of each Camp made travel difficult. Limited transportation options significantly hindered incarcerees as they tried to find their way home.

The WRA provided incarcerees with $25, known as "gate money," to help cover travel expenses and a one-way train or bus ticket to their residence or another destination.

The gate money didn't come close to covering the costs of reintegrating and restarting their lives. Many incarcerees had to rely on their resilience and community support to rebuild their lives after the incarceration ended.

Local organizations, such as the Quakers, provided incarcerees with clothing, food, temporary housing, and other necessities as they reintegrated into their communities.

Caucasian veterans, on the other hand, returned and established homesteads on former Camp property. Some purchased barracks for a dollar each and converted them into starter homes.

The WRA sold a barracks building from the Heart Mountain Camp to the Town of Greybull, Wyoming, 60 miles away. Later, Iowa State University (ISU) acquired the building and moved it 15 miles east of Greybull to Shell, where the school's Geology Department converted it into a field station.

ISU donated the building to the Heart Mountain Foundation in 2015 and covered the $150,000 in relocation and historic preservation refurbishment costs. It is now part of the Heart Mountain Interpretive Center collection.

Like many incarcerees, Grandpa and Uncle George returned to a community indifferent to their plight. They arrived in Cheyenne, only to find their storefront shuttered and business at a standstill.

With no truck and no produce to peddle, Grandpa worked as a custodian at Stockgrowers National Bank and washed dishes at the Mayflower, both on West 17th Street, to make ends meet. Mrs. Shuto hired my grandmother to cook at the City Café.

Suspicious people may have stereotyped Grandpa and Uncle George as Japoteurs, but xenophobia and stereotypes led to their incarceration. Superman embodied the American Way. If he had a choice, I doubt he would have allowed his persona to symbolize the protection of American technology and military might.

18

Entrepreneurship

Life became a little more stable for my family after the War. Grandma quit cooking at the City Café in 1951. Grandpa and Grandpa Ohashi moved from the Westside when Uncle Rich purchased a newer home with GI Bill assistance.

They opened the Highway Café on the South Greeley Highway. Uncle George moved into an apartment behind the Café, continued the truck-farming business, and set up a fruit and vegetable stand next to the Café.

He asked me to help him organize the point-of-sale by setting up rudimentary aisles between the makeshift tables and displaying the produce with price signs. The stand faced the sun, so I built a shelter from the green canvas tarp my family used on our camping trip to Lake Marie in the Medicine Bow National Forest.

I spent my first summer working in the family restaurant business. That opportunity gave me, a shy kid, more confidence in sales and helped me develop my entrepreneurial tendencies.

Uncle George let me help "tend the store" and use a big kitchen knife. When a customer wanted a watermelon, I "plugged it" by slicing a trapezoidal wedge through the rind and removing it for the patron to see.

The customer could tell immediately whether they wanted the fruit. If the customer rejected it, I replaced the plug for the next curious buyer. If we didn't sell the plugged melon by the end of the day, it would go from the fruit stand to the Café, an early version of a farm-to-table restaurant.

My grandparents first opened their Café farther south, but the Wyoming Highway Department forced them to move a few blocks north when I-80 came through. The move worked out because the Café then sat in the heart of the Southside motel district, where most CFD rodeo cowboys stayed.

Cowboys staying at the nearby motels brought steady breakfast business during the Daddy of 'em All. Lorinda waited tables, and I washed dishes. The novelty of being served by my sister humored the friendly Highway Café patrons.

Uncle George welcomed our help, even though Lorinda and I worked without a permit. She kept her tips. George compensated me with candy and got rid of my Little League Pancake Breakfast tickets.

My grandmother asked me to write the daily specials on a blackboard that hung next to the counter. I don't think she could write English very well. I scribbled the menu items with a piece of chalk. Grandma served short-order favorites like hamburger steaks or meatloaf, with a scoop of canned green beans or corn and a mound of mashed potatoes or rice. I don't know what happened, but my handwriting has gone downhill since then.

The restaurant catered to a diverse clientele. A Filipino fellow named Carl came in every night, wearing a dark suit and porkpie hat. He worked at the Plains Hotel on Central Avenue, north of the railroad viaduct. The Plains hired many Filipino men as bellhops and restaurant staff. Carl always ordered half of the daily special.

Frank Omoto, a tall, jolly sort, used to come in and sit at the far end of the counter, wearing a big smile. I think that's because he caught a lot of fish. He and Uncle Rich fished together. Hank sometimes brought in part of his catch, which Grandma cooked for him.

I don't know how much work I did, but I had plenty of time to play around with the neighbor kids. Marvin Goldhammer owned the Corral Motel directly across the highway, the Lariat, a few blocks to the north.

One of his sons, Randy, around my age, spent quite a bit of time hanging out at the Café with me because Uncle George generously handed out candy.

Grandma had slowed down, and Uncle George began working at Laramie County Community College. My dad, the heir apparent, had no interest in taking over the business when it closed after my grandfather died in 1966. An Asian woman most recently painted the Café bright pink and converted the business into a doughnut shop. I stopped by and asked if I could look around. The layout hadn't changed.

Dad went in after his day job at the Coke plant and flipped steaks until closing. He had the chance to keep the Café open when Grandpa died. Dad had a steady job and family obligations. Mom likely would have had to go to work, which would have been disruptive.

I've often wondered what might have happened if he had decided to take over the restaurant. My life would have taken a major turn. Having inherited the entrepreneurial gene, I would have gladly taken on the challenge of owning and operating it.

My experiences at the Highway Café would serve me later in life. If I had a résumé back then, "no queasiness around dirty dishes" would have been a valuable job skill when I landed my first real summer job at the Hitching Post Inn.

19

Snappy Answers and Stupid Questions

Sam Contos, one of my Carey Junior High teachers and a neighbor, lived on the corner of Windmill and Old Trail roads with his wife, Stella; his son, John; and daughter, Marti. Mr. Contos helped me secure my first job as a busboy at the Hitching Post Inn. This regional resort hosted movie stars and politicians and served as the unofficial headquarters of the Wyoming State Legislature.

My dad must have talked to him about getting me out of the house. I would be entering 8th grade at Carey Junior High. I removed my blinders, which exposed me to people different from my family and neighbors.

I gained an appreciation for jerks at an early age at the Hitching Post. Occasionally, I felt openly discriminated against. Later, I realized that out-of-towners, whether rednecks or big-city folk, based their remarks on their privilege and entitlement, treating menial workers like me as inferior.

"Hop Sing, bring me more coffee," a skinny guy with a handlebar mustache and a Texan drawl hollered at me, referencing Ben Cartwright's Chinese servant and cook (Victor Sen Yung) on the TV show *Bonanza* (1959 to 1973). The show's producers paid him considerably less than others in similar supporting roles.

The show centered on Ben Cartwright (Lorne Greene), a three-time widower, and his three sons, each born to a different wife. The eldest, Adam (Pernell Roberts), an engineer, designed the stately Ponderosa ranch house. Hoss (Dan Blocker) stood 6'4" and weighed 325 pounds, which fit his nickname. Michael Landon played Little Joe, the youngest son.

My lowly busboy job placed me in the Perpetual Immigrant stereotype. I didn't have a snappy answer to the Texan's obnoxious request. Crafting clever responses is a skill I've had to develop over the years. *Mad Magazine* featured a recurring department called "Snappy Answers to Stupid Questions."

When I first moved to Boulder and browsed around at the local camera store, a woman approached me at the display counter.

"Can you read this?" she asked, pointing to one of the Asian-language *kanji* versions of a camera operation manual.

"No, I don't know Spanish," I responded with a snappy answer.

Another time, on an airplane, I sat in one of the emergency exit row seats, you know, the ones with extra legroom.

"CAN YOU SPEAK ENGLISH?" the flight attendant loudly and slowly enunciated her stupid question while staring at me, making sure I could see her lips move.

"I'm Japanese, not deaf," I snidely retorted.

****

The Hitching Post Inn had humble beginnings. Petter and Nathan Smith followed the American Way and emigrated from Russia in 1921 with their nephew, Harry. President Warren G. Harding signed their Homestead Act land grant for property 20 miles west of Cheyenne.

The brothers originally planned to grow potatoes on the dusty prairie, but they sold the property and bought land on the western edge of Cheyenne. In 1927, the brothers built the Lincoln Court along the Lincoln Highway (U.S. Highway 30).

Western expansion continued as the American public became more mobile. Car ownership became more affordable, and motor hotels like Lincoln Court popped up along major highways, including the transcontinental Lincoln Highway, which runs from Atlantic City, New Jersey, to Astoria, Oregon. Motels along Route 66 from Chicago to Los Angeles remain popular stops.

Harry Smith and his wife, Harriet, eventually owned the Lincoln Court, which later became the Hitching Post Inn. Their son, Paul, managed the property.

I knew the popular hot spot as the "Hitch," the "Post," and the "HP." The Hitch became my home away from home for three summers. I sometimes worked 50 or 60 hours per week, mostly at night, because I had nothing better to do.

A veteran busboy trained me during the breakfast and lunch shifts at the coffee shop. He taught me the pecking order. As I gained experience, my tips improved significantly during dinner hours in the Carriage Court, the Beefeater, and Patio dining rooms, from 4 p.m. to midnight.

The CFD day shifts differed from other days by the steady flow of customers until the rodeo started at 1:00 p.m. I remember clearing a table in the coffee shop during the lunch rush when a frantic mom approached me. Her son had left his dental retainer on the paper placemat and asked if I remembered clearing it from the table. As a braces wearer myself, I identified with the kid's angst.

I pushed my bus cart to the dishwashing area, dug through the paper trash, and, sure enough, found his retainer. That mom must have paid my favor forward, which could explain the good luck I've had over the years. After the lunchtime rush, things quieted as the crowds headed to the rodeo at Frontier Park.

My favorite CFD shift began at 10:00 p.m. and ended at 6:00 a.m. I ran booze and glassware from the main bar to the Coach Rooms in the conference center, for the big shows. I sneaked in for a closer look at some of the big parties.

I would have stood out in my red HP uniform jacket over a white shirt and a black bow tie. The tips would have been good, especially if I had played Mr. Yunioshi. I wore black horn-rimmed glasses and could have been his *doppelganger*.

"*Herro* (Hello), *Hawry* (Hawry) *Gorightry* (Golightly)," says Mr. Yunioshi (Mickey Rooney) in *Breakfast at Tiffany's* (1961).

The buzz and the merry crowd provided me with plenty of entertainment. Popular acts, including the Sons of the Pioneers, performed at the Hitching Post during CFD. I didn't know any of the bands and didn't pay attention. Country-western music didn't suit my fancy.

Jody Miller, a well-known lounge singer, played the Hitch. In 1966, she won the Grammy for Best Female Country Vocal Performance for "Queen of the House," her answer to Roger Miller's "King of the Road," which reached number 12 on the Billboard Hot 100 and number 5 on the Country Singles chart.

I brought her room service from time to time. She never tipped me. Maybe she left tips when she checked out, but the cashier didn't give them to me.

An actor named Victor Jory showed up during one of my shifts. He wore a jungle field jacket and sat at the end of the coffee shop counter, having breakfast. How Jory could eat and smoke a cigarette at the same time mystified me.

His roles include that of Injun Joe in the movie version of *The Adventures of Tom Sawyer* (1938) by Mark Twain. Jory played the part of Jonas Wilkerson, who managed the enslaved workers at the Tara plantation in *Gone with the Wind* (1939).

He co-starred with cowboy actor Hopalong Cassidy in seven films from 1941 to 1943. I hadn't heard of him, but the servers sure had. He graciously scrawled a few autographs on paper coffee shop placemats before digging back into his eggs.

The Hitching Post introduced me to older people. I hit it off with a funny guy named Mark Samansky there.

He attended Central High School. We both preferred the late CFD shifts. I only had a learner's permit, and he gave me a ride home if my dad couldn't pick me up.

Mark introduced me to my favorite meal: two turkey sandwiches with mayo and iceberg lettuce on white bread. The food at the Hitch tasted better than at other places. Most places allowed smoking back then, so maybe the secondhand smoke permeating the bread gave the sandwiches an extra appetizing flavor.

When our shifts ended, Mark and I leisurely dined in the coffee shop under a fake tree decorated with white twinkling Christmas lights, which protruded from the center of the round Formica table in the staff break area.

The banquet setup crew pulled back the inner walls, transforming the three spacious Coach Rooms in the conference center into a single vast space. One early morning after a CFD show in 1968, Mark climbed behind a drum kit and played the drum solo from *Inna Gadda Da Vida* by the acid rock band Iron Butterfly.

"Nice drum solo," Paul said after summoning us to his office, reminding us that even if nobody saw, the walls had ears. He didn't fire either of us. Mark became a well-known radio personality in Denver.

****

CFD or not, the Hitching Post hosted visiting celebrities in Cheyenne. On October 3, 1964, the Lincoln Theater hosted the press premiere of *Cheyenne Autumn* (1964). I hadn't started working at the Hitch, but star Carroll Baker disembarked from her train in front of the hotel and walked along a red carpet across the tracks and the Lincoln Highway to the front entrance.

The movie plot has nothing to do with Cheyenne, Wyoming. Mayor Bill Nation, with an eye for public relations, arranged the Cheyenne event.

Author Mari Sandoz's novel *Cheyenne Autumn* (1953) tells a fictional story through the eyes of Cheyenne Chief Lone Wolf. The tale recounts the experiences, struggles, and cultural heritage of tribal members as they journey from Oklahoma to their fictional homeland in Northern Wyoming. In real life, the Northern Cheyenne ended up on a reservation in Lame Deer, Montana.

Typical of Hollywood Anglo-centrism, the *Mexicano* actor Ricardo Montalbán played Lone Wolf in a supporting role. The film adaptation, directed by John Ford, shifts the perspective to non-Native characters, Captain Thomas Archer (Richard Widmark) and Deborah Wright (Carroll Baker).

****

My first taste of up-close retail politics shaped me and deepened my long-term relationship with the Hitching Post Inn. U.S. Senator Robert Kennedy (RFK) (D-NY) ran for President in 1968. On April 26 and 27, he whistlestopped in Cheyenne, the first stop on a long train trip through Nebraska that would end in Omaha before the Nebraska primary in mid-May, a critical state for his presidential bid.

Wyoming, politically purple back then, meant that Red and Blue candidates regularly campaigned for votes in the Equality State. The local Democratic Party hosted a reception for RFK at the Hitching Post in the afternoon, followed by his speech that evening at the Pavilion in Lions Park.

The 1968 presidential election piqued my interest in politics. I knew about the 1964 election between LBJ and Barry Goldwater, but I didn't take a personal interest in it at the time.

"Accordingly, I shall not seek, and I will not accept, the nomination of my party for another term as your president," President Johnson declared. LBJ won the 1964 general election by a landslide. His withdrawal as a candidate led to a wide-open primary season with enormous fields from both parties.

During the tumultuous year, I noticed political symbols, which marked the beginning of my political memorabilia collection. Collecting each candidate's bumper sticker and button became my mission.

I mailed handwritten letters to the campaigns to request their campaign materials. Since then, I've scrounged buttons for each major party nominee and their running mate, starting in 1896. My collection eventually dated back to 1789.

By the time I sold my collection in 2022 to a political memorabilia dealer, I had accumulated an Andrew Jackson clothing button and two George Washington clothing buttons, the 18th- and 19th-century precursors to modern buttons with pins attached to the backs.

My Carey Junior High School pal, Mike Whitehead, had deep Democratic Party roots through his parents. His mom, Janet, served as Laramie County Clerk, and his dad, Ed, represented Laramie County in the Wyoming State Legislature alongside Ellen Crowley, the wife of War hero and Assistant U.S. Attorney Tosh Sueymatsu.

Mike and I staunchly supported RFK. We decided to go see him. We taped six pieces of poster board together and stapled them to two sticks of lathe. I wrote "Kennedy Is Our Man" on the sign with a Magic Marker, a new writing medium at the time. As the cartoonist for the school paper, *The Tumbleweed*, I drew a decent caricature of RFK on the bottom of the placard.

Mr. Whitehead drove Mike and me to the Hitching Post Saturday afternoon for the reception before the Senator's speech that night. I didn't work that night because I wanted to attend the rally. After the reception, Mr. Whitehead handed me a business card autographed by RFK.

We returned to my house, rolled up the sign, shouldered it, and hauled it four miles to the Pavilion in Frontier Park. RFK, his wife, Ethel, and some of their kids stood onstage and welcomed the crowd. The crowd treated him like a rock star. I couldn't hear a word he said over the noise.

RFK noticed our sign. He came over, shook our hands, and autographed a "Join Now" campaign card I picked up at the door, which I still have. I realized that events like that capture the essence of old-fashioned politics. A *Wyoming Eagle* story estimated that 2,000 supporters and the curious packed the place.

At that rally, I also learned how accessible politicians can be at any level of government. I didn't realize it then, but the rally gave me my first taste of federalism, the system of relationships among the national, state, and local governments.

I studied political science in college and graduate school, which led to a public service career in local, state, and tribal government in my first past life. That experience has stayed with me to this day, as has my fascination with autographs and political buttons.

RFK continued his train trip through the Cornhusker State and won the Nebraska primary. A few weeks later, on June 6th, my clock radio turned on early in the morning to a live broadcast from the Ambassador Hotel in Los Angeles about RFK's murder. A man named Sirhan Sirhan shot him at close range.

20

Southern Discomfort

Before RFK's murder, James Earl Ray assassinated Martin Luther King, Jr. (MLK) in Memphis on April 4th as MLK stood on a balcony at the Lorraine Motel. His death didn't affect me much at the time, in my insular world in Wyoming. My parents didn't discuss civil rights at dinner. I don't recall any talk about race at school.

Maybe the rest of the state played it down. The April 5th CST headline had nothing to do with the assassination. It read, "President Calls Leaders to Deal with Tensions."

Compare that to the June 6th CST headline "Sen. Kennedy Dies—Victim of an Assassin's Bullet." Having shaken RFK's hand in Cheyenne made his death feel more tangible.

I knew about problems with civil rights and race relations, but they felt distant from me. It wouldn't be until a road trip through the Deep South that new experiences would open my eyes.

****

Raymond Candelaria, one of my friends in Lander, also had roots in Laramie. I worked with his brother, Don, at the Laramie Coke plant. Ray and I took a road trip in his Mazda RX-7 to San Diego to watch our alma mater, the UW Cowboys, play in the 1987 Holiday Bowl. UW lost a nail-biter to the University of Iowa, 20-19. The game turned out to be the tamest part of the trip.

"You never been to Tijuana?" he asked.

"It's a big tourist trap." I responded.

"It's not the tourist trap you may think," Ray said as he buckled up.

I hadn't been south of the border before. Raymond knew his way around. He showed me places where only locals went and no tourists. The attractions included a dark, dingy bar where women sat on benches around a sunken floor. Patrons paid a few pesos to dance.

Mexico comes alive late at night. We stood on the street, eating tacos and washing them down with *horchata*, a beverage made from rice, sugar, water, and spices.

After a night of revelry, we crossed back into the United States, and an INS border guard profiled Cheech and Chong, waving us to a waiting station. He opened the RX-7 hatchback and poked his baton into one of the plastic bags, releasing a plume of white powder.

"Remember to use a little lard," he said as he slammed the lid closed. "That's the secret to a good corn *tortilla*."

Raymond had purchased a few Mexican kitchen staples unavailable in Laramie for his mother, not a kilo of cocaine. I wrote *Stardust*, my first screenplay, based on our brief visit to Tijuana, which won an award in the Denver Screenwriters contest.

My experience in that underbelly of Mexico would prove helpful a decade later, when I lived off and on for six years in Sombrerete, Zacatecas. My mother warned me to be careful when I traveled to Mexico. She didn't want to get a phone call from the U.S. Embassy informing her that thieves had abandoned me in a fleabag hotel with one less kidney.

****

Because Wyoming didn't play in a post-season football game in 1990, we organized a Cheech and Chong bowl-a-thon. Ray and I met in Laramie and flew to New Orleans on Christmas Day. We picked up a rental car at the airport for our 3,000-mile road trip through the Deep South.

The hotel clerk noticed two brown guys checking in together and assigned us a room that housekeeping had not yet made up. We stayed in what turned out to be one of those "rent-by-the-hour" hotels. That night, the temperature dropped below freezing, and the pipes froze. The hot water ran again the following morning.

We headed to Memphis after a night in New Orleans marked by gunshots in the streets. We had to be there by December 28th for the Liberty Bowl game between Ole Miss and the Air Force Academy Falcons.

I didn't know what to expect in Memphis and Orlando, where Raymond built extra time into our itinerary. I became an Elvis fan because of Raymond's obsession. He insisted we stop at The King's childhood home in Tupelo, Mississippi, and at Graceland in Memphis.

In 1990, developers converted the Presley family's two-room home, built by his father, grandfather, and uncle, into a small, free museum. Vernon and Gladys Presley had Elvis on January 8, 1935. His twin brother, Jessie Garon, died in the womb. Elvis grew up in Tupelo, surrounded by his extended family, including his grandparents, aunts, uncles, and cousins.

The grounds now charge a $25 admission fee, which includes several sculptures and his childhood church. One benefit of getting older is having visited tourist attractions before they became commercialized.

In Memphis, we made an obligatory stop at Graceland, the 14-acre estate Elvis purchased in 1957 for a little over $100,000 after he became rich and famous at age 22. Exhibit curators arranged items The King touched and the clothes he wore alongside his Grammy Awards and Gold Records in the display cases. The display cases at Graceland made me more aware of Elvis's unmatched fame.

I didn't pay attention to Elvis or rock 'n' roll. My parents set the radio to KFBC, which played easy listening. My dad, an early adopter, brought home a record player with stereophonic sound from Garvalia's.

We had records by Frank Sinatra and Tony Bennett around the house. I owned a Beatles 45-rpm with She Loves You and *I Wanna Hold Your Hand.*

Raymond had experienced more diverse cultures and more blatant racial discrimination than I had. Being more aware of MLK, he wanted to find the balcony at the Lorraine Motel where MLK stood when an assassin gunned him down.

The civil rights leader traveled to Memphis to support a strike by African American sanitation workers, advocating for better wages and working conditions. King's assassination on the balcony of the Lorraine Motel marked a pivotal moment in American history, sparking nationwide mourning and intensifying civil rights efforts.

The Lorraine, originally the Windsor Hotel, opened in the 1920s as a Whites-only establishment. In 1945, Black businessman Walter Bailey purchased the hotel and renamed it after his wife, Loree, and the famous jazz song Sweet Lorraine. The Green Book listed the Lorraine, which became a prominent destination for Black travelers.

In the years after King's death, the Lorraine struggled financially and eventually closed. In the 1980s, local business leaders and activists formed the Martin Luther King Jr. Memorial Foundation, purchased the motel, closed it in 1988, and cordoned off the area.

We met Jacqueline Smith, who lived at the Lorraine until a judge ordered her to move in 1990. She erected a tent from a blue tarp on the sidewalk outside the chain-link fence that blocked the Lorraine from the public.

She gave us her canned speech about how Reverend King would have preferred the motel to be converted into housing for homeless people rather than repurposed as the multi-million-dollar National Civil Rights Museum, which opened on July 4, 1991.

Raymond taught school and filed an internal civil rights complaint against one of his colleagues for making disparaging racial remarks to his face.

I felt safe growing up in the sheltered life of the East Cheyenne suburbs until I took that extended road trip with Raymond. Talk about stepping out of my comfort zone. Raymond took me to some different places. I learned that there are both wet- and dry-rub barbecues. We caught the Blues at Lou's Place, a converted cotton warehouse on the Mississippi River, where I tried dry rub for the first time.

A dry-rub BBQ pit master rubs a mixture of spices and herbs directly onto the meat hours in advance, then grills or smokes it, creating a crusty exterior.

After my 40th-class reunion at Hastings College, I extended the trip and drove to KC to interview the Thomas Hart Benton Home Site Administrator, Steve Sitton, for a documentary about abstract painter Jackson Pollock, who spent his childhood in Cody, Wyoming, and painter Thomas Hart Benton. Both had ties to Saratoga, Wyoming. Pollock appears in one of Benton's paintings, *The Ballad of the Jealous Love of Lone Green Valley* (1934).

On my way out of town, I stopped at Jack Stack Barbecue in KC. I read some reviews and thought this would be a good time to try wet BBQ. Wet barbecuers apply a liquid marinade or sauce as a coating before cooking or as a baste while grilling or smoking to create a moist, sticky exterior.

I found Stack's thick, tomato-based sauces to be too sweet. Sauce makes the ribs too sloppy. Give me dry any day.

Compared with our Memphis adventure, Ole Miss defeated Air Force in a lackluster Liberty Bowl game. We pulled out of the parking lot and headed to Jacksonville, Florida, via Orlando.

Raymond liked to embed himself in neighborhoods and took me on a hunt for menudo, a soup made with tripe (cow stomach). Ray, a connoisseur of animal innards, wanted to find a place to try chitterlings (chitlins). Chitlins are a Southern soul food made from hog intestines. There are Japanese versions of chitlins, but nobody has offered them to me.

We traveled long before Yelp, TripAdvisor, and Google, so we had to ask around. A local directed us to a small café in Orlando. I don't recall the name, but I remember a wooden, spring-loaded screen door painted white that slammed shut behind you.

The house didn't have chitlins that day, but it offered fried hog maw made from a pig's outer stomach wall. We ordered the breakfast special: hog maw and eggs. The unappetizing maw crunched more than crispy bacon. I learned the cook may not have seasoned it properly.

What we did for the rest of the day escapes me, but we hunted for the Gator Bowl in Jacksonville. On our way to Miami, the Clemson Tigers defeated the West Virginia Mountaineers 27-7.

Raymond and I chose our bowl-a-thon lineup to coincide with the Orange Bowl, where two undefeated teams faced off for the national championship on January 1, 1990.

The University of Colorado finished the season with an 11-0 record. Notre Dame had an unblemished record until the final week of the regular season, when the Irish lost to the Miami Hurricanes. That loss deflated the hype balloon.

The Fighting Irish prevailed 21-6 over the Buffaloes in an anticlimactic game. Rather than stick around for post-game partying, we decided to drive toward New Orleans.

I got sleepy and pulled over at a rest stop to catch some shuteye. A rap on the window woke me before dawn's early light. One of Alabama's finest rousted us. I didn't know what to expect after being caught "parking while brown." I didn't know what to think, since I only knew the redneck stereotype of redneck sheriff Roscoe Coltrain from *The Dukes of Hazzard* (2005) (M.C. Gainey) dancing in my head. The officer ordered us to get back on the road. We dropped off the car and made it back to Laramie without incident.

****

I had been to Florida before my trip with Raymond, but not to experience racial diversity firsthand. My first time came when I enrolled in a month-long Hastings College Interim class on the Ecology of the Southeast, led by Professor Gilbert Adrian.

Hastings scheduled classes on a 3-1-3 rotation, with three months in the fall and spring and one month in between, called the Interim. Students would take one concentrated class. I stayed on campus for two Interims. In my first year, I took a Cosmology class. The trip to Washington, DC, happened my sophomore year.

As a junior, I signed up for piano lessons with all the voice majors. It surprised me that many didn't know how to read music. My mission, which I decided to accept: to learn, you guessed it, "The Happy Farmer" by Robert Schumann. That year I enrolled in a second class about the politics of the Vietnam War with a bunch of veterans, a timely follow-up to being tear-gassed at the antiwar demonstration in DC the year before.

A December 1975 drive to Florida marked the inaugural road trip for my graduation present, a brand-new base-model 1974 pea-green Ford Pinto station wagon. I didn't have much luck with the Pinto, the economy cousin of the Mustang.

I began in Laramie and made my first stop in Denver, where I picked up my classmate Brooke from her parents' house. We then drove to pick up Lynn from his place in Nebraska and headed south through Kansas. We probably should have waited until the next day.

I drove into a white-out blizzard and slid off the road in the dark of night. We camped out in a ditch after spinning out on U.S. Highway 20. A friendly fellow pulled us out with his pickup truck. Being stranded in Kansas would be the first harrowing incident in my Pinto.

The Florida Keys offered a welcome change from winter in the Midwest. Spending extended time in the Deep South in the mid-1970s opened my eyes. Maybe my friends didn't notice, but the stares from locals made me uneasy as the only raisin in my ecology class's oatmeal. My trip with Raymond reinforced all of that.

****

I didn't experience much diversity growing up in the homogeneous state of Wyoming. I had seen African American people before, but always from a distance on a football field or basketball court. My dad graduated from Cheyenne High School, now Central, where he played basketball. At 5'11", he stood tall for a Japanese player and had a pretty good left- and right-handed hook shot.

Once in a while, Dad took my sister and me to watch his alma mater, Cheyenne High School—now Central High—play at Storey Gym. In 1964, I followed two well-rounded students, Barry West and Percy Johnson. They played in a rhythm-and-blues band.

I recently befriended Barry's brother, Grant, on social media and learned that Barry had passed away and that Percy is a minister in Illinois. He also mentioned that his grandmother owned one of the restaurants at 420 W. 17th Street.

We would occasionally drive to Laramie to watch UW basketball games. In 1964, the Cowboys' Flynn Robinson eventually played in the NBA for the Cincinnati Royals and the Milwaukee Bucks. He missed out on winning the NBA championship with the Bucks in 1970-71, when Milwaukee traded him back to the Royals for guard Oscar Robertson.

Robinson would play on the great Lakers team that won the 1972 championship with Jerry West, Elgin Baylor, and Wilt Chamberlain.

I met Flynn in 1994, when the UW Athletic Department inducted him into the Hall of Fame. I covered the on-field ceremony, taking photos. He autographed a basketball card for me.

Also, on that Wyoming team, 6'6" center and small forward Leon Clark dominated the boards. The Boston Celtics drafted Clark, which converted me into a Celtics fan.

The dominant Celtics generally had one of the last picks in the NBA. The Celtics selected the best of the remaining players from smaller conferences, such as the Western Athletic Conference, including Leon Clark. Sports pundits hailed Clark as the next Bill Russell, but he faded after a couple of seasons in Beantown. He finished his career in Europe.

Later, the Celtics drafted Charles Bradley from UW, as well as Danny Ainge and Greg Kite from rival BYU. In my opinion, I witnessed the best basketball game between the Cowboys and BYU on February 26, 1981, at the UW Fieldhouse.

When I worked for the City of Lander, Barry Cook, a friend and local government colleague, and I drove from Cheyenne to Laramie. During the day, we lobbied the state legislature on behalf of the Wyoming Association of Municipalities.

The Memorial Fieldhouse, known as the "Barn," gave Wyoming a significant home-court advantage because mulch-like woodchips covered the surface, the perfect substrate for growing mushrooms.

The UW rodeo team competed indoors there as well. Crews assembled the basketball floor in sections over the mulch. Visiting teams had to play at 7,200 feet and breathe the moist, musty, and thick Fieldhouse air.

I had forgotten the game's details, but here's the play-by-play from UW Sports Information Director Kevin McKinney. BYU led 68-64 with 1:28 remaining in regulation.

Mike Jackson hit a jumper, then a monster slam-dunk, to tie the game at 68-68. BYU guard Danny Ainge missed a one-and-one, then a jumper at the buzzer, sending the game to overtime (OT).

BYU led 76-72 in the first OT before Bill Garnett and Mike Jackson each made two free throws, sending the game to the second OT. The Dallas Mavericks picked Garnett fourth overall in the first round of the 1982 NBA Draft. The Kansas City Kings selected Jackson in the 4th round a year later.

In the second OT, with BYU trailing 85-81, Ainge converted a three-point play after being fouled, narrowing the gap to 85-84 with 19 seconds left. BYU fouled Charles Bradley. He made the first free throw but missed the second, extending the lead to 86-84. BYU grabbed the rebound, and Ainge had a last-second shot that banged off the rim. Bradley grabbed the rebound, and the game ended.

The stands emptied. Screaming fans stormed the floor and trampled past Danny Ainge, who crumpled after missing the last shot.

Ainge signed with the Toronto Blue Jays during college. He had a so-so-professional baseball career. The Celtics selected Bradley as the last pick in the year's first round of the NBA draft. The Celtics also drafted Ainge in 1981.

They played roles on the Celtics' 1980s dynasty teams alongside teammates Robert Parrish, Larry Bird, Kevin McHale, and Dennis Johnson. Charles Bradley played only one season before becoming a college coach at Loyola Marymount.

****

Wyoming experienced its share of civil rights unrest. The University of Wyoming had a hostile sports rivalry with BYU. The relationship with Mormons went beyond sports. My earliest memory of the rivalry dates to 1967, when it led to the infamous "Black 14" incident. If you Google it, there's plenty of information online.

In 1967, I followed Wyoming football religiously. The Cowboy gridders went 10-0, finishing the season as the nation's only undefeated team and ranked No. 5.

The Pokes lost 20-13 to unranked Louisiana State University (LSU) in the Sugar Bowl, played in Baton Rouge. I wrote a newspaper story about the UW Sugar Bowl appearance for the Carey Junior High School *Tumbleweed*.

Paul Toscano, the quarterback on that team, taught my 8th-grade PE class. He showed off his Sugar Bowl watch. The Houston Oilers drafted Toscano, but he opted to coach high school football and basketball.

The 1968 season brought high hopes for the Pokes, but the team finished 7-3 and won its third consecutive Western Athletic Conference (WAC) championship.

Racially charged unrest plagued the country following the assassinations of Bobby Kennedy and Martin Luther King Jr. The political upheaval from those events spilled into Wyoming.

The team began the 1969 season strong, posting four straight wins and ranking 16th in the nation. Before the BYU home game, the campus Black Student Alliance (BSA) met with the 14 African American football players and asked them to wear black armbands to protest BYU's religious ties to the LDS Church, which did not allow African Americans to join the priesthood.

Governor Stan Hathaway mobilized the National Guard to enter Laramie as a show of force. *Sports Illustrated* buried the story on page 26 of the November 3 edition. The headline read, "No Defeats, Loads of Trouble."

After a team meeting, coach Lloyd Eaton booted the 14 players. Short-handed Wyoming soundly defeated their rivals 40-7. The Cowboys lost four of their five remaining games and, in 1970, nine of their 10 games.

As a high school student, I intellectually understood the controversy but didn't fully grasp it emotionally until years later.

In 2019, UW apologized to the former students to commemorate the 50th anniversary of the Black 14. Wyoming's football program has never fully recovered from the controversy.

I didn't meet an African American adult until I attended a professional baseball game in Denver. I had late-blooming exposure to diverse people during college and early adulthood.

21

Baseball and Assimilation

Unlike Superboy, I had sub-mortal baseball skills. After the 1966 Cheyenne Babe Ruth League season, the year I broke my ankle, I didn't advance any further in baseball. We wore uniforms and cleats, but played on dusty, hard clay dirt. I would have liked to play at the American Legion level, but my rehab left me physically underdeveloped compared with other players. The public schools didn't sanction baseball as a school sport, as they did in Smallville.

Young Clark Kent, secretly Superboy, plays on the Smallville High School baseball team. In *Superboy #55* (1957), the strain of living as an undocumented immigrant on Earth, fitting in with humans while possessing Kryptonian superpowers, frustrates him.

Smallville High School plays a crucial baseball game against a rival team. Clark faces challenges during the contest, where he must subtly deploy his powers. Rather than relying on his super speed, he runs under fly balls as a human would, and when at bat, he is careful to avoid hitting a home run on every swing.

The central conflict arises when a player on the rival team is determined to win at all costs. Despite his opponent's attempts to cheat, Clark leads his team to victory through skillful play and good sportsmanship. He demonstrates his leadership and athletic abilities without revealing his secret identity as Superboy.

The story ends with the Smallville High players celebrating their victory. Clark reflects on the importance of collaboration and civility, emphasizing fair play, using his powers for good, and blending in with his peers as an ordinary teenager.

****

The Ohashi family reunion marked the end of a summer of activities. I broke my ankle sliding into 2nd base and spent the July 4th picnic on crutches. After that, I lost my desire to improve at hitting the curveball and quit Babe Ruth baseball at the end of the season. I didn't like abandoning baseball, but I realized the world wouldn't end. It became a new starting point.

Auntie Elsie became a good sports role model for me, my only Nisei relative who competed in organized leagues. She started at 2nd base as the sole Japanese raisin in her softball team oatmeal, which had won a state championship in the women's fast-pitch tournament. Games moved quickly because of good pitching.

In Lions Park, across from the CFD rodeo arena, the City of Cheyenne maintained a regulation grass ball field with bleachers, a backstop, a scorer's booth, an announcer, and an outfield fence adorned with signs advertising local businesses. The women played under the lights, wearing uniforms and metal spikes, which impressed me as a young ballplayer.

****

Japanese baseball has a long history in the United States. World War II cut short the baseball careers of many prominent Nisei players, including the Miyamoto brothers.

Japanese baseball originated in the United States when the Fuji Athletic Club of San Francisco founded the first Japanese baseball league in 1903. By the end of the decade, the Japanese Pacific Coast Baseball League had formed, with teams in eight West Coast cities.

Jim Crow laws and customs segregated all-Japanese leagues, much like the Negro Leagues. The Rocky Mountain Baseball League expanded to 20 all-Japanese teams by 1920.

The WRA allowed baseball at the incarceration camps, facilitating the Japanese adoption of the American Way.

Four of the 10 camps fielded traveling teams: Gila River and Poston in Arizona, Camp Amache in Colorado, and Heart Mountain in Wyoming.

A Japanese-born professional baseball player, Kenichi Zenimura, emigrated to Fresno, California, in 1920 and founded the Nisei Baseball League. In 1934, Zenimura organized a baseball tour of Japan featuring American All-Stars, including Babe Ruth and Lou Gehrig.

Zenimura organized a 32-team Gila River baseball league that played at a 6,000-seat baseball field next to Butte Sub-Camp High School, where he coached the Eagles baseball team. He invited the Tucson Badgers, three-time state high school champions, to play a game at Gila River. The Eagles won an 11-10 slugfest.

The Heart Mountain High School team played an epic 13-game series against Gila River in 1944. The Arizona players paid for their 1,200-mile bus ride to Wyoming with money earned from odd jobs around the Camp. The old bus broke down several times en route.

The players wore their uniforms during the journey rather than street clothes. When law enforcement officers stopped them, they explained they played baseball and not Japanese spies. Gila River won the Series, which took about a month to complete.

****

Wyoming also fielded an adult Nisei team. Minol Ota, the Heart Mountain Camp veterinarian from Cheyenne, had moved to Powell. He and his brother, Joe, played on the Wyoming team that won the 1943 Tristate Japanese Baseball League tournament. The Baseball Hall of Fame in Cooperstown, New York, enshrined that team, which had strong ties to the West 17th Street neighborhood.

Bill Matsuyama, the owner of the California Fish Market, managed the Nisei Nine. His players included his son, Harry; Tom and Bill Miyamoto, who later owned Baker's Place; Kaye, Harry, and

George Hashimoto; Paul Tani, who lived above the City Café; and Fred Futa, who lived down the block.

Japanese baseball in Wyoming had ceased by the 1960s. A Cheyenne team competed in a Northern Colorado league. The Denver Nisei team included a player named Art Arita, who, as a child in the 1940s, lived on West 17th Street before moving to Colorado. The WRA spared him, like other Japanese living in the interior before Pearl Harbor, from incarceration.

****

I had no idea about Japanese baseball leagues during World War II. I loved baseball, the New York Yankees, and the only Japanese player in the Little League. People ask me how I became a third-generation Yankees fan in Wyoming.

I'm third generation. My grandpa and dad are Yankees fans. Now me. The AAA Denver Bears, from the Pacific Coast League, affiliated with the Yankees.

The Cheyenne Little League sponsored an annual summertime pancake breakfast to raise funds. In 1964, the League tasked players with selling tickets, and the team that sold the most received tickets to the game between the Yankees and the Bears. The second-place team received tickets to a regular-season Bears game.

I had a solid network of potential pancake eaters. My dad took a few and sold tickets at his workplace. Sales in my neighborhood didn't go well because all my friends played on other Little League teams.

My ticket-selling secret weapon? Uncle George at the Highway Café kept them in the cash register drawer. Instead of counting out change for his customers, he handed them my tickets. When the League announced the final ticket tally, my Red Sox team took second place. I went to the AAA Bears game. What a letdown compared with seeing the Yankees.

One of the Coke truck drivers, Tony Rizzuto, a relative of former Yankees shortstop Phil Rizzuto, organized a carload to attend the game. The Hall of Famer played shortstop for 13 years with the Yankees from 1941 to 1956 and appeared on seven World Series-winning teams.

Tony made all the arrangements. Dad bought an extra ticket and invited me to the Bears vs. Yankees exhibition game. On that outing, I met and talked baseball with my first adult African American.

Danny picked everyone up in his black-over-powder-puff-yellow 1963 T-Bird convertible. We pulled up to the turquoise-painted concrete-block Fix 'n Mix bar and liquor store.

Tony's friend walked out the front door wearing a light olive-green satin bomber jacket and climbed into the backseat beside me. I assumed he and Tony knew each other from the Fort Warren Coke business.

The airman, also a big Yankees fan, deployed from New York City to Wyoming. I thought it odd that we met him at a liquor store, but it makes perfect sense now. Integrated Baker's Place had moved out of downtown, and Fix 'n Mix, on the Westside near the airbase, became a place where Black residents could safely gather.

When I said "met," we sat beside each other in a car driving to a game in Denver. My new pal knew a lot about baseball.

Like me, he looked forward to the Yankees game. My first pro game in Denver is a highlight of my life. Minor league exhibition game or not, it didn't matter.

When our baseball party arrived at Mile High Stadium, we sat together in the right-field bleachers by the foul pole, near the fence. I wanted to watch Roger Maris (9) in Right Field and Mickey Mantle (7) in Center.

I thought about my grandfather's disparaging *kuronbo* nickname. I sat between the airman and my dad, out of my comfort zone for the first time, hanging out with my dad's adult friends. I had no preconceived notions about the airman except that we both supported the Yankees.

Later, I thought Tony had assigned me to sit next to the airman because the others would have felt uncomfortable with that in public, even though they fraternized at work.

Mantle and Maris played half the game, but to this day, seeing 9 and 7 play remains a highlight of my life. Sitting in Yankee Stadium for the 2001 World Series games is a close second.

By 1964, the Yankees had traded Moose Skowron to the Dodgers, and Joe Pepitone had taken over as the everyday 1st baseman. After the game, Joe walked across the outfield.

"Hey, Joe, how ya doin'?" my baseball pal yelled out as if he knew him, and maybe he did. Pepitone hailed from Brooklyn. Joe waved back at us.

We got back to Cheyenne late and dropped my new baseball friend off at the Fix 'n Mix. I never saw him again.

****

My mom not-so-subtly encouraged me to keep up with my sports card collection. When I took off for my first job in Gillette, Wyoming, she sorted through my childhood stuff from the basement, including a cardboard box of trading cards dating back to 1962, which I carted around for the next 40 years.

The hobby made a comeback in the 1980s and 1990s. Many mothers of Baby Boomer boys must have liberated their sons' collections. I compiled a complete set of 1961 and 1962 Topps brand card sets by attending shows and trading on eBay.

My colleague from the Lander WSJ, John, also collected cards. We opened a sports card store in Riverton called "Pine Riders." Any memorabilia business is great for collectors because it lets them buy wholesale. I traded for a program from the 1964 Yankees-Bears game, which I still have.

During my childhood, the Yankees made five consecutive World Series appearances, beginning with a 1960 loss to the Pittsburgh Pirates that I first saw on TV, deepening my Yankee fanaticism.

One of the low points of my baseball fandom came while watching Bill Mazeroski's walk-off homer at Forbes Field, which won Game 7 and the Series. I'm still not much of a Pirates fan today, and don't get me started on Mazeroski being in the Hall of Fame, but I digress.

The Yankees bounced back to win in the 1961 World Series. The news media focused on Roger Maris and Mickey Mantle in a friendly competition to break Babe Ruth's single-season home run record. Maris won the contest with an end-of-the-season blast off Boston Red Sox rookie pitcher Tracy Stallard.

That would be his 61st home run of the season, surpassing Babe Ruth's longstanding record of 60. MLB marked Maris's record with an asterisk because his feat occurred over 161 games, whereas Ruth played in 154 games during his record-setting season.

Former Yankee Bud Daley lived in Lander after retiring. He pitched the decisive Game 5 to win the 1961 championship. Bud spent a lot of time on the golf course and owned a landscaping business. John and I invited Bud to stop by and sign autographs for our card store's grand opening.

We asked another major leaguer, Woody Held, who played for the Cleveland Indians, to attend as a special guest. He lived nearby in Dubois. Bud and Woody knew each other from their playing days. Bud wore one of his World Series rings. We gathered a bunch of Bud and Woody cards for the occasion.

I chatted with Bud in front of a slot machine at the Northern Arapaho Tribe's Wind River Casino. Another tall, lanky baseball guy named Joe Lanham dropped him off. Joe played semi-pro ball in Georgia.

When I worked in Lander, Joe and his son owned a contracting business. He brought me back a Mason jar of moonshine. Over a few sips of "white lightning," Joe told a pretty good hidden-ball trick story.

After the catcher returned the ball to him, he lobbed a white object into the crowd. The runner on 3rd, a little confused, took off for home. Joe nailed the guy at the plate. He fooled the runner by throwing a peeled potato into the stands.

The Yankees won the World Series again in 1962 but lost back-to-back, first to the Los Angeles Dodgers in 1963. In the off-season, Ralph Houk took over as General Manager and named catcher Yogi Berra the new Manager. St. Louis won the 1964 World Series, with Bob Gibson on the mound, pitching a complete Game 7 and winning 7-5. The Yankees traded Maris to the Cardinals and won another ring that year.

Elston Howard became the full-time catcher after Houk promoted Berra to manager. Howard became the Yankees' first African American player, joining the team in 1955. The Yankees integrated shortly before the the Red Sox. In 1960, Boston pulled up the rear and added Pumpsie Green. He's no longer alive. I should contact his brother, Cornell, to ask about both of their experiences breaking into professional sports.

The Yankees signed Howard on July 19, 1950, and assigned him to their Central League farm team, the Muskegon Clippers. He served in the U.S. Army and missed the 1951 and 1952 seasons.

After his discharge, Howard played for the Class AAA Kansas City Blues in the American Association. The following season, the Yankees invited Howard to spring training in Florida.

****

My broken ankle ended my baseball career until I started playing softball as an adult. Dad and I played for the First Presbyterian Church slow-pitch softball team when I came home to Cheyenne during my first year at Hastings.

Dad, at age 50 and the oldest guy on the roster, played 1st base and catcher. Nobody liked to catch, so he always had a spot on the team.

"If you want to play, learn how to catch," he advised. "In slow-pitch, it's easy."

Dad's knees and back could no longer handle the position, but he could still bat. He always got on base and often led off. He could put the ball in play with shallow bloopers to the opposite field.

He relegated himself to the 1st-base coach role. I put on the mask and have been a catcher ever since, and I have always played.

I caught for my Lander slow-pitch softball team. Elston Howard from the Yankees' 1960s dynasty and my dad became my role models. I traded for Howard's rookie card, an oddball 1955 Bowman. Bowman designed its the Mid-Century Modern cards featuring colorized pictures of each player on a TV screen, bordered by a wooden cabinet complete with an on-off knob and a channel dial.

****

I'm a hands-on guy who likes to experience life firsthand. MLB postponed the end of the 2001 season to allow the dust to settle after the 9/11 terrorist attacks and rescheduled the playoffs. MLB delayed the World Series between the Yankees and the Arizona Diamondbacks to October 27–November 4.

My to-do list included watching the Yankees in the World Series. 2001 would be the year. The prospect of more airplane hijackings scared the traveling public, and airline ticket prices plummeted. World Series game tickets glutted the market well before counterfeiting became a growth industry.

I picked up ducats for close to face value on eBay for Games 3 and 4 at Yankee Stadium. I had them FedExed to my favorite Midtown Manhattan dive, the Hotel Pennsylvania. The Glenn Miller Orchestra's rendition of *Pennsylvania 6-5000* made the hotel's phone number famous. Vornado Realty Trust razed the Hotel Pennsylvania in 2023 to make way for the 56-story Penn15 skyscraper. That marked the end of an era. I'll have to find a new hotel in New York City.

I'd been to Lower Manhattan several times. On October 29th, I walked to the Downtown Deli, the walk-up restaurant's first day back after it had shut down because of the dust and debris that had shut down the neighborhood after 9/11. I ordered my usual Reuben sandwich and ate it at the front counter, smiling at the reunion of longtime customers and workers.

The Downtown Deli has also permanently closed, so I'll need to find a new Lower Downtown eatery.

After lunch, I wandered around and caught glimpses of the devastation. I'd never seen such damage. Each time I visit New York City, I walk along Greenwich Street and take a few photos.

****

After the Diamondbacks dominated the first two games in Phoenix, play resumed in the Big Apple. I met my Hastings College Eta Phi Lambda fraternity brother, Tom Crisp, for coffee before taking the subway to the Bronx. I stayed in Tom's apartment on the Upper West Side during the Robert McKee *Story* seminar in 2004.

Another transition: Tom fell on the sidewalk, hit his head in a freak accident, and never woke up. His sisters removed life support a week later, and Tom died on August 26, 2024.

I arrived in the Bronx early to soak up the atmosphere, stopped at Stan's Sports Bar for a beer, and then walked to Yankee Stadium for a hot dog. The Yankees won three games in dramatic fashion.

During those three days in New York City, every baseball fan wore pinstripes. The Yankees' 2001 World Series run unified Americans.

Suddenly, race, ethnicity, and social class didn't matter. I sensed civic solidarity and patriotism with everyone around me.

Before Game 3, the Stars and Stripes that had flown over the World Trade Center fluttered in the center-field autumn breeze. Lee Greenwood stood on the field, singing "I'm Proud to Be an American," and President George W. Bush, wearing a flak vest under his navy blue Presidential jacket, threw out the first pitch.

After Arizona won the first two games in Phoenix, Roger Clemens took the mound for the Yankees in Game 3. He threw seven innings of one-run ball before closer Mariano Rivera pitched the eighth and ninth for the save. Catcher Jorge Posada homered, and 3rd baseman Scott Brosius drove in the game-winning run with an RBI single in the sixth. The Yankees won, 2-1.

Game 4 ended in dramatic fashion. Derek Jeter hit a home run in the early morning of November 1st, adding to the sweep. Because of his heroics, Jeter became known as "Mr. November." The Yankees won, 4-3.

I watched Game 5, which ended after 12 innings at Diana's sister's house in Concord, Massachusetts. The Yankees won, 3-2.

The Bronx Bombers took a 3-2 game advantage back to Arizona. The 2001 World Series provided an emotional lift, even though the Diamondbacks won the Series in seven games on a blooper hit into shallow center by Luis Gonzalez off Yankees closer Mariano Rivera, scoring Craig Counsell to end Game 7.

Visiting New York in the aftermath of the terrorist attacks to watch the Yankees electrified me in a sobering kind of way.

A dark side emerged as patriotic civility waned. According to Human Rights Watch, FBI statistics show that hate crimes against Muslims rose from 28 in 2000 to 481 in 2001. Since then, Muslim hate crimes have become normalized and politicized. Conservative politicians and pundits accused Barack Obama of being a non-citizen and demanded that he produce his birth certificate.

Hate crimes against Muslims spiked from 2016 to 2020, fueled by political rhetoric during the COVID-19 pandemic. The October 7, 2023, Hamas terrorist attack didn't slow the rise in hate crimes.

****

The 2001 World Series took me back to my childhood, when I first saw the Yankees in 1964. My dream of playing shortstop for the Yankees never came true. The manager always gave the job to someone else. There have been few Asian players in MLB.

I liked Lenn Sakata from Hawaii, who is unrelated to my mom's family. Sakata played his best years at shortstop and second base for the Baltimore Orioles, the team that won the 1983 World Series. He played his final season with the New York Yankees in 1987.

Lenn gave me hope that I could have played middle infield for the Yankees. During the heyday, the list of World Series Champion years included Tony Kubek (1961-1962), Bucky Dent (1977-1978), and Derek Jeter (1996, 1998, 2000, 2009).

After Jeter retired, the Yankees have had a revolving door at shortstop. The scouts passed me over again. I should have kept up with piano lessons instead of playing Little League.

I might have had a better chance of banging out *Take Me Out to the Ball Game* on the Yankee Stadium organ than of diving for hot ground balls up the gap.

Grandpa Sakata visited his daughter, Hisako, in Washington, DC. On one trip, he brought me back a Washington Senators cap with the red W emblazoned on the front.

That must have been around 1960, before the Senators became the Minnesota Twins. While I appreciated his gesture, my mom helped me embroider a Yankees *NY* on the cap.

There's a photo of me wearing that makeshift hat after the neighborhood kids toured the Plains Dairy. Mr. St. Clair, of Roman Candle battle fame, and his family lived across the alley. He organized tours of local places, including the dairy, and took us to the movies.

****

My dad treating me to the Yankees in Denver cemented our relationship. We bonded over baseball. He bought me the first baseball glove I saw at Ben Franklin in the Cole Shopping Center. I played with it until I signed up for Little League.

One summer, while playing catch with one of the older neighbor kids, Nick, he burned one to me. My glove didn't have a very deep pocket, and the ball ricocheted off and bonked me on the cheek, knocking me out. After that, I looked for a different glove. I couldn't afford a new, higher-quality one.

Mom's Presbyterian Women's Circle sponsored a giant rummage sale in the fall. I liked to help sort out the piles of clothes and sundries. Mostly, I looked through all the merchandise and picked out a thing or two before the doors opened.

At the 1963 sale on Saturday, November 23rd, I dug out a Rawlings baseball glove from a box in the inventory room. The glove fit my tiny hand perfectly. For a dime, I used it throughout my Little League and Babe Ruth baseball years.

Wally Moon, the 1954 National League Rookie of the Year, played for the dreaded Los Angeles Dodgers and endorsed it. Moon played on three Los Angeles Dodgers World Series championship teams in 1959, 1963, and 1965.

I remember the rummage sale date because the Friday before, on November 22nd, Lee Harvey Oswald assassinated JFK in Dallas.

"It served him right," one of the Women's Club members growled, apparently a Nixon supporter. She stormed into the church kitchen, disgusted by the assassination conversation, while the others in the room stood stunned and silent. The disdainful woman in my mom's church group lived across from the community pool in the Cole Addition.

JFK made stops in Wyoming, including Cheyenne, Laramie, and Jackson, shortly before Lee Harvey Oswald assassinated him in 1963. Local newspaper mogul Tracy McCracken arranged the visit.

There's a frequently used TV news clip of McCracken barking out the Wyoming delegation's votes, which put JFK over the top and secured the nomination for President. That moment played on a hotel room TV in the movie *LBJ* (2016), with Woody Harrelson in the starring role.

The school district dismissed school so students could go to the Cheyenne airport to see JFK. My mom took my sister and me. We arrived late and watched from behind the perimeter fence, past the airport terminal, at a distance far from the stage. The President gave a brief speech before driving over Sherman Hill to Laramie, where a capacity crowd greeted him in the Field House on the UW campus, which had a mulched floor.

The mitt I bought at the Presbyterian Church rummage sale held more memories of that day in November than did those around the Little League baseball field.

****

I brought my Wally Moon glove to the Yankees-Bears game in 1964, hoping to catch a home run ball hit by Mickey Mantle. Little did I know that same year, Masanori "Mashi" Murakami would become the first Japanese player in MLB.

He began his professional baseball career with the Nankai Hawks in Japan's Nippon Professional Baseball (NPB). NPB is Japan's top baseball league, comprising the Central and Pacific Leagues.

In 1964, the Nankai Hawks sent Murakami to the United States as part of an exchange program between Japanese and American baseball teams. He initially played for the Fresno Giants, a minor-league affiliate of the Giants.

His impressive minor-league performance, including a 1.78 ERA and 104 strikeouts in 11 starts, earned him a call-up to the San Francisco Giants. Murakami debuted on September 1, 1964. In his rookie season, he appeared in nine games, posting a 1.80 ERA and earning one save. The following season, he appeared in 45 games, going 4-1 with a 3.75 ERA and eight saves.

A contractual dispute between the Nankai Hawks and the Giants prompted Murakami's return to Japan after the 1965 season. Mashi's journey paved the way for other notable *nihon jin* players, including Hideo Nomo, Ichiro Suzuki, Hideki Matsui, and Shohei Otani, to succeed in MLB.

****

In 1995, I treated my dad to the first game, an exhibition matchup at the brand-new Coors Field in Denver between the Colorado Rockies and the Yankees.

The game took place at the start of the strike-shortened season, between the replacement Yankees and the replacement Rockies. Colorado made the playoffs that season as the first-ever Wild-Card team.

The Rockies lost to the eventual World Series champion Atlanta Braves three games to one in the best-of-four Series (Best of Three+One). The extra game extended the shortened season. In the event of a 2-2 tie after four games, the winner of a fifth game, hosted by the team with the better regular-season record, would break the deadlock.

I gave up my Rockies season tickets after the 1998 MLB All-Star Game at Coors Field. The Rockies held little interest for me after my fantasy baseball league disbanded, even during the 2007 World Series, when the Boston Red Sox swept the Rox in four games.

****

I volunteer at the National Baseball Park Museum on Blake Street near Coors Field. The Museum houses Bruce Hellerstein's collection of artifacts from 14 classic ballparks, including Wrigley Field and Fenway Park, the only two still standing.

In 2019, Bruce asked whether I would record interviews with several former Nisei players about Japanese baseball. He partnered with the Japanese American Resource Center of Colorado (JARCC) to mount an exhibit titled "Japanese American Baseball: A Shared Experience" that showcased the growth of baseball in Colorado. Alan Suzuki, a Sansei, is researching Japanese baseball history in the Denver area. He and Millie King handled much of the JARCC preproduction and coordinated the panel of players.

A panel discussion at the Colorado History Museum highlighted the exhibit. Panelists included Japanese American baseball expert Kerry Yo Nakagawa, author and PBS documentary director; Dan Evans, former GM of the LA Dodgers; and Rowher Camp and baseball player Masaru "Mas" Yoshimura.

Mas ended up in Denver after stints at the Rowher and later at the Jerome camps. He became the starting 1st baseman for the Denver Nisei Baseball Club.

A train transported Mas and his family from the Fresno Assembly Camp. The train stopped at the Cheyenne depot for a break. The Military Police allowed the detainees off the train for a stretch break. A host of soldiers stationed along the railway platform greeted the passengers, aiming .50-caliber machine guns at them.

When the War ended, the WRA paroled Mas and his family to Denver, where he joined a Nisei league team. Many northern Colorado teams existed, including those in Fort Lupton, Greeley, and Brighton. Teams also had formed in Wyoming.

****

MLB suddenly moved the 2021 All-Star Game and the baseball draft from Atlanta to Coors Field in Denver in response to Georgia's newly enacted voting law that restricted voting access for minority groups.

"Do you want to help out at the Ball Park Museum during All-Star week?" my baseball-fan neighbor, Henry Kroll, asked. "All we do is sell tickets and answer questions."

"Yeah, sounds like fun. When's the first day?"

Senate Bill 202 introduced changes to Georgia's voting procedures, including new ID requirements for absentee ballots, limits on ballot drop boxes, and restrictions on providing food and water to voters waiting in line. Critics argued that these measures disproportionately affected voters in minority communities and would suppress voter turnout.

MLB Commissioner Rob Manfred announced the decision on April 2, 2021, stating that the League supports voting rights for all Americans and opposes restrictions on ballot access.

Posing for a photo with former Red Sox player David "Big Papi" Ortiz highlighted my All-Star break. I asked him to sign an All-Star Game baseball. The Museum arranged with MLB for the Hall of Famer to greet fans and pitch Papa John's Pizza.

Big Papi looked good, considering he nearly died after a jealous drug dealer shot him in 2019. He's one big dude.

Every year, All-Star Week is a big festival around the host ballpark. In Denver, former players signed autographs. Topps gave out baseball cards. Kids swung in batting cages. I took my dad to the 1998 All-Star Game at Coors Field. MLB gave away a limited edition Beanie Baby. My mom avidly collected the plush bears.

The 2021 event featured similar attractions.

Civil rights groups and voting rights advocates praised MLB for acting decisively. Still, the decision drew criticism from political figures and others who argued that politics motivated the change and unfairly penalized local businesses and fans in Atlanta. Despite the controversy, MLB stood by its ruling, which favors communities that support fair voting access. I doubt Georgia will change its evil ways.

I spoke with a Museum guest from Cheyenne. Based on our conversation, I surmised that he lived in one of the Lotus townhouses on West 17th Street.

"I had no idea it used to be a Japanese community," he said, surprised. "I'll buy your book and watch the documentary. It's *Beyond Heart Mountain*? Amazon and PBS Passport, you said?"

I had no intention of going to the game. I didn't want the hassle of fighting through the crowds at the hot dog and beer lines. Besides, the game wouldn't have meant as much as the one I attended with my dad. I refuse to pay outlandish prices for a tickets to any big-time sporting event. I had more fun talking with museum-goers. The American League defeated the National League 5-2 for the eighth consecutive time.

****

After the bombing of Pearl Harbor, MLB Commissioner Kenesaw Landis wrote to President Roosevelt seeking his opinion on whether professional baseball should continue to play games during wartime.

FDR responded with the Green Light Letter, stating that baseball is a tightly woven fabric binding Americans together. He recommended that professional baseball continue on the home front.

Over 500 professional ballplayers from the white cheese melting pot served in the military during the War. Baseball didn't integrate until 1947, when the Brooklyn Dodgers signed Jackie Robinson. The military assigned notable stars to light duty.

New York Yankee Joe DiMaggio enlisted in the U.S. Army Air Force in February 1943. The Yankee Clipper spent most of his time playing baseball for military teams and teaching PE classes.

Ted Williams took leave from the Boston Red Sox. He enlisted in the U.S. Navy in 1942 and later became a Marine Corps pilot. Ted "The Splinter" served as a flight instructor and did not see combat during World War II. The U.S. Army recalled him to active duty during the Korean War, during which he flew 39 combat missions.

St. Louis Cardinal Stan Musial enlisted in the U.S. Navy in January 1945. Stan the Man served as a sailor stationed in Hawaii, where he played baseball for Navy teams.

The U.S. Military didn't offer a clear-cut option for the incarcerated Japanese men to serve their counry.

22

Draft Avoidance

President FDR signed the Selective Training and Service Act into law on September 16, 1940. The legislation marked the first peacetime conscription in United States history. I read a conjectural account in which Clark Kent registered for the draft. He reported for his physical, and because of his X-ray vision, he recited a different eye chart in the next room and flunked the vision test. The Smallville Draft Board classified him as 4-F.

Clark does his part and supports the War effort from the home front. He embraces his role as Superman with a strong sense of duty and responsibility. From a young age, his parents instilled in him the importance of using his extraordinary abilities for the greater good.

Throughout the War years, Clark struggles with the pressures and personal sacrifices that come with being a superhero but doesn't shy away from his dedication to truth, justice, and protecting the American Way.

****

Dad turned 18 on March 17, 1941, but his doctor diagnosed him with a heart murmur. The Cheyenne Draft Board classified him as 4-F, unfit for service. He supported the war effort by founding the Skyline Nisei Club from scratch. The Club offered a safe space for the Cheyenne Japanese community amid overt and subtle racism.

Like Clark Kent, I had no family pressure to serve. Uncle Rich said nothing to me about enlisting. As a high school student, all I knew about war came from reading Sgt. Rock comic books.

Young men who served in the military embodied the American Way on their path to the American Dream. When I turned 18, Mom watched from the front doorway as I stepped into my red Ford Falcon. I drove to the Cheyenne Selective Service Office to register for the draft, with the possibility of being sent to Vietnam.

The recruitment officer sat alone at his desk when I opened the office door. He had me fill out some paperwork, my tangible, personal act of patriotism.

My parents had a better sense of what that would entail than I imagined. We had the TV news on during dinner. They preferred CBS news anchor Walter Cronkite.

The correspondents embedded among the troops reported on the casualty count, which sparked a few family discussions about the Vietnam War around the dinner table but nothing about me enlisting.

My draft card arrived in the mail, indicating my 1-H deferred status. By the time my first day at Hastings College rolled around, the Vietnam War had begun to de-escalate, while President Nixon ordered the secret bombing of Cambodia.

In 1969, the U.S. Selective Service replaced the traditional draft with a birthdate lottery system. The Lottery Board assigned a number to each day of the year. Critics argued that the original draft system disproportionately affected certain demographic groups, particularly lower-income individuals and minorities.

Wealthier individuals could avoid service through college deferments or crony connections. Public outrage over the draft's perceived unfairness fueled widespread protests and social unrest in the 1960s and early 1970s.

As public sentiment shifted against the Vietnam War and concerns about the draft grew, policymakers recognized the need for a system that could restore legitimacy to military conscription. A randomized selection process, based on birthdate, gave each eligible person an equal chance of being drafted, helping to create a perception of fairness in the selection process.

Advocates believed the lottery fostered a more transparent and equitable process. I lucked out when the Selective Service drew lottery number 275 on Groundhog Day, February 2, 1972, for those born on May 2, 1953.

****

As a sophomore, I enrolled in a Hastings College Interim field trip course titled "Legislators and Lobbyists." My roommate, Sam, and I joined a busload of classmates who traveled to President Richard Nixon's Inauguration on January 20, 1973, in Washington, DC.

My road trip highlight: I saw Colonel Harlan Sanders, of Kentucky Fried Chicken fame, shaking hands on a Chicago sidewalk as the bus drove through the Windy City.

We stayed at the Alban Towers, a hotel that also rented rooms to long-term tenants, which caught fire during our stay. The lingering smell of smoke that permeated the drapes and rugs gave us a great reason to get out into the field.

The coursework included lectures from legislative staff, lobbyists from Common Cause, and government agencies.

My roommate, Sam from Cody, had arranged for us to have lunch with a family friend, U.S. Senator Cliff Hansen (R-WY). He's the same "Cliff" who drove Roy and Joanne Takeda from the Jackson Airport to the Wort Hotel. We met for lunch of Navy bean soup in the Senate dining room.

We had a full Inauguration Day. My Hastings group arrived early and found a spot to watch, relatively close to the action. Sam boosted me up a light pole, giving me a higher vantage point for unobstructed photos. In this day and age, I wouldn't have been able to do that without getting arrested.

After the ceremony and parade, we returned to the Alban Towers. Law enforcement officers caught us in tear gas crossfire while dispersing a demonstration against the not-so-secret bombing of Cambodia. We walked back, coughing, to the Alban Towers.

The Inauguration headlined the week, but other noteworthy events also occurred. SCOTUS decided *Roe v. Wade*, and former President Lyndon Johnson died on January 22nd. I stood in line to view LBJ laying in state under the Capitol Rotunda.

Shortly after our return to Hastings, the U.S. Selective Service held the draft lottery for Sam's birth year, 1954, on March 8, 1973. Sam drew a not-so-lucky number below 20. He had to report for a pre-induction physical. Sam recounted a scene to me that sounded like Bill Murray's induction scene in the movie *Stripes* (1981), in which he and Harold Ramis enlisted.

****

Maybe I would have felt more patriotic had I known that former Secretary of Defense Robert McNamara, who served during the JFK and LBJ administrations and the Vietnam War, had conceptualized my red Ford Falcon.

McNamara, a young upstart executive at the Ford Motor Company, designed the Falcon after the mid-size Edsel debacle. The compact proved an enormous success in 1957, competing with the VW Type I Bug, the Chevy Corvair, and the Plymouth Valiant.

The politically unpopular Vietnam War, as evident from the tear gas in DC, had no clear enemy. As such, the U.S. had no chance of winning through traditional warfare against ideological guerrillas who didn't follow the rules of engagement.

The U.S. began training the Army of the Republic of Vietnam (ARVN). When the Easter Offensive began in March 1972, the scale and intensity of the North Vietnamese assault initially surprised ARVN forces.

U.S. military advisors provided extensive training and financial support to the ARVN. American military strategy relied on capable

South Vietnamese forces to assume primary responsibility as American troops withdrew.

Raw, local troops, compounded by command-and-control issues, sustained heavy losses during the Battle of Two Cities in Quang Tri and Hue. Despite their training, they struggled in urban warfare, in part because of inadequate preparation for an aggressive, coordinated enemy offensive. ARVN casualties totaled 5,400, compared with around 200 U.S. deaths. Quang Tri and Hue fell to North Vietnamese forces.

After nearly 20 years of U.S. military presence in Vietnam, Nixon planned to withdraw. Henry Kissinger, Nixon's Secretary of State, negotiated the final departure on March 29, 1973, leaving out-of-work veterans on the streets. Soldiers bravely earned Purple Hearts, Bronze Stars, and Silver Stars, but not all of them received a hero's welcome when they returned home.

Instead, disenfranchised veterans faced unemployment, alcohol and drug abuse, and mental and physical health issues caused by PTSD. Vets claimed that protesters blamed the troops rather than the U.S. government's poor decisions.

Eliminating the draft meant military duty had become a job. Draftees in World War II worked as meat cutters, railroad workers, and teachers. After the War, they returned to their civilian workplaces. Captain Miller (Tom Hanks) in *Saving Private Ryan* (1998) eagerly wants to return to teaching, but the enemy kills him after he saves Private Ryan (Matt Damon).

Serving in the armed forces is now a career, given the all-volunteer military. The macroeconomic phrase "Guns or Butter" is an analogy for the trade-offs between defense and civilian spending and how the two can best balance the country's economic needs. When soldiers give up their guns, they can deliver butter, such as building roads and bridges or constructing affordable housing.

****

On January 23, 1973, the week after President Nixon's Inauguration, the United States and the Democratic Republic of Vietnam signed the Paris Peace Accords. The accords allowed the U.S. to withdraw from Vietnam and repatriate American prisoners of war. Nixon called the agreement a way to "end the war and bring peace with honor in Vietnam and Southeast Asia." In my view, Nixon's reelection motivated him more than his pursuit of peace.

The last U.S. combat troops left South Vietnam on March 29, 1973, though about 7,000 civilian employees remained to assist South Vietnam. In March 1975, North Vietnamese forces launched a major offensive in the Central Highlands. Fighting between North and South Vietnam continued until Saigon fell in 1975.

After my trip to DC, I enrolled in an intensive Hastings College Interim class during my junior year, alongside several Vietnam veterans, to study the history of American involvement in Southeast Asia. By 1974, the U.S. had withdrawn its military presence. The veterans shared cathartic stories and experiences from combat and from their return home.

In retrospect, I could have enlisted in the military, knowing that three of my uncles fought in Italy. Still, I don't regret staying on the sidelines after witnessing the anti-war unrest at Nixon's inaugural, his subsequent impeachment, and his resignation.

"You didn't miss anything," Tom, my Gillette housemate, would say. Tom served in the 101st Airborne, known as the "Screaming Eagles." The North Vietnamese called the 101st the "Chicken Men" because its emblem featured an eagle. The Vietnamese had never seen an eagle before. Enemy commanders warned their troops to avoid the 101st, which earned a reputation as the most feared U.S. unit in the Vietnam War.

Tom's stories about being a "Comic Book Hero" and about how he earned a Purple Heart and a Bronze Star brought me close enough to the action. President FDR signed Executive Order 9419 on February 4, 1944, establishing the Bronze Star retroactive to December 7, 1941.

****

I ardently supported Bobby Kennedy and have wondered how the world would have turned out if he had been elected president in 1968. The Vietnam War might have ended sooner, and Watergate and the subsequent political upheaval wouldn't have occurred.

If the military drafted me, like Muhammad Ali, I would have resisted or applied to be a Conscientious Objector. It made no sense for me, an Asian, to travel thousands of miles to kill other Asians.

Baby Boomer men had mixed military experiences that I missed because of the lottery system. I didn't enlist because of how TV news portrayed the bloody realities of the Vietnam War. One of my Fairview Elementary classmates enlisted and saw combat during the Easter Offensive and the Battle of Two Cities, while I sat as a draft avoider in college.

During World War II, patriotic citizens upheld the American Way. Traditional war defined "good guys" and "bad guys." The American Way cast my parents and family as bad guys on the home front because they looked like the enemy, even though they did their best to assimilate into mainstream society.

23

Reluctant Heroes of the 442nd

Japanese Americans went above and beyond what society expected for minimal acceptance as Model Minorities. DC Comics cast Superman as the underdog outsider destined to keep America safe. Similarly, many Japanese American men sought to rid the world of totalitarian regimes by demonstrating their loyalty to the United States amid the suspicion and prejudice they faced after Pearl Harbor.

The U.S. had an image problem when it entered World War II to fight the Nazis and Fascism, while ironically incarcerating Japanese Americans.

Before Pearl Harbor, international tensions between the United States and Japan escalated. The U.S. Department of War trained Americans as Japanese-language interpreters and translators in anticipation of war.

By 1940, the U.S. Army had enlisted or drafted more than 5,000 Nisei, mostly Hawaiians. In November 1941, the Military Intelligence Service Language School (MIS Language School) assigned 60 students, including 58 Japanese Americans. My uncle Rich joined its first class in San Francisco.

The U.S. military gave individual commanders the option to discharge Japanese American soldiers who served on the mainland, to take away their weapons, and to assign those who remained in the U.S. Army to desk jobs or menial tasks such as latrine duty.

Some local draft boards refused to accept any Nisei, even American citizens, due to their Japanese ancestry. Meanwhile, the Hawaii National Guard secretly organized its Nisei soldiers into the Hawaii Provisional Infantry Battalion. The U.S. Army transported 1,400 soldiers to San Francisco and then to Camp McCoy in Wisconsin, where they formed the 100th Infantry Battalion.

The U.S. Army formed the Board of Military Utilization of U.S. Citizens of Japanese Ancestry, composed of military brass and the WRA, which recommended against forming an all-Japanese American fighting unit because of "universal mistrust" of the Japanese.

The Office of War Information disagreed and sent President Roosevelt a letter stating that Japanese Americans in the Army would counter allegations of racism. FDR subsequently formed the 442nd Infantry Regiment (IR).

****

In February 1943, authorities activated eager Nisei enlistees from Hawaii and incarceration camp volunteers, and a quarter of 442nd IR soldiers volunteered from Minidoka. By serving in the 442nd, Nisei men wanted to prove their dedication to the United States and improve the status of Japanese Americans. They hoped their service and sacrifices would help alleviate the distrust and discrimination their families and communities endured.

The 442nd IR caused conflict between its 1,500 Yes-Yes members and the wider Japanese community over the Loyalty Questionnaire. Many No-No boys resisted the draft and believed that the enlistees had caved to authoritarian U.S. military pressure and had ended up in jail.

The recruits joined the 100th Infantry Battalion's training at Camp Shelby, Mississippi. The 442nd IR, the 522nd Field Artillery

Battalion, and the 232nd Combat Engineer Company formed the 442nd Regimental Combat Team (RCT), which served as a self-sufficient and effective combat force. In June 1944, the 442nd deployed to Italy alongside the 100th Infantry Battalion.

The Caucasian commissioned officers selected noncommissioned officers from among mainland Japanese troops already in the U.S. Army. Soldiers from Hawaii on active duty before Pearl Harbor resented the Army brass for passing them over for noncommissioned officer positions.

Military commanders struggled to maintain morale in the new regiment, particularly among the Japanese American soldiers from Hawaii and those in the U.S. Army before the War who resented recruits from the incarceration camps. Arguments and fights broke out between "buddhaheads" from Hawaii and "kotonks" from the mainland.

The Hawaiian soldiers coined these monikers, referring to their dominant religion, claiming that kotonk sounded like a mainlander's hollow noggin when they smacked the ground.

While they had differences within their ranks, they, like Black Americans, shared a struggle against racism in the Jim Crow South. The Japanese soldiers occasionally intervened on behalf of African Americans, prompting reprimands from their superior officers.

****

The 442nd RCT participated in the invasion of the South of France in September 1944, liberating Bruyères and Biffontaine and rescuing a battalion that had become separated from its division.

The "Lost Battalion" is a story arc behind the movie *Go for Broke* (1951). "Go for Broke" is the 442nd's motto. Lt. Michael Grayson (Van Johnson) is a bigoted commanding officer who changes his tune after fighting alongside the 442nd RCT. Robert Pirosh directed the movie and also created the TV show *Combat!* There is no *Combat!* episode about the 442nd in France, which surprised me.

In March 1945, the 442nd RCT and the 100th Battalion finished the War by joining forces with the African American 92nd Infantry Division, also known as the Buffalo Soldiers, to drive the Nazis out of northern Italy.

By the end of the War, the 442nd RCT suffered the following casualties: 650 men dead, 3,700 wounded, and 67 declared Missing In Action. The Regiment earned the following awards:

- 7 Presidential Unit Citations
- 2 Meritorious Service Plaques
- 36 Army Commendation Medals
- 87 Division Commendations

442nd RCT individuals awarded:

- 21 Medals of Honor
- 29 Distinguished Service Crosses
- 560 Silver Stars
- 4,000 Bronze Stars
- 22 Legion of Merit medals
- 15 Soldiers Medals
- 9,500 Purple Hearts

The MIS Language School recruited more linguists to join the 442nd. Uncle Rich never mentioned a special citation from the school or a Purple Heart. When I saw the medals at his funeral, I wondered about the circumstances behind his decorations.

"You fought the enemy abroad and prejudice at home, and you won," said President Harry Truman, who invited the 442nd RCT to a ceremony on the White House Ellipse in 1946. He also inspected the unit and presented it with its seventh Presidential Unit Citation. April 5th is "Go for Broke" Day, honoring Japanese World War II veterans.

The Department of War awarded Toshiro "Tosh" Suyematsu of Casper, Wyoming, the most decorated soldier of the 442nd, the Purple Heart, the Purple Heart with an Oak Leaf Cluster, two Silver

Stars, and the Bronze Star. The citation for one of Tosh's Silver Stars notes his role in the liberation of the "Lost Battalion."

By the direction of the President, the Silver Star was awarded to Toshiro Suyematsu for gallantry in action on 22-24 October and 28-29 October 1944, near Biffontaine, France. Sergeant Suyematsu was a forward observer with the 100th Battalion during the unit's isolation near Biffontaine. When he was directed to lay a creeping barrage on the reverse side of a hill to forestall the barrage from his observation point until the rounds were just clearing the trees above him. Despite the ever-present danger of the tree bursts and a subsequent counter barrage by the enemy, which came in over the ridge and bracketed him between two curtains of fire, he continued his fire mission.

****

Tosh moved with his parents, Tsuchio "Ben" and Masa Suyematsu, from Oakland, California, where Ben repaired shoes. The family came to Casper in 1919, where Ben worked for the CB&Q railroad until the 1922 railroad strike, when 400,000 workers walked off the job in protest against a national wage decrease. After quitting the railroad, Ben returned to his previous trade and set up a shoe repair shop in North Casper.

The Suyematsus and my mother's family knew each other because my grandfather Sakata and Ben Suyematsu worked for CB&Q at or near the Powder River and Arminto sections in Natrona County. Tosh had two brothers, King and Taro, whom I didn't know very well. I met their kids but saw them only on rare occasions in Casper.

Auntie Hisako befriended Tosh's sisters: Sara, a nurse in Casper, and Kiyo, a music professor at Mankato State University in Minnesota. Like my aunt, they never married and often visited Cheyenne. My family frequently traveled to Casper. Sara and Kiyo took me on my first ski outing on Casper Mountain, where I had to lace up heavy leather boots.

Tosh had enrolled at UW before World War II. He ran out of tuition money and left school to join the U.S. Army. He attained the rank of sergeant, but on November 30, 1941, his superior officers demoted him to buck private.

Japan bombed Pearl Harbor a week later. The U.S. Army assigned him and other Japanese soldiers, including his brother, King, to desk jobs until they volunteered for the 442nd Infantry Regiment.

Tosh returned to UW after the War, completed his undergraduate degree, and then attended law school. He remained in southeastern Wyoming, where he practiced law with his wife, Ellen Crowley, in Cheyenne. She served in the Wyoming State Legislature. Tosh served as Wyoming's Assistant U.S. Attorney General during the Nixon, Gerald Ford, Jimmy Carter, Ronald Reagan, and George H.W. Bush administrations.

The U.S. Army awarded Ted Miyamoto of Baker's Place, a member of the 442nd RCT, the Bronze Star for his role in France, where he supported the Lost Battalion. His citation reads:

For extraordinary heroism in action on Oct. 29, 1944, near Biffontaine, France. When the forward elements of Sergeant Miyamoto's company were pinned down by fire from an enemy machine gun and supporting snipers, he fearlessly worked his way forward to the enemy emplacement. While so engaged, he was wounded in the forearm by a sniper, but disdaining medical treatment, he continued to advance until he reached a point within 25 yards from the emplacement; exposing himself to get a better observation, opened fire with his submachine gun, killed the two gunners and thus neutralized the position in the two-hour firefight that followed, Sgt. Miyamoto accounted for five more of the enemy and refused to be evacuated until the initial objective was reached.

I'm grateful to the men who enlisted and put their lives on the line to join the 442nd and prove their loyalty until I began researching this book. Their perseverance in combat allowed me to participate in once racially segregated activities, such as playing baseball in the Cheyenne Little League and softball in town leagues rather than on Japanese-only teams.

24

First Harvests and Rites of Passage

My high draft lottery number meant I could sit out the Vietnam War. I also avoided a rite of passage that had been a male tradition since America's founding. I could have enlisted, but my parents dissuaded me because of how the U.S. government treated the Japanese during World War II.

Cool and calm Superman didn't kill anyone, but he came close in "The Stolen Costume," the 13th episode of the first season of the *Adventures of Superman* (1952) television series.

The Rope Burglar threatens Superman's secret identity when he breaks into Clark Kent's apartment, discovers Superman's costume, and delivers it to a fence named Ace (Dan Seymour) and his girlfriend, Connie (Veda Ann Borg). The two threaten to blackmail Kent.

Superman captures Ace and Connie, abandons them at a remote mountaintop cabin, and promises to bring firewood and food. They try to escape but fall to their deaths.

The episode occasionally streams on cable TV. I've always thought Superman's decision to let them die didn't fit his character as a virtuous superhero, even though the two criminals took a big risk by trying to escape during a snowstorm.

The difference between Clark and me is that he had an alter ego that expressed his aggressive tendencies, assailing bad guys.

****

My dad's brother, Rich, subsisted on hunted game. I decided that hunting would be a way to play out what I viewed as a barbaric rite of passage.

After Pearl Harbor, police tracked down Japanese families in town. Federal agents confiscated the hunting rifles when they stopped by Grandpa Ohashi's. I don't know whether the law enforcement agency returned them, but Rich had a well-stocked gun cabinet where he kept various long rifles and shotguns.

I knew little about Uncle Rich's subsistence hunting. I still haven't developed a taste for venison, but I liked the elk steaks and the hamburger he brought over following a big hunt.

He worked as a meat cutter at the Stop 'n Shop grocery store, a sister business to Fix 'n Mix, where we picked up the airman on our way to watch the Yankees play in Denver. I imagine Uncle Rich drew on that experience when field-dressing big game.

My mom made it clear she forbade me from joining Rich's hunting trips, a stark contrast to Wyoming's gun culture. In the Cowboy State, hunting is a way of life.

When hunting season opened in the fall, schools excused students from classes. I saw hunting as a rite of passage I had missed during my childhood.

****

The Lander softball season had ended, and local volunteers had begun preparations for the Lander One Shot Antelope Hunt, scheduled for mid-September. In 1939, Harold Evans and Hank Dahl established the annual competition in Lander.

The One Shot became one of the oldest and most prestigious hunting events in the United States. The competition originally comprised two teams from Wyoming and Colorado. The Hunt issues each participant a single bullet to harvest a pronghorn antelope.

Now organizers invite teams of three hunters representing specific groups, such as astronauts or movie stars. One year, I sat in the Union Bar when Roy Rogers and Little Jimmy Dickens wandered in, turned around, and left.

The One Shot initially limited participation to Caucasian males. I lived in Lander in the 1980s. The losing hunters participated in an Eastern Shoshone "squaw dance." Women hunters took part in the event for the first time in 2021. Advancing through the One Shot Antelope Hunt hierarchy required paying penance by volunteering for menial tasks, such as setting up tables. I'm not much of a joiner and had no interest in the annual planning, but others did, including my friend Mike.

Like mine, society challenged Clark Kent to straddle two worlds and be "one of the boys." Clark conceals his superpowers, appears weak, and struggles with this duality. I think that hunting allows men to get violent aggression out of their systems. I didn't serve in the military and missed that adrenaline rush.

"You can't live in Lander and not be a hunter," Mike said with surprise.

"I've always wanted to try hunting," I said. "I haven't had the opportunity. My mom didn't allow guns in the house."

"That's on account of the War," Mike added. "I get that."

He sold me a .243-caliber Winchester with open sights for $200, and Wendall at the local camera store sold me a scope.

I had some prior experience with guns. Tom, my Gillette housemate and Vietnam vet, owned an AR-15 semi-automatic that we would take to the back lot to blast Commie tin cans back to the Stone Age. Our target practice took me back to my youth, imagining myself as Sgt. Saunders on *Combat!*

When you consider a guy like me who could get a hold of an unregistered rifle, firearms are very accessible. Mike helped me calibrate the scope at the local gun range south of town.

He recommended that I take a hunting safety class to become as knowledgeable as any other first-time hunter. Mike guided me, but he had rules: I couldn't shoot from the vehicle or the road, and I had to pick an animal and stalk it.

We spent all morning following around an antelope buck. The spiked critter finally stopped and stared back at me from 100 yards ahead. I aimed and squeezed the trigger. His knees buckled, and the lifeless antelope dropped to the dusty prairie.

Mike showed me how to field-dress the animal. I waited while he brought the truck around. We dropped the carcass off at the processing place in Lander. Antelope meat has always tasted gamey to me, but this tasted very mild compared to some I have tried.

Mike at least made a day of it with his stalking rule. Otherwise, we could have been home hours earlier. An animal has no chance against even a small-bore rifle like mine. Taking this antelope would be the first and last game animal I would stalk, shoot, and kill. I'm glad I got that measured violence out of my system.

I moved my rifle around, from closets to crawl spaces to basements. Many years later, I traded it to a guy for some tile work on a condo remodel in Boulder.

Men who fought in World War II or the Vietnam War faced difficult times upon returning home. Killing that antelope paled in comparison to the heroics of anyone who saw combat. I wonder if there is a streak of violence that people, particularly men, have pent up and need to release?

My hunting uniform of choice included an orange vest while carrying my rifle. I looked like all the other hunters. Since stalking and gunning down that antelope, I felt like part of the club when I exchanged stories with others wearing the same clothing.

"What was your first kill?" I ask as an icebreaker, even among my "polite" circles, to get a reaction.

I didn't hunt again after that, but another form of hunting became an activity that required less equipment and brought me closer to my cultural heritage.

******

"Where are the forks?" I wondered when I visited my parents' new home for Thanksgiving in 1973. During my sophomore year at Hastings College, they moved to Laramie. I didn't know then that Laramie would be where an unexpected rite of passage would lead me to become more Japanese.

My mom had a seamless move to Laramie, but not so much for Dad. Most of our family activity centered on my dad's family and coworkers. Mom left Cheyenne in her rearview mirror. The Coke company changed hands, which is why we moved. As part of the sale, the new owners had to keep my dad on as plant manager.

He rented an apartment at the Spanish Walk Apartments in Laramie during the summer transition before my sophomore year of college, before they sold the Cole Addition house. Dad and I commuted to Laramie for the workweek and returned to Cheyenne on weekends. I've always been a homebody and didn't mind staying in Laramie on my own, even without a car.

Mom needed a change of scenery. I think she grew tired of her family life revolving around my dad's circle. After she retired, Mom nurtured her watercolor art business and reinvented herself by hyphenating her name to Sumiko Sakata-O'Hashi.

On the other hand, I had trouble leaving behind familiar surroundings, friends, and family in Cheyenne. Going away to college and then moving to Laramie left me with culture shock.

Summers in Laramie are always pleasant and one of academia's best-kept secrets. Like most other college towns, Laramie sees most students go home. In the 1970s, the UW administration invited everyone on campus to an all-school steak fry at the UW Science

Camp in the Medicine Bow National Forest. I became one of the summer school students. Being terrible at math, I took two physics classes in summer school at UW and earned two As, which helped my GPA.

I'd been in summer school before. I took high school world history because of the accelerated schedule. That lightened my school-year load. I slacked off a bit and looked forward to a few months off before college.

My parents gave me a Smith-Corona electric typewriter as a graduation present. Mom insisted I spend three months learning to type from Mr. Halverson in summer school. I reluctantly went along. Learning to type benefited me more than any class I took in high school, including this moment.

****

The Laramie move allowed my parents to build a new Japanese niche. I continued working for my dad during the summers until I graduated from Hastings, watching him adapt to the rapid changes in his work life.

Even though we moved only 50 miles over Sherman Hill to Laramie, the bottling line with newer equipment and more bells and whistles operated similarly to the one in Cheyenne but didn't run as efficiently.

The new job stressed Dad out because he had to work with a co-manager who happened to be the owner's son. The co-manager had a business degree but little mechanical knowledge. He eventually left the company after Dad made changes to the production line.

After his first 30 years with Coca-Cola in Cheyenne, he now had to carve out a niche for himself in a new town, had no familiar community to provide a safety net or support network, and had to restart his trajectory. Dad had ingrained in him the American Way of rugged individualism, which emphasized struggling to the top.

Laramie is much smaller and more socially accessible than Cheyenne. The Rotary Club invited him to join. He became active in the Cowboy Joe Club, the UW Cowboy sports boosters group.

Mom had excellent typing skills and secured a good job as the Accounting Department Office Manager at the UW College of Commerce and Industry. She became well known for her creative business, Sumiko's Art.

Right after the internal management of the Coke plant stabilized, it became a turbulent period for him because of changes brought about by mergers and acquisitions across many businesses, including hospitals and the beverage industry.

First, a company in Wichita Falls, Texas, bought the Laramie Coke plant, which proved beneficial because it had a retirement program, at least while it lasted. Rapidly expanding Swires, based in Hong Kong, acquired a large plant in Bonneville, Utah, in the late 1970s and soon gobbled up smaller bottling operations like Laramie, converting them into distribution points.

He thrived in his tedious job in exact production management. That changed to organizing product delivery, which required less precision but more heavy lifting.

Dad would have been in his 50s and would have had a tough time reinventing himself if he had quit. In the fledgling digital era, he never turned on a computer, let alone looked at one, or used a cell phone.

He retired shortly after, but the owners couldn't find a suitable replacement and hired him back for a few more years because the company didn't want to hire and train new workers. The wear and tear from delivery work took its toll on him.

When Dad finally retired, I gave him a copy of *From Age-ing to Sage-ing* (1995) by Rabbi Zalman Schachter-Shalomi. I didn't know much about the book until I became acquainted with the good Rabbi and his wife, Eve, in Boulder.

The book reframes aging, from a period of decline to one of growth and wisdom, by exploring "sage-ing" as a conscious transition into later life.

Schachter emphasizes the importance of spiritual development and the cultivation of inner peace. He says that aging is a time to share accumulated wisdom and experience with younger generations. Schachter encourages active participation in community and social life to foster meaningful connections.

The book addresses the inevitability of death with a sense of acceptance and preparation. I became intentionally aware of death. He inspired me, and I continue to serve many communities as a do-gooder, trying to save the world.

Dad aged and saged. He supported my mom's art business behind the scenes after she retired from UW. My gregarious mom enjoyed group activities, such as joining a quilting club and taking clogging dance classes.

She survived breast cancer, volunteered for Relay for Life, and participated in fundraising benefit events for the local arts community and the Presbyterian Church. Dad followed along with all that.

****

We had the big family thing going in Cheyenne, but we held an uncertain place in Laramie until we broke into the mushroom-hunting scene. The Matsuyamas, who owned the California Fish Market, had a reputation for being the best Cheyenne-based mushroom hunters. Old-time Cheyenne Japanese families formed cliques. They never disclosed their coveted hunting areas and had the market cornered.

When we still lived in Cheyenne, my family took a Saturday drive to Laramie, looking around for mushroom hunting grounds. We sensed the mother mushroom lode from telltale signs. At one stop, I found disposable chopstick paper wrappers on the side of the road. We saw a carload of Japanese from Colorado rumble down the dirt road towards us.

Infringing on other hunters' mushroom claims didn't seem honorable. Our hunting would have to wait. That would be years later, when my parents first moved to Laramie.

Being 50 miles from the rest of the clan in Cheyenne might as well have been 500 miles away. That sense of isolation changed when my dad staked claims to a couple of prime mushroom-hunting areas.

Albany County is allegedly among the best hunting grounds for the elusive pine mushroom, *Tricholoma matsutake,* a delicacy in Japanese cuisine.

The mushroom season didn't open until late summer and early fall. The ground in August and September couldn't be too wet or too dry. It may be wet one week, but the conditions would be perfect the following week.

The altitude and humidity create ideal conditions for many kinds of mushrooms, and many hunting areas are ripe for exploration. *Matsutake* are tasty when freshly harvested, cleaned, and sautéed in butter and *shoyu.* I like their chewy texture.

Armed with small gardening trowels, our hunting party spread out and wandered across every square foot of the Ponderosa Pine (*Pinus ponderosa*) pungent needle detritus where the mushroom caps would poke up.

I developed a pretty good eye for *fungi.* I remember how triumphant I felt when I spotted my first *matsutake* cap barely peeking through the Ponderosa Pine needles. I knelt, used my trowel to flick off the residue, and gently pried the mushroom free. I dusted it off with my gloved hand, gazed at it as if I had discovered a nugget of gold, then placed it in a cloth bag.

It felt better than when I pulled a 1962 Roger Maris card from a wax pack. Mushroom hunting required intuition and skill, not luck. It exhilarated me more than killing an antelope.

Hunting *matsutake* fostered togetherness among family and friends. My mom treated the hunts as epic social events that required planning: preparing lunch, gathering tools, sorting and cleaning the finds, and cooking some up as a treat.

Our cabin near Centennial became the home base for mushroom hunting, skiing, summer parties, and family gatherings. The O'Hashis had tapped into the *matsutake* world. Our new status drew kin from Cheyenne for the hour-long drive to our place in the North Fork Subdivision.

Rich came out later in the summer to scout potential deer and elk hunting areas. Sometimes he hauled his boat and went fishing at Lake Hattie or Rob Roy Reservoir. If he had a successful outing, we'd have grilled trout with rice and pan-fried *matsutake* on the side.

After our grandparents and parents passed away, interest in *matsutake* hunting waned among the Sansei generation. I observed my elders, learned the techniques, and learned to distinguish the odors associated with finding matsutake, but I didn't follow through. Mushroom hunting is a group activity, and I couldn't persuade any of my non-Japanese friends to take on the challenge.

We hunted *matsutake* as part of my intra-Cheyenne Japanese cultural practice. I couldn't tell you where we hunted, except in general terms. I'm not even mentioning where I think the mushroom troves might be. The mental maps are going with me to my grave.

Whenever I see Ponderosa pines at elevations of 7,000 to 9,000 feet, I look for signs of *matsutake* hunters, such as multiple tire tread marks where they shouldn't be. These days, I've read that places in Scandinavia have entered the *matsutake* market.

The social aspects of the mushroom hunt are gone, at least in my Japanese circles, but someone is still hunting them. The Pacific Mercantile grocery store in Denver sells them. At one time, the Granada Fish Market, which had its roots in Camp Amache in southeastern Colorado, also sold them.

25

Amache and the Sand Creek Massacre

I haven't checked around lately, but Safeway doesn't carry matsutake mushrooms. Most mainstream grocery stores have rudimentary *sushi* bars. As Americans have become more globalized, these stores now stock Asian foods such as South Asian, Chinese, and Japanese rice, *udon,* and *phō* noodles, along with a variety of marinades and sauces.

Japanese rice isn't available in 80-pound bags, though. Years ago, mills packed in cotton bags. During the Great Depression, my grandmothers repurposed the sacks into dishtowels and aprons.

Grandma Ohashi ran her household and cooked three meals for her sons Rich, George, and Roy, as well as my grandfather, both at home and at the Highway Café. She grilled *teriyaki* steak for dinner, baked meatloaf for lunch, and flipped Denver omelets with onion, bell pepper, ham, cheese, and egg for breakfast.

Chinese immigrant railroad and mine laborers made the first Denver omelets for sandwiches in the 19th century. Workers could easily carry omelets, a complete meal, and eat them with dirty hands.

The egg sandwiches are comparable to pasties that Cornish miners brought to Wisconsin in the 1830s and 1840s, where they became a family tradition and a dietary staple. Miners filled flattened dough with meat and vegetables, then folded it into a pasty (pahstee). They easily fit into a pocket for meal breaks.

Whenever family members dropped by Grandma's house, she always had plenty of food ready. She went through a lot of rice. My dad's responsibilities included driving her to the Granada Fish Market and Pacific Mercantile in Denver to pick up Japanese food supplies, especially around the winter holidays.

Both stores carried delicacies unavailable in Cheyenne, such as *tako* (octopus). The shopping list always included the most exotic item: canned *awabi* (abalone). Abalone bottom-feed in the coastal waters of California and Baja, Mexico. They are also called "sea snails" and are a delicacy, priced at $200 a can. Give me a rubbery slice of octopus any day.

The WRA built the Granada Incarceration Camp in southeastern Colorado, which became informally known as Camp Amache. Granada means pomegranate in Spanish. The fruit is associated with the Jewish religion and with the Crypto-Jews who settled in Southern Colorado in the 15th century. Whether there is a Jewish connection is only my speculation.

Granada is one of many small farming towns in the Arkansas River Valley, designated in 1873 by the Atchison, Topeka, and Santa Fe Railroad.

Despite anti-Japanese attitudes, regional business owners viewed Camp Amache incarcerees as valued customers. Compared with the others, Camp Amache had a relatively more relaxed and informal leave request process, especially as the War progressed.

Colorado had a robust agricultural economy and high demand for labor. The WRA followed general guidelines for granting leave, but implementation varied by camp. The Amache administration issued leave passes less formally.

Frank Tsuchiya, a former Amache incarceree from California, owned and operated a fish market in town near the Camp after his parole.

Tsuchiya owned a similar business in Los Angeles and maintained the connections he had formed before being forced to leave California. He sourced shellfish, sashimi-grade tuna (thinly sliced, fresh, raw fish or meat), and a variety of Japanese pantry staples, such as *shoyu* and *udon* noodles, which he had trucked to Granada.

Denver University conducted archaeological digs and uncovered evidence of these connections, including abalone shell fragments and the remains of a *sake* (rice wine) distillery.

****

Amache is the nexus of two tragic events in American history. The U.S. Postal Service named the Amache Post Office after the daughter of Cheyenne tribal Chief One Eye. Amache married John Prowers, a Colorado cattle producer credited with introducing the first Hereford cattle to the Colorado Territory. The county bears his name.

Chief One Eye negotiated a truce in 1864 between the Cheyenne and Arapaho tribes and the U.S. government. The agreement guaranteed tribal members safe winter camping at Sand Creek.

Despite the pact, soldiers from the Colorado 3rd Cavalry stormed the Prowers Ranch and held Prowers and Amache hostage on the morning of November 29, 1864.

The now-infamous Colonel John Chivington ordered his troops to attack the Cheyenne and Arapaho at their encampment along Sand Creek. The raid, now known as the Sand Creek Massacre, killed 150 tribal members, including Chief One Eye.

The 2024 Amache Pilgrimage featured a cross-cultural exchange between surviving Camp Amache incarcerees and Cheyenne-Arapaho tribal members. Each group recounted the injustices of the Sand Creek Massacre and of Japanese incarceration.

****

Geographically, Granada lies in a rolling prairie basin nestled between the Rocky Mountains and the Great Plains. Despite the region's aridity, the lush fields receive ample irrigation water from the Arkansas River.

Severe summer thunderstorms and tornadoes disrupt the semi-arid climate. Winters are cold and dry, though they can bring heavy snowfall. High winds sweep across the land year-round, kicking up dust storms.

The Dust Bowl and the Great Depression hit Granada hard. The area remained economically depressed until World War II, when Camp Amache sparked an economic revival.

The WRA purchased private property encompassing more than 10,000 acres of the Koen and X-Y ranches. The WRA condemned a dozen other private farms and ranches, including them in the project area, creating a contiguous perimeter that bred ill will between the WRA and the locals.

Amache's population reached 8,000 incarcerees, making it the 10th-largest city in Colorado. The U.S. Census Bureau estimated Granada's population at 494 in 2022.

Contractors built the barracks on a low-lying hill that, during heavy rains, broke up the fast-moving water and prevented erosion and flash flooding. Like other Camps, the barbed-wire fence marked the perimeter, with eight guard towers and soldiers with machine guns.

The first incarcerees arrived from the Central Valley of California, the northern coast, and southwest Los Angeles. Later, over 900 loyal Yes-Yes incarcerees from Tule Lake Camp arrived. When the Jerome Camp in Arkansas closed, another 500 transferred to Amache.

Amache incarcerees had to complete the loyalty questionnaire and reported a higher percentage of Yes-Yes responses than the other nine camps.

Colorado Governor Ralph Carr supported the establishment of the incarceration camp in his state. Carr welcomed the incarcerees, and as a result, earned their respect. Denver's Japanese American citizens honored Carr by placing a bust of the former Governor in Sakura Square near the Tri-State Denver Buddhist Temple.

The Camp police department hired 60 incarcerees as police officers, and the Amache Fire Department had three crews of incarceree firefighters. In 1943, the Camp established a print shop staffed by 45 workers, which produced internal program flyers and calendars. The U.S. Navy contracted for more than 250,000 color posters and training materials.

The WRA reserved most of Camp Amache's open space for agriculture. The Camp became self-sufficient through its agricultural operations. In 1943, Amache farms produced about 4.0 million pounds of vegetables. The WRA delivered 600 bushels of surplus spinach to the Poston and Gila River camps in Arizona and sent 1,000 bushels to the U.S. Army.

In 1943, Tsuchiya and the Granada Fish Market purchased a truckload of Christmas trees from Portland, Oregon, and donated them to all mess halls.

Tsuchiya opened a store in Los Angeles after the War and another in Denver at 1919 Lawrence.

Frank's family moved the store to Sakura Square and it is no longer in business. However, its memory is alive as the Granada Fish Factory, a seven-unit condominium complex built in 1980 in the River North (RiNo) area at 2400 Broadway. RiNo is gentrifying into a newly developing art district.

Pacific Mercantile still flourishes in Sakura Square, next to the Buddhist temple. It's like a regular grocery store that stocks Japanese food and dry goods, including dinnerware, chopsticks, and my memoir, *Beyond Heart Mountain* (2022).

******

I always liked to tag along on the ride to Denver with Dad and Grandma, hoping to be treated to gooey mochi balls filled with *anko* (sweet bean paste). Back then, stores sold fresh *mochi*. These days, it's available frozen, including versions with ice cream in the center.

Grandma liked a restaurant called the Mandarin on 20th Street, across from the Buddhist temple and west of the 20th Street Café. That's where we stopped for lunch when we had extra time before returning to Cheyenne.

The Mandarin offered a menu similar to the City Café's, with short-order Asian food like chop suey and my favorite, pork noodles. The *tsukemono* (pickled cucumber salad) tasted as good as my grandmother's, except it didn't include sliced abalone.

As abalone became more expensive, she substituted octopus, also a delicacy but not as pricey, or *kamaboko*. In a pinch, she added *surimi* (fake crabmeat).

My grandparents Sakata had two mouths to feed. My mom checked with them for a list before Dad made his periodic trips to Denver.

We lived in two worlds. Japanese assimilated and adopted the dominant cultural American Way but kept our Japanese lifestyle alive through traditional food.

"I like making *sushi* rolls. I didn't know other kinds of *sushi* existed until I went to a *sushi* place in San Francisco," is my usual answer when curious people ask what I like most about Japanese cuisine. "What's your favorite American food?" I ask. My Caucasian friends usually give me a blank stare.

I worked at the Hitching Post as an employee and never went there with my parents. My family dined out only at the City Café during the Skyline Nisei Club's Friday night gatherings.

Kids didn't join their parents when they went out to restaurants. One time, my mom must not have been able to find a sitter. She had lunch at a coffee shop called The Trail on West Lincolnway. I sat in the waiting area and sipped a Coke through a paper straw, no doubt sold to the restaurant by Pioneer Printing.

As I got older, my culinary experiences in Cheyenne expanded to include Petersen's Buffet, where the pricing structure encouraged families to dine there. Petersen's served only American food, including red and green Jell-O that stayed solid at room temperature.

When I sold pop at the Cheyenne Frontier Days parade, I wondered about several Downtown Cheyenne watering holes, including the Wigwam dive bar in the Plains Hotel and the legendary Mayflower Café and Tavern.

"Got one left?" a drunk cowboy standing outside the Wigwam asked. He handed me a five for a can of pop. I fished his change from my apron. "Keep it. You been workin' harder than me today."

I didn't go into the Mayflower until I served as a state legislative intern. During my first year of grad school, the Mayflower burned down in January 1976. The Cheyenne Frontier Days mainstay briefly returned in the 1980s, later became Grand Avenue Pizza, and is now Bejo Sushi and Asian Cuisine.

I've been to Bejo once but prefer *sushi* and pork noodles at Hi Sushi on East Lincolnway near the Cole Addition. Talk about bicultural straddling: In the morning, it's a donut shop, and in the afternoon, it's a Japanese restaurant.

26

Kimono Kowboy

My antelope-hunting garb identified me as a hunter, and I could spin a good yarn because I had succeeded in my Wyoming male rite of passage. Like Superman, I needed costumes to give me an identity.

From my youth, Cheyenne Frontier Days has been a big deal to me. Even though I felt like a raisin in the rodeo oatmeal, I decked myself out in a straw cowboy hat, Lee jeans, Acme boots, and a Western-cut snap shirt.

As an adult, I've been a Japanese cowboy trying to buck the farmer-and-gardener stereotypes. I didn't quite fit the look, as evidenced by my conversation at the Log Cabin Saloon in Jackson. I try to mix up my garb with a T-shirt or hat for my peace of mind, since members of the dominant culture don't notice.

"The Daddy of 'em All" is Cheyenne's most economically important and high-profile event. Sales during CFD make or break most local businesses. CFD features a daily outdoor rodeo, held annually since 1897 during the last full week of July, plus an extra weekend. The event draws over 200,000 celebrants from around the world to a variety of events of interest to everyone, from cowboys to flatlanders.

If you're a vegan, a health-conscious eater, or an animal rights advocate, CFD probably isn't the place you'd want to spend your vacation days. I usually do some videography at CFD and am required to request permission from the Professional Rodeo Cowboys Association (PRCA). The PRCA wants to ensure that I, or any other professional producer, won't use the footage for blatant anti-rodeo propaganda.

The daily rodeos feature contests pitting men against steers, bulls, and horses, followed by the night shows. A carnival offers rides, games of skill, and food vendors who hand out tasty turkey legs, deep-fried funnel cakes, and cotton candy.

Downtown Cheyenne hosts three parades featuring floats, antique automobiles, horse-drawn carriages with riders in period dress, and top marching bands.

The local Kiwanis Club offers free breakfasts to 40,000 hungry rodeo-goers, serving 100,000 pancakes and 3,000 pounds of ham over three mornings between the parade days.

The CFD Indian Committee invited Native American tribal members from South Dakota and Oklahoma to participate in the Indian Village, which the dancers set up downtown starting in 1898. In 1960, the CFD moved the event to Frontier Park near the rodeo arena. Northern Arapaho tribal dancers and oral historians from the Wind River Reservation now lead the CFD's tribal culture programs.

As long as I've been old enough to pay attention, I've attended CFD every year except 2020, when the organizers canceled all events because of the COVID-19 pandemic.

****

My mom's friends in her X-JWC volunteered for CFD, which meant they brought their kids, too. Every July, we gathered at the ranch owned and operated by Doran and Enid Lummis, along with their children: Chris, Claudia, and Cynthia—we all went to high school together—and their brother Del, who is a few years younger.

We assembled the parade float in the barn at their ranch on the east edge of town. My dad provided the Coca-Cola flatbed trailer, which my mom's X-JWC transformed into a parade float, skirted with chicken wire and stuffed with paper napkins.

Mom rode on that one with her Dearies singing group. Their *a cappella* voices carried pretty well over the street noise from their parade float. They sang popular songs from the turn of the 20th century: *Five Foot Two, Eyes of Blue, Blue Moon, Toot, Toot, Tootsie, etc.* The Dearies entertained around town, wearing long hoop skirts and wide-brimmed floppy hats.

My sister and I climbed onto one of the gender-specific hay wagons, the "entry-level" float for youngsters. The float wranglers at the head of the parade directed us into traditional gender roles, telling the boys to be boisterous by yelling "Yeehaw!" along the parade route while the girls sat quietly, smiled, and waved hankies to the adoring crowd.

The parade featured a wild and crazy Hell's Half Acre float. The beer kegs began flowing before the parade got underway at 10 a.m. sharp, signaled by a cannon blast. The bar floozies, flaunting heavy makeup, alluring satiny can-can dresses, and fishnet stockings, partied through Downtown Cheyenne. The boldest parade watchers earned a badge of honor by jumping onto the float from the street.

Hell's Half Acre had nothing to do with Cheyenne. The name came from an advertising campaign by Casper business boosters seeking to attract more tourists to the area with a roadside attraction.

A developer built a motel and restaurant west of Casper, near a 960-acre geological badlands formation that the U.S. government granted to Natrona County in 1924. They settled on the name of a rough-and-tumble red-light district in Fort Worth, Texas, that catered to cowboys in the 1880s.

The float riders arrived at the Hell on Wheels tent town in Holliday Park after the parade. The would-be drunken railroad workers, cowboys, and prostitutes reveled and entertained city-dude tourists.

They staged vignettes of men arguing over women, money, or both. The ensuing gunfights left bad guys on the ground, feigning death after being shot with a hail of blanks.

****

Cousin Matthew visited from Utah most summers when our extended family gathered. He, my sister, and I teamed up with a neighbor, Pat, to sell pop at three parades during CFD. That continued through the 1980s until my grandparents and our Nisei parents passed away.

I viewed selling pop as what is now known as a "cottage industry." Most of the sales crews lived on the Westside, near the parade route. They viewed Eastside entrepreneurs like us as carpetbaggers.

Over the past few months, we saved our weekly allowances and stocked up on store-brand soft drinks like Shurfine, Cragmont, and Shasta during the school year. We could have bought Coke products from my dad, but didn't want to lower our profit margin. Thirsty parade-goers didn't care about brands.

We provided ice in cups upon request, a service none of the other wagons offered. Dad gave us cups, so Coke got free advertising, anyway. Dad parked the family's Pontiac early on parade day near Brannen's grocery store on Carey Avenue, an excellent resupply depot location.

I'm glad I sold pop at CFD before it became over-regulated. These days, the City of Cheyenne requires young vendors to obtain a permit, sell only on the sidewalk behind the crowd, and be accompanied by a responsible adult. What's the point of all that? I'm glad my parents trusted us enough to keep us safe.

The most practical life skill I've still retained from our business venture is counting back change. That courtesy rarely happens now with digital cash registers. We had fun while it lasted. Matthew married, had kids, developed a full life, and seldom visited Cheyenne.

****

After the parade, Mom drove us to the carnival, where we spent our hard-earned cash on cotton candy, foot-long hot dogs, and funnel cakes. Maybe greasy fast food is what exemplifies American cuisine.

I preferred the mystery exhibits to the rides, including the bearded lady and oddities such as two-headed sheep. Polio had become a public health threat in the 1960s, and one attraction featured a woman lying in an iron lung.

Iron lungs are obsolete in modern medicine. A large, cylindrical stainless-steel chamber encased the polio patient's body, leaving only the head protruding from one end. A collar sealed around the patient's neck, creating an airtight chamber that provided mechanical ventilation for patients unable to breathe independently because of paralysis of the respiratory muscles.

The machine adjusted the pressure inside the chamber to simulate natural breathing. The lung created a vacuum that expanded the patient's chest cavity, drawing air into the lungs. When the chamber pressure returned to normal, the chest cavity relaxed, expelling air from the lungs. The contraption made a noise like Darth Vader's breathing.

Downtown Cheyenne lost its retail storefronts to urban sprawl, including Brannen's, Miller's, and Safeway grocery stores. The State of Wyoming purchased all three properties for office space.

****

My next CFD Parade phase came in high school. Jan Benton, my East High School classmate, organized patients who rode in the horse-drawn Civil War-era field ambulance. Jan's mom volunteered on the CFD Parade Committee, which helped. My East High pals Tad Leeper and Eddie Frye and I played wounded soldiers, and Jan played our Florence Nightingale.

"Bedpan! Bedpan!" we yelled from the ambulance windows during our PG-rated personal hygiene act, which involved flinging a urinal filled with water and a dash of yellow food coloring. In between, we moaned in the back of the wagon as battle-weary soldiers bandaged up in ripped-up bedsheets.

When the parade ended, the crowds headed for Frontier Park and the rodeo in the afternoon, the midway carnival, and night show entertainment.

CFD night show fans didn't expect extravaganzas in the 1960s. Superstars such as Kiss, Garth Brooks, Winona Judd, Florida Georgia Line, Charlie Daniels, and Chris LeDoux headlined from the 1990s to the 2000s. The 1960s show talent included TV stars such as Milburn "Doc Adams" Stone and Ken "Festus" Curtis from *Gunsmoke* (1955–1975).

"Safer than chitlins on a city folk's supper plate," Festus would observe with an exaggerated country twang. He broke out of his "aw shucks" Festus persona and crooned with his golden voice. From 1949 to 1952, he sang lead with the Sons of the Pioneers western quartet.

****

In the summer of 1976, I worked as the Glacier Basin Campground ranger at Rocky Mountain National Park, also known as RoMo, the radio designation for the park dispatcher.

I stayed with Rick Thamer for the last weekend of that CFD. Saturday, July 31, would be the last ride for my pea-green Pinto. Rick and I taught political science together at UW. He and our mutual friend John Accardo tried to get me to stay over, but I decided to head back to RoMo that night because I had to work at 11:30 a.m. on Sunday.

The Accardos lived in Cole Addition on White Cloud Road. His dad, a dentist, collaborated with my dentist, Dr. Carson, on a complicated molar extraction that required a chrome-plated chisel and mallet, but I digress. I recount the epic dental surgery in my memoir, *A Twinkle at the End: Living Seven Decades in the Healthcare Industrial Complex* (2025).

I exited I-25 after an uneventful drive from Cheyenne into Colorado and headed west on U.S. Highway 34, with a black ribbon of clouds stretching beneath the crimson sunset.

"Why are all these cars and RVs driving away from the park?" I thought while winding my way through the "narrows" at the mouth of the steep-walled Big Thompson Canyon.

A law enforcement officer waved me down and told me, "There's some bad water ahead," and that I'd best turn around in the small town of Drake. I heeded his warning.

The weather cooled and started to sprinkle when I made it to Drake. I reined in the Pinto when I came upon a stream of water trickling across the road. Before I knew it, the rain poured down in buckets. My little steed slammed into a wall of water that gushed down the hillside and into the riverbed. The torrential rain soon flowed over the hood of the Pinto.

My headlights reflected off the LV license plate on the car coming toward me. The passengers had the interior dome light on, and I watched the current carry the frantic Loveland family over the edge and into the canyon.

I sat in the car as if a tornado had picked up Dorothy and whisked her away to the Land of Oz. I looked out the windshield in wonder. The wipers couldn't keep up with the rain, but my headlights lit up giant uprooted trees and large propane tanks as they bobbed by. I kept thinking Miss Gulch on her bicycle would float across the road through the deluge pouring down the canyon face.

I could feel bowling-ball-sized boulders clanking against the fenders. My back bumper caught a floating port-a-potty, which acted as a rudder, steering me toward the canyon wall rather than into the rushing water.

I rolled down the window, climbed out, and waded up to the highway's crest. A Colorado Department of Transportation truck picked me up and dropped me off at a high spot called Rainbow Lodge, where I spent the night.

While exploring the following morning, I came across trophy-size trout washed up on what remained of the highway. Someone had covered the body of a not-so-lucky tourist or resident with a blue tarp, like the one Jacqueline Smith used for her tent on the sidewalk next to the Lorraine Motel in Memphis.

Rumors spread that Lake Estes up the road had crested and would soon overflow the dam. A group of us climbed the side of the canyon and waited. A Chinook helicopter eventually airlifted my fellow survivors and me to a gymnasium in Loveland, where I picked up a dry pair of socks and a cup of coffee.

The flood had destroyed the phone lines, and I couldn't call my family in Laramie. Not a Good Samaritan, but a Great Samaritan gave me a ride to Cheyenne and dropped me off at Tad Leeper's house. My parents eventually found me after first driving to Loveland to look around.

The 1,000-year Big Thompson Flood would be the last time I saw my Pinto. I'm reviewing my old slides. One photo shows the Pinto in Boca Raton, Florida, during a Hastings College field trip to the Keys. I ironically parked it between two Cadillacs. The insurance settlement covered enough to replace it with a new sky-blue Pinto featuring better rims, a bigger engine, and an AM/FM radio with a cassette player.

I drove that car when I moved to Gillette in 1977. By this time, Ford had recalled the Pinto because it could explode when involved in a rear-end collision. I had left the office and slowed down at the light near Ole's Pizza on Highway 14 when an oil-field water truck rammed me from behind.

I inspected the damage underneath and noticed that the threaded end of a bolt holding the transmission differential halves together had crimped against the gas tank. If punctured, the tank could have sparked an explosion.

Rick Thamer bought that car from me. He drove it to Lubbock, Texas, where he attended law school at Texas Tech. I stopped buying

American cars, and my obsession with VWs began with a sporty 1977 white Scirocco with black pinstripes. My first flirtation with death came when I narrowly escaped with my life in Big Thompson. I like a close call every 20 years or so to hedge my bets.

****

CFD once kept Downtown Cheyenne a happening place. I thought about the ragtag laborers who built the Transcontinental Railroad and how decadent Cheyenne must have been when the construction crews got out of control at the Hell on Wheels tent.

Now that I had a job and disposable income, I came to Cheyenne and partied like a railroader in 1868. In the 1970s, crowds spilled from the bars onto the streets, stalling traffic. Police closed West 17th Street from the Elks Club and Blue Bird at Central Avenue, past the Mayflower, to the Cheyenne Social Club on Capitol Avenue. Everyone got along during CFD.

I remember standing in front of the Mayflower, holding a Miller beer can. A cop came by and whacked it out of my hand. It clunked, half-full, onto the sidewalk, covered with a layer of cans.

Bikers had taken over the Pioneer Hotel flophouse on West 17th Street. I had visited my family's grave plot at Memorial Gardens east of town. I slowed down and gave a hitchhiker a ride. He had no bags, so I figured he had been working on a farm. I dropped him off at the Pioneer. Curious, I walked him inside to check out the place.

William Moffatt originally purchased what is now the Pioneer Hotel and named it after himself. The Moffatt Hotel had noble beginnings as the Gilded Age arrived in Cheyenne. Over the years, as Cheyenne bust, much of the downtown core did as well. The Pioneer also declined to its current state, but it still fills a housing need for a sector of the community.

Today's CFD Downtown Cheyenne crowds are a shadow of their former wild and crazy selves. Not everyone in Cheyenne is as CFD-obsessed as I am. Many locals plan their vacations for the last week of July and leave town.

The following year, I drove the Scirocco to CFD. I met some friends from Gillette at the Atlas Motel, a block from the Hitching Post. I can now say that, because new owners razed the Atlas, we tore that room to pieces.

As much as I enjoyed the company of my Gillette friends, I kept my distance at my parents' place in Laramie, a throwback to heeding my mother's advice to be good. Even though I tried to blend in, I still stood out.

27

The Gillette Syndrome

When my parents cut me loose after high school, I wanted to make it in the outside world but didn't know where to start. I only worked for Paul Smith, clearing tables at the Hitching Post, and for my dad at the Cheyenne Coke plant during my high school years.

I didn't have a family business to fall back on, except for my grandparents' restaurant, which I should have pursued more aggressively. Some students majored in business or accounting, while others studied pre-med or pre-law. Me? I had no employment prospects in mind.

Following Superman's American Way would be necessary if I wanted to broaden my horizons. A few months before I went to college, Grandpa Sakata gave me a $1,000 check and a speech.

"Alan doesn't understand Japanese," my grandmother prompted. He then translated and told me that being a hardworking Japanese person wouldn't be enough.

"Get a good education. Learning is important, but you will be more successful if you get to know people," Grandpa advised.

He based his grandfatherly advice on his days with the railroad, when he kept his job after Pearl Harbor. I took him at his word. I worked hard, paid attention, and graduated from Hastings with a well-rounded education and a Bachelor of Arts degree.

Hastings emphasizes a range of disciplines through its liberal arts approach to learning. I studied the Old Testament and Art History and majored in political science and biology. I didn't anticipate honing my critical thinking skills or becoming a more effective communicator.

I still had no idea what I wanted to be when I grew up, even though I benefited from my curiosity and vast stores of general knowledge. A full-time job after college kept swirling in the back of my mind, but I didn't know how to find one.

I've always been pretty good at change management, so my lack of planning didn't freak me out about having student loans to repay with no income, no roof over my head, and being stuck between Nebraska and Wyoming with no vision for my future.

After graduating during the post-Vietnam War recession with degrees in biology and political science, no employers offered jobs involving identifying mammal teeth or discussing whether the confederation is a better form of government than a federation.

I applied to graduate programs. The University of Wisconsin-Green Bay accepted me into one of the country's first environmental politics programs but offered no financial aid.

As a procrastinator, I submitted my paperwork to the University of Wyoming graduate school late. The College of Arts and Sciences accepted me, but the Registrar placed me on the waiting list for a teaching assistantship.

"We had a student back out. Do you still want the poli-sci spot?" the Registrar asked me over the phone. "Let us know because the fall semester is beginning soon. We pay your tuition and also a housing allowance."

I took the open slot immediately, which also resolved my housing situation. I considered moving back to Cheyenne, but my parents invited me to boomerang back to live with them and my sister.

They didn't ask for any rent. I think they appreciated having me around, but they soon realized that another full-sized adult in the house took up a little more space than young Alan David did when he cleared the dinner table and ran outside to play Army in the dark shadows around the neighborhood.

I mentioned that when my cousin Milton from San Francisco ran into one of his high school classmates at the Buckhorn, we stumbled into my parents' house tequila-drunk that night. That didn't go over well.

The last-minute political science teaching assistantship brought me closer to solving the mystery of my career path. I compounded my academic missteps by creating a new-fangled discipline. I merged my two undergraduate degrees into "environmental politics."

American conservationist and marine biologist Rachel Carson wrote a book titled Silent Spring (1962). It's about the food chain reaction caused by pesticides entering ecosystems.

In January 1969, 1,000 gallons of crude oil spilled over 10 days from an offshore Union Oil well platform near Santa Barbara, California.

The news media provided extensive coverage, including photos of black beaches and some of the 3,500 seabirds coated in oil, sparking public outrage. Over time, news stories broadened to other topics. You name the ecological harm: raw sewage in waterways, toxic waste dumps, and pesticides appearing in babies.

Nixon engaged with civility when planning public policy in response to the environmental movement, garnering support from diverse groups: Republicans and Democrats, the wealthy and the not-so-wealthy, urbanites and rural farmers, business executives, and union leaders.

President Nixon signed the National Environmental Policy Act (NEPA) into law on January 1, 1970. NEPA established the Environmental Impact Statement process to evaluate projects and propose various solutions.

Environmental activists celebrated NEPA's broad support, joined by millions of concerned citizens, at the first Earth Day on April 22,

1970. Spontaneous and organized groups gathered on the streets, in parks, and on college and high school campuses.

NEPA also established the Council on Environmental Quality (CEQ). In July 1970, the CEQ coordinated environmental and energy policies by merging antipollution, pesticide control, and air and water quality programs administered by the USDA and the DoI, which led to the formation of the EPA. Auntie Hisako transferred to the EPA, where she retired.

After attending St. Louis Park High School's Earth Day activities in 1971, I spent the next couple of years in Laramie completing the coursework for my environmental politics concentration. My research design paper, *The Earth Day Legacy: Environmental Attitudes Among College Students*, found that at one end of the spectrum, college students supported efforts to keep the environment clean. At the other end, respondents reported an unwillingness to do their part by changing their consumption habits, as reimagined in Superman's American Way.

I balanced my classwork by teaching Intro to Political Science, Wyoming Government, and Social Statistics. Social research and design continue to interest me, and I still design surveys.

My grandfather advised me to build a network. Easier said than done. I didn't know many people in Laramie beyond my parents' church friends. I became acquainted with my fellow graduate students, but most had families and established lives in Laramie. I couldn't relate to the younger undergrads, though they had more free time after hours.

In my first year at UW, I focused on securing a job. All my elective courses included an internship or hands-on experience. Bill Roepke taught Introduction to Public Relations, which provided the most practical classroom content to support my internship at the UW Federal Energy Research Center.

I still refer to the *Effective Public Relations* (1952) textbook by Scott M. Cutlip and Allen H. Center, which is in its 11th printing and remains in use in classrooms. Cutlip and Center define public relations as "the management function that identifies, establishes, and maintains mutually beneficial relationships between an organization and the various publics on whom its success or failure depends."

I spent my most valuable UW internship meeting several Wyoming state legislators during two legislative sessions, commuting to Cheyenne each day. That experience as a 21-year-old had the greatest long-term value, consistent with my grandfather's advice to get to know people.

The department assigned me to two members of the Joint Appropriations Committee: easygoing Gus Fleischli from Cheyenne and stodgy Speaker of the House Warren Morton from Casper. He eventually ran for governor in 1982 and lost to Ed Herschler.

I met Gus at his office, Fleischli Oil, each morning, and we had breakfast at the Husky Truck Stop before he drove us to the state capitol building in his white-over-red Cadillac Coupe de Ville. I ran into Gus now and again, but learned that he had passed away at 98 during Cheyenne Frontier Days in 2024.

Morton's son, Bob, taught alongside me in the UW political science department. He pulled an envelope from his backpack and showed me a letter from his dad. A Legislative Service Office secretary typed the letter on official letterhead using an IBM Selectric typewriter and signed it, "Sincerely, Warren Morton, Speaker of the House."

At the time, I met Al Simpson, the Wyoming House of Representatives Majority Whip. Al got along with everyone and could collaborate adeptly across the aisle.

After a committee meeting, he rounded up a group of his colleagues and me and took us to the Mayflower Café and Tavern in Downtown Cheyenne, where I had my first French Dip sandwich, for whatever that's worth. He took a liking to me, and we stayed in touch over the years. I think his experience as a Boy Scout meeting the Japanese Troop at Heart Mountain had a profound influence on him.'

My high school, college, and grad school years blended into a potpourri of experiences. On the surface, the mixture didn't make sense. It turned out that it all fit together as collaborative, civil problem-solving.

I wouldn't be where I am today without practical internships at the Wyoming State Legislature and hustling carnival patrons into giving me a dollar for nothing during CFD. I didn't realize then that I had learned to close deals by building strong, often fleeting relationships that fostered my entrepreneurial spirit.

****

My fortunes changed during my second year of grad school when I walked through the Student Union and spotted a sign-up table.

"If You Want a Job After Graduation, Join the Wyoming Human Services Project (WHSP)," it read. The WHSP would be my ticket, eliminating the need for job hunting and interviews. I wouldn't have to compete with anyone. Plus, I spent my first two semesters in classes that offered practical internships.

Wyoming began to recover from an oil-and-gas bust in the mid-1970s. Congress enacted the Clean Air Act in 1977, and President Carter signed it, tightening sulfur dioxide emission standards. Al Simpson had advanced through the political ranks, and Wyoming voters elected him to the U.S. Senate.

He joined a bipartisan effort to pass federal legislation that tightened emissions standards. Wyoming soft coal became more desirable than high-sulfur eastern hard coal. In addition to the regulatory changes, soft, low-sulfur coal became a desirable fuel because of its relative ease of extraction through surface mining.

Wyoming boomed again.

The WHSP curriculum taught students a multidisciplinary approach to developing creative and effective social programs to mitigate the negative effects of rapid population growth in rural areas during the coal boom in the Powder River Basin, which includes parts of southeastern Montana and northeastern Wyoming.

The region supplied about 40 percent of the United States' coal, but this has since tailed off due to competition from less expensive oil, natural gas, and renewable resources such as wind and solar power.

The WHSP team devised strategies to eliminate social ills that contribute to the "Gillette Syndrome," a typical boomtown stereotype of a bunch of rough-and-tumble single guys from Texas who lived out of their beat-up pickup trucks, dug coal by day, and partied hard at night in a tiny town where they fought over eligible women: single moms living in trailers or still in high school.

The Planning Director, Joe Racine, asked me to reverse the anecdotal stereotypes about Gillette Syndrome. My public relations internship helped me with this assignment. I clawed through the weeds, parsed empirical data, and came up with a pretty good story. For example, the divorce rate is high because it's easy to dissolve a marriage in Wyoming because of the short residency requirement.

The multidisciplinary WHSP team drew on diverse academic backgrounds. Our varied perspectives led to well-rounded strategies to mitigate impact and advance community development. We avoided "groupthink" by creating an early form of analog crowdsourcing. The job exposed me to consensus decision-making before it became trendy.

My cohort included an attorney, a social worker, a parks and recreation staff member, and me, a political scientist working in the city administration. We spent half our time on our agency job placement. For the remaining half, we collaborated with community-based organizations to address problems resulting from rapid population growth.

****

Soon after I started my job, Phil, the WHSP team lawyer, and I became housemates at 611 Kendrick, along with his friend Tom, a

Deputy County Attorney. He grew tired of living in close quarters.

"I served in 'Nam and have GI benefits. Let's buy a house," Tom suggested. "The down payment will be low."

The three of us chipped in to buy a new split-level house at 3003 Foothills Boulevard. The U.S. Treasury guaranteed the loan. We became joint tenants in common and agreed to a buyout agreement.

Our domicile became known as "The 3003 Club: Where Mom Is Never Home." As bizarre as that sounds, that would be my first taste of intentional living in a "cooperative" house, or co-op. We each had a bedroom, and we finished the basement to create a fourth bedroom. We made club decisions by consensus: "BBQ or Tacos," and, believe it or not, we had disagreements.

"Who eats Cheez Whiz on tacos?"

Our Club shared the kitchen, living room, and bathroom, prepared meals together, and divided household chores, though we had differing interpretations of "clean" and "cooking." Each of us owned an undivided third of the property and contributed to the household's day-to-day operations.

Upwardly mobile young professionals gathered at the 3003 Club. Our lifestyle centered on watching sports on TV, playing strategic board games such as Risk, and listening to music.

I had lived a sheltered life in the suburbs of Cheyenne and at a conservative Presbyterian college. Maybe the world had immersed me in self-indulgence, but I hadn't paid close enough attention to it.

Reverend Leland Rubesh, the pastor at the Gillette UPC, volunteered to serve on the Council of Community Services. WHSP helped stabilize the project, which continues to operate today. The Council coordinates social services across Campbell County. It originated with an idea from a tall, rotund police officer named Tiny, who wanted to maximize the amount of charitable food and cash given to transients to encourage them to leave town.

After a meeting, Rev. Rubesh and I made small talk. Because the Cheyenne UPC had anointed me as an Elder, we had acquaintances in common. He invited me to check out his church.

Rapid community growth didn't spare the Gillette UPC. I felt obligated to get involved because Rev. Rubesh urgently needed more volunteers to teach Sunday school classes. I agreed to teach junior high students.

I stood out in Rev. Rubesh's UPC as a single brown-skinned young raisin, living with two fellows and teaching Sunday school in Gillette's conservative oatmeal.

I again had to straddle two worlds and felt conflicted about teaching teenage Sunday school students. My staid upbringing as a Model Minority in one realm. The other, a risky lifestyle in the 3003 Club, practiced by 20-somethings.

****

Growing up, my Mom and Dad lived a far from rowdy lifestyle. Once in a while, the owner of Cheyenne Beverages would invite them over. His business included Coors beer distribution and soft drink manufacturing. My parents felt uncomfortable with the Country Club crowd but attended, anyway. Many of that ilk went to college and subsequently adopted drinking and partying habits.

My parents did their share of entertaining, though. Japanese food attracted the neighbors. My mom prepared Japanese food, such as the ever-popular *teriyaki* wings and *maki sushi,* both very labor-intensive. One summer, our Cole Addition house teamed with guests having a good old time.

I wondered about the fuss. I poured some "76" lemon-lime pop, the local brand bottled by Coca-Cola, into a glass of ice.

By this time, Bill Fisher had finished the basement, and Dad stored liquor behind the bar he constructed from two bar-height Coors can display stands topped with a wooden door.

I took my glass downstairs and poured myself a High Ball from the bottle of Seagram-7 on top of the small fridge. It went to my head quickly. I had more fun than usual with the Shinmori kids. The next day, I woke up with flu-like symptoms and slept it off for the rest of the morning. My parents suspected nothing because Alan David never got in trouble.

****

I eased into the rowdy life at the 3003 Club. We had quite a membership.

Bob O'Neil, an attorney from South Boston and a law school classmate of my housemate Tom, avoided the draft. His family pressured him to join the Army because his father had served in World War II. To fulfill his rite of passage, Bob enrolled in Officer Candidate School. When I hit a major bump in the road, Bob kept me from careening into the barrow ditch.

He and I have a love-hate relationship that persists because he's a Red Sox fan and I'm a Yankees fan. He went home to visit his family and watch the Bosox play.

"They sell those in Fenway?" I asked. He held his nose as he handed me a Yankees cap, which dropped to the floor. He and I meet at Coors Field whenever the Red Sox are in town to play the Colorado Rockies.

Bob is the only person I know who has seen the Beatles live. His dad worked at the Suffolk Downs racetrack in 1966, and Bob got in to see them. He and I spent hours mixing music onto cassette tapes. I don't know whether Wyoming radio stations played the songs Bob liked: Patti Smith, Steely Dan, Boston, Styx, Talking Heads, Grateful Dead, New Riders of the Purple Sage, etc.

I wish I had kept those tapes, which I lost after three moves. Who knew technology would be widely available in the 21st century to convert analog data from tapes into digital form? Something about the recorded sounds of scratches, pops, and skips gave the tape mixes character.

Jim moved in after Tom, and I bought out Phil. He coached high school football and played linebacker for the UW Cowboys. I moved from Gillette, and he returned to his roots in Detroit, Michigan. We've kept in touch over the years. In 1981, I told him I'd be in Detroit for the National League of Cities Conference and asked if he'd like to grab a beer. He called back and said he had tickets to see the Rolling Stones at the Pontiac Silver Dome.

Jim introduced me to White Castle hamburgers. A rat the size of a cocker spaniel sat up in the shadows waiting for crumbs to fall onto the ground.

We had a grand reunion. It was a gas, gas, gas.

My pals and I embodied the "Gillette Syndrome." I earned more money than I'd ever made and had nowhere to spend it.

We lived the rural version of *St. Elmo's Fire* (1985). We all had way too much fun for a gang of young professional whippersnappers in the state's most conservative county. The wild lifestyle I led back then is now legal in some form in most states, but not in Wyoming.

I'll leave it at that. To paraphrase the tagline from an Oscar-winning movie, "The events conjured up for this tale took place in Gillette, Wyoming. At the request of the living, their names have been changed. The story is retold precisely as it happened, out of respect for the deceased."

In 2016, I went to Gillette for the annual Donkey Creek Festival. Many of my friends from Razor City still live there 40 years later. I drove up to the 3003 Club. The house is still the same but now in the old part of town.

****

Superman inspired my fascination with other worlds. He came to Earth from the planet Krypton with "powers and abilities far beyond those of mortal men." He grew up as a typical boy in Kansas, where his parents taught him to be American, including attending church.

In Sunday School, I learned that angels spoke to biblical figures like Moses through burning bushes, pillars of fire, and other supernatural means. God whisked Elijah away in a chariot of fire. The Bible says that Jesus will return in a cloud.

I didn't understand it until I took an Old Testament class at Hastings College. I read *Chariots of the Gods* (1968) by Erich von Daniken. His books describe beings aboard Unidentified Flying Objects (UFOs) from other dimensions who, according to the author, are angels based on literal interpretations of the Bible.

According to some accounts, Good Angels and Evil Angels have been engaging in a perpetual, invisible conflict. Seraphim, Cherubim, and Thrones constitute the highest order of angels, closest to God, and administer divine matters.

The second order comprises Dominions, Virtues, and Powers, which govern creation and the cosmos and oversee the natural order.

Principalities, Archangels, and Angels constitute the third order of angels. These angels are closest to humans and are concerned with guiding nations and individuals.

Good angels occupy angelological hierarchies. Evil angels emerged from a heavenly rebellion instigated by a fallen angel. Scholars think Lucifer/Satan is a Cherub.

Cable TV channels run programs about the UFO-Bible nexus. Since I'm more into the tangible, the model made some sense. In 2022, the National Aeronautics and Space Administration (NASA) referred to UFOs as Unidentified Aerial Phenomena (UAP). I'm sticking with the more familiar UFO acronym.

Then there are the animal mutilations. In the 1960s, my family took a road trip to Mesa Verde National Park in southwestern Colorado. Uncle George subscribed to a UFO magazine that published an article about horses and cattle killed and mutilated near Montrose and Buena Vista, Colorado, which I read as we drove through the area.

Witnesses continue to report similar incidents in which ranchers find livestock with precise cuts and missing organs, prompting various theories about the causes, including UAP-naut involvement.

I'll skip through time.

****

While in grad school, preparing for the WHSP job in Gillette, I had put all this supernatural stuff to the back of my mind. I hadn't given it a second thought until a June 29, 1980, story in the CST reported strange lights bouncing around the sky at the Morton Pass Farm, owned by Pat McGuire and his family.

The farm is at the mouth of Sybille Canyon on Highway 34 between Laramie and Wheatland. I called the reporter about it, and even as a journalist, the sightings freaked him out.

"We have to go there," I told a group of friends at the 3003 Club. *That's Incredible* (1980–1984), a TV show hosted by actress Cathy Lee Crosby, singer John Davidson, and Fran Tarkenton, the former New York Giants and Minnesota Vikings quarterback, sent a crew to southeastern Wyoming to cover the UFO phenomenon on the remote high plains.

The story is wacky and more involved than I'll write here, but hold on to your aluminum foil hats. A world-renowned paranormal psychologist at the UW, Leo Sprinkle, specialized in alien-abduction experiences and, through hypnosis, regressed McGuire to the moment he said aliens had taken him aboard their UFO.

He claimed to have been in touch with the Archangel Michael and to have received instructions to drill a large well on his property and to begin farming. The State of Wyoming approved Pat for a low-interest loan to purchase irrigation equipment, even though hydrology studies indicated he'd have little chance of striking groundwater beneath the land. He drilled a well that gushed more than 8,000 gallons per minute.

His lush alfalfa fields spanned the horizon.

Pat flew the Israeli flag over the water-well pumping station in homage to Archangel Michael and his colleagues. He said the aliens wore Star of David belt buckles and had one on the belt holding up his Wranglers.

My UFO entourage drove down and met the *That's Incredible* crew. The nocturnal light sources made infrequent, distant appearances, compared with their activity a few weeks earlier, but some with red, green, yellow, and white lights bounced around the night sky, which I photographed. Those who didn't witness it can explain the phenomenon away, but I believe my own observations, and I saw some weird stuff.

Through the early 1980s, on my way from Gillette to visit my parents in Laramie, I usually stopped at the McGuires' place. I lost touch with Pat and his family. I heard that UW ended up with the farm. Pat died in 2009.

****

WHSP placed me in the Gillette city administration as a grant writer. My boss, Mayor Mike Enzi, had a vision. Rather than let rapid growth reshape Gillette at random, he assembled a team of young, upstart professionals to manage the transformation.

Enzi progressed through the state legislature before winning a seat in the U.S. Senate. He suddenly passed away in late July 2021 after a freak bicycle accident. My friends and I got our band together and enjoyed reminiscing about the good old boomtown days.

Governor Ed Herschler appointed Mike's wife, Diana, and me to serve on the Wyoming Private Industry Council for a couple of terms. The council distributes U.S. Department of Labor workforce training funds.

Everyone liked the gruff and personable Gov. Ed. He answered his own phone and smoked Philip Morris Commanders. Bars stocked Cabin Still whiskey, not knowing when Gov. Ed might stop by to chat.

Mayor Enzi directed me to bring in as much federal and state funding for Gillette as possible.

"If Gillette doesn't apply, other places will," he advised. I've been a fundraiser since the Jimmy Carter administration, and I continue to refine that philosophy and life skill today.

While working to reverse the negative public perception of Razor City, I had to use the compelling Gillette Syndrome story to make a case for obtaining grants.

"Not only does Gillette have bad drinking water, it has the worst." I spouted off that familiar refrain when asked whether the stories about Gillette are true. "We have a high level of domestic violence, and in some months it's the highest."

****

My life circled back to the Hitching Post Inn, where I lived for a month and ate more than my fill of sliced turkey sandwiches. Serving as a legislative intern proved to be a valuable life skill. Because of my familiarity with the Hitch, I felt confident, knowing my way around from my days as a busboy. Many of the same people I knew still worked there, including my former boss, Paul Smith.

I ended up back in Cheyenne as a lobbyist for the City of Gillette. Mayor Enzi counted on me to raise $30 million for the Madison Water Project. As a lobbyist, I persuaded lawmakers to approve the funds because they had to serve the good people of Gillette. Wyoming thrived when Gillette, the "Energy Capitol of the Nation," did.

Gillette became the headquarters of the fossil fuels industry, which paid millions in severance taxes that funded schools and public infrastructure throughout the state.

Convincing the lawmakers took a little doing. I camped out in Gov. Ed's office to ensure he would sign the legislation.

Ed Herschler, an FDR Democrat from Kemmerer on the southwestern edge of the state in Lincoln County, typified politically purple Wyoming. No other governor has served three terms. He first defeated Dick Jones in 1974, riding the Blue Wave that swept the country after Watergate.

His "growth on our terms" mission during the 1970s energy boom led to some of the country's most stringent state-sanctioned environmental impact regulations. In 1978, John Ostlund of Gillette defeated

Gus Fleischli in the Republican primary. Herschler narrowly defeated Ostlund. He won his third term four years later, defeating my legislative mentor, Warren Morton.

Representative L.J. Hunter, a pharmacist at Murphy's Drugstore, sponsored the Madison Water Project bill. He provided me with boxes of medicine bottles, which I filled with water that reeked of rotten eggs, with bits of scaly carbonate floating in the fizz. I placed a sample on each legislator's desk.

Those amber bottles did the trick.

Despite legislative support, the railroad remained the bison on the tracks. I had to convince UP lobbyist Jack Knott that the City of Gillette wouldn't sell or allow others to use the Madison formation water to transport coal via a slurry pipeline, a low-cost alternative to coal cars rumbling to Texas power plants. I had a crush on Jack's daughter in high school.

Energy Transport Systems, Inc. (ETSI), led by Frank Odasz, wanted to build a massive pipeline between Wyoming and Texas to deliver a slurry of pulverized coal mixed with brackish Madison Formation water to power plants.

The City of Gillette drilled a test well that showed the Madison water is drinkable. Securing adequate water would be the least of ETSI's worries, compared with obtaining rights-of-way through four of the country's largest landmasses: Wyoming, Colorado, Kansas, and Texas, and with disposing of contaminated water at the end of the line.

I kept looking through a tunnel. The gates finally stayed open at the same time. I remember sitting at the Hitching Post bar, sketching out the funding flow on a bar napkin, which ended up consisting of a loan from the Wyoming Permanent Mineral Trust Fund and state and local grants. The legislature eventually forgave the loan.

As a young guy, I knew my way around Wyoming state government and became pretty good at lobbying. I did so during subsequent legislative sessions on behalf of the Wyoming Association of Municipalities, including in 1981, when Barry Cook and I watched the greatest University of Wyoming basketball game ever.

I heeded my grandfather's advice. Getting a job or any advantage had more to do with "who I knew" than with "what I knew."

Remember our family friend, Secretary of State Thyra Thomson? Wyoming operates under the commission form of government. The top elected officials, including the Governor, Secretary of State, Superintendent of Public Instruction, State Treasurer, and State Auditor, serve on various boards and commissions that ultimately decide on multiple aspects of state government.

Back then, the Farm Loan Board disbursed state funds for local government capital projects, including roads, fire stations, and water plants. Whenever I appeared before the board, Mrs. Thomson invariably asked about my grandparents' and family's well-being, much to the chagrin of the other local government representatives in the room. I could always count on her support for my projects.

My mom always invited Thyra over to our summertime family gatherings so she could meet my relatives visiting from out of town, including Auntie Amy. Auntie Amy took me to the theater in Salt Lake City, where I saw my first production of *The Music Man.*

28

Lander's Music Man

Life moved much more slowly in Lander, nestled at the foot of the Wind River Mountains in Fremont County. I left Gillette's fast-paced, free-wheeling life in 1981, with enough professional success to be hired by Lander Mayor Del McOmie to shore up the Planning Department. An internal conflict-of-interest scandal had created political problems.

I got a little carried away trying to blend into mainstream America in Gillette. My mom's warnings registered with me. If I couldn't be good, I should at least be careful.

Because of a housing shortage in Lander, I rented one of the Faust Apartments above the Ace Hardware store. Japanese residents of Downtown Cheyenne walked everywhere. Flash forward a generation. After World War II, owning a single-family house on a plot of land became the norm.

Living in an apartment downtown? Not desirable, but I could walk two doors down to McRae's Drugstore, the Grand movie theater across the street, my bank at the end of the block, and Safeway a block away, behind my City Hall office.

I didn't drive around town much for a year. I now realize how my past living arrangements, including a Lander mixed-use apartment, a Gillette co-op house, and the Altman Hall dorm, along with close extended family life during my formative years, influenced why I became hooked on the high-density urban lifestyle.

Then, the Great Fremont County Depression hit, and life slowed down.

The 1979 Three Mile Island nuclear power plant meltdown in Pennsylvania curtailed further uranium mining in Fremont County. Seven years later, the Chornobyl reactor melted down in Ukraine. That disaster didn't help shift public perceptions of the harms of nuclear power.

During the Cold War, Jeffrey City, Wyoming, located 60 miles southeast of Lander, grew significantly due to the uranium-mining boom of the 1950s and 1960s.

The uranium mines in the Gas Hills and Crooks Gap districts, northeast and southwest of Jeffrey City, respectively, produced more uranium than any other region during the boom of the 1950s and 1960s.

The founding family homesteaded in the early 1930s and named the town site "Home on the Range," after Brewster Higley's poem about a place with blue skies all day. An abandoned motel, also named "Home on the Range," still stands.

Western Nuclear renamed the town in honor of Dr. Charles W. Jeffrey, a prominent advocate for uranium mining during the Cold War.

By the late 1970s, Jeffrey City had a population of about 4,000. At its peak, the Western Nuclear uranium mine employed about 1,000 people. The community thrived, with a bank, a bowling alley, a newspaper, and restaurants. It also had a school district, an emergency medical clinic, and a volunteer fire department.

When the uranium industry collapsed in the 1980s, the downturn led 95 percent of the population to leave town. The 2020 census lists the population at 146.

The U.S. Steel laid off 500 workers when it closed the taconite mine south of Lander in 1983, compounded the softening uranium market. The U.S. Steel Geneva Mill in Vineyard, Utah, became a potential strategic target following the bombing of Pearl Harbor. The U.S. military believed that building an inland mill would protect America from an enemy *Japoteur* attack.

The main iron ore mine near Cedar City, Utah, produced raw material, but its output soon proved insufficient to keep the Geneva mill operating at full capacity. The Lander Atlantic City taconite mine became a secondary source of raw material. The Wyoming open-pit mine and the short-line railway to Utah began construction in 1960.

My job description shifted from strictly city planning to facilitating economic development and crafting a compelling story for Lander.

Thanks to Auntie Amy, who dragged me to the Salt Lake City theater, I chose film-flam *Music Man*, Professor Harold Hill, as my economic developer role model. Raisin James Shigeta played the lead role in the bowl of River City oatmeal.

Hill convinced the good people of River City, Iowa, to purchase musical instruments for the boys to play in the newly formed town band. The young players would learn the music using the "think method."

"You got trouble in Lander City, and what you need is economic development." The paraphrased Professor Hill lyric became my self-imposed tagline.

****

For the "think" method to work, a project needed a quick turnaround and a tangible outcome, such as a centennial celebration. Most cities, including Lander, could choose among multiple founding dates. To gain the most traction, the successful Music Man convinces the unsuspecting mark that the good idea is theirs.

It could have been when the Fort Bridger Treaty designated the bounds of the Wind River Reservation in 1868, too early for this time around. The Lander incorporation in 1890 would have been a big competition with Wyoming's statehood date and too far out.

Captain William A. Jones led the 1873 Jones Expedition, a significant military reconnaissance mission to explore the Wind River Mountains and the Yellowstone region. The expedition mapped the area, documented natural resources, and recorded interactions with Native American tribes. The date had passed.

In 1875, Eugene Amoretti purchased a large tract of land that would become Lander. He bought it from the original homesteaders, seeing an opportunity to establish a new town. That date didn't help, either.

How about Dr. Howard Lucas, who discovered the Dallas Dome oil field and drilled Wyoming's first oil well in 1884?

The unsung commemoration worked and fit a "back to the past" economic downturn narrative. The Centennial began in 1983 with a save-the-date kickoff. Lander celebrated for 20 months, ending in July 1985.

The City Council appointed the Lander Centennial Committee. The Centennial brought short-term success and long-lasting effects. The celebration fostered a high level of entrepreneurship.

The Committee sponsored a contest to select a product-licensed Centennial logo that emblazoned commemorative plates, silver and bronze coins, a limited run of Coca-Cola cans with the logo, Centennial Winchester rifles, and T-shirts.

Local artist Jerry Antolik painted the Centennial poster. I preferred doing business with Uncle Jake. Pioneer Printing produced the limited-edition lithographs. I drove to Cheyenne to pick up the order.

"I'm compiling my newspaper columns for an anthology titled *Wyoming Grafitti*," I asked Jake. "Do you know anyone who might publish them?"

"I print books for a small publisher in Texas. When you have it finished, I can send it to her."

The Centennial Committee sold the high-value prints, its primary source of revenue. I still have one in a plastic box in the basement.

The year culminated in a massive celebration in the City Park. I convinced Al Simpson to sit in the dunking booth. He wore a suit and tie for the underwater activity.

During the Centennial year, the City of Lander began a survey to designate the Main Street core area as a historic district. Nancy, a seasonal weed and pest control employee, remained on staff to develop and process the district survey.

The Wyoming State Historic Preservation Office and the U.S. National Park Service (USNPS) added the Lander Historic District to the National Register of Historic Places in 1987.

A few Main Street business owners protested "creeping socialism" and the government's seizure of property rights. Despite the protests, the City Council approved the application, and the rest is history.

I remember revisiting Lander for the first time 20 years after I left. I saw banners and signs on streetlight poles welcoming tourists to Historic Downtown Lander. I later learned that the Wyoming Department of Transportation funded significant Main Street improvements, partly because of the historic district designation.

My friend Robin, who works at the Lander Pioneer Museum, came across a box of centennial memorabilia 40 years later and is seeking additions to the collection. The Lander 150th anniversary will be in 2034, and it's time for another celebration!

****

The "think" method also aligned well with the WHSP collaborative problem-solving approach I brought from Gillette. To this day, my decision-making methods revolve around the multidisciplinary "think" method.

In Lander, that included two groups of dedicated citizens. The City Council appointed the Economic Development Commission in 1983, and the private sector established the LEADER Corporation a year later to match the grants by loaning small amounts of seed money to project applicants.

Both groups helped with smokestack chasing to entice businesses to relocate, but the most success came from local companies expanding and counseling aspiring entrepreneurs.

I applied for grants from the Economic Development and Stabilization Board (EDS Board), an appropriate acronym given that Ed Herschler served as Governor. The EDS Board awarded the City of Lander the highest percentage of grant funds it had approved during Wyoming's bust cycle.

Modeling the "think" method for the Lander community seemed to work. People would stop me on the street to explain a business idea or tell me about a guy they knew who wanted to move his company.

I became a Music Man.

****

The 3003 Club opened my eyes to a broader world, and part of that came from staying in touch with my fellow Club members. After I moved to Lander, Jim returned to Motown, where he taught school.

"I'll be in Detroit for a meeting and would like to meet up for a beer," I suggested after calling Jim. The National League of Cities planned its 1981 conference at the Renaissance Hotel. I shared a room with my hunting buddy, City Councilor Mike.

Jim got tickets to see the Rolling Stones at the Pontiac Silver Dome. I consider that the "Disco Stones" era. "Start Me Up" and "Hang Fire" are two tracks from that album. Iggy Pop and Santana opened. Carlos Santana rocked the house. The crowd booed Iggy off the stage.

Jim showed this small-town kid around the big city of Detroit. He took me to a White Castle hamburger stand. "Buy 'em by the sack." Now I buy 'em in the frozen-food aisle. We snacked as we walked, and I came across urban wildlife. A rat the size of a cocker spaniel rose from the shadows, waiting for hamburger-bun crumbs to fall onto the sidewalk.

I've since seen the Stones six more times in Denver. On June 20, 2024, the "Greatest Rock and Roll Band in the World" brought its Hackney Diamonds tour to the Denver Broncos' stadium.

A Stones show is always a gas, gas, gas.

****

I researched a WSJ newspaper column for a first-person account of working at the CFD carnival a decade after the Big Thompson Flood. I didn't know what to expect, but my weekend experience enhanced my Music Man "think" method skills.

I drove to Cheyenne, picked up my credentials at the CFD Media Trailer, and wandered over to the carnival grounds. The rodeo had let out, and the late-afternoon crowd streamed from the grandstands, looking for the next activity. I followed the crowd toward the carnival grounds.

I walked around and took in the atmosphere before negotiating past the gatekeepers. I didn't want to pay the $5.00 cover charge. After some cajoling, my media pass got me in. I hadn't been to the Midway in years.

"Do you know where I can find Dozer?" I asked one of the carnies.

"Over there," she said, pointing toward the administrative office trailer.

I pounded on the door. Dozer answered, and I pitched my newspaper story idea to him. He hired me on the spot for the Bill Hames Show.

Dozer and his wife Angelyn operated half a dozen privately owned games and rides for Kelley's Concessions, based in Alabama. I don't think he thought a city slicker like me could cut it standing and talking nonstop for a 12-hour shift.

Money by Pink Floyd blared from the loudspeaker by the Ferris wheel. I slipped on the navy blue acetate polo shirt with a circular orange-and-white logo over the left breast. Dozer paired me with a blond-haired carny named Anice, a born-again Christian who had lived a hard life.

"The object of the game? Buy a dart for a dollar and bust a balloon for your choice of a small mirror. Five wins for a large mirror," Anice explained. "Mirror" is a misnomer because the prizes are non-reflective square pieces of glass with pictures silk-screened on the back.

"I'm part-time, a couple of nights a week. I live in Englewood and work at a print shop in Denver. I share a motel room in Cheyenne with one of the other women and her boyfriend. I used to work full-time, but the guy I was with beat me up, so I left the show a couple years ago. Dozer asked if I'd work for him again," she said, tying a knot in one of the spare balloons.

The game is rough on the fingers. Each mirror slips into a cardboard sleeve to protect the paint and prevent patron injuries. I tried to be careful, but still managed to slice minor cuts in places I never thought had any useful purpose, like the index finger cuticle, which gets irritated each time I tied off a balloon stem. My hands bled the entire weekend.

A woman named Amber joined us.

"I'm trained as a nurse and working here until something opens up in town," she said, tenderly limping around the area, clearly in pain.

"It's not my foot. It's my back. I was shot in the abdomen, and it hit a disc on the way out," she said before pulling up her shirt and showing the scars. "I ruptured another disc moving a box of these mirrors and have to have surgery again."

Anice divided up the counter.

"Amber takes the first third. I'll take the middle, and you take the other end," Anice said with authority since it's her joint. As the newbie, she assigned me at the end of the line. An imaginary line separates each section. Common courtesy is to avoid cross-hawking. Taking a fellow carny's business is counterproductive.

"If you pull that stunt on one of the guys traveling with the show, he'll knock the hell out of you. I'm telling this for your own good if you decide to do this again," Anice advised.

My experience selling pop at the parade gave me thick skin and made me unafraid of being told "No." Offensive remarks from jerks, based on my appreciation for them at an early age at the Hitching Post, bounced off me like bullets off Superman.

I kept my guard up, being the only dark-skinned fellow there, staying aware of potential problems that could arise, even though all the carnies I met seemed civil despite their cussing and smoking. Luckily, the carnival management and the CFD didn't allow beer or alcohol on site.

I learned how to build relationships with potential customers by feigning politically incorrect character traits. Purveying those mannerisms improved my business.

"That's a nice Kiss t-shirt you're wearing. How about winning a matching mirror for your girl?" or "Looks like you spent a lot of money winning that huge panda for the little lady. Pop a balloon for a Gene Simmons mirror. Costs a dollar. A winner every time."

Occasionally, a youngster would toss the dart in between two balloons. Nothing scattered a crowd faster than a loser, as if we somehow rigged the game: under-inflated balloons, too much space between balloons. I held young kids inches from the target to have a "winner every time."

To this day, I break into carnival mode whenever I have to close a deal or sell books at Barnes & Noble.

Multitasking is a job skill for a carny.

"You're from Beatrice? I went to Hastings," I'd say, my back to the crowd, as I put up more balloons or fetched a mirror for a winner. "How do you like Frontier Days so far?"

As an introvert, I found keeping up with endless personal chatter and building relationships with those waiting their turn exhausting. I didn't want my attention to wander, since all players are potential return customers. It bugs me when I'm in a store waiting for help from a clerk who doesn't at least make eye contact or nod. I walk away and find someone else.

"See you at 10," Dozer called out at closing time on Saturday night. He paid each of us a percentage of our take. I inflated 150 balloons, and my jaw ached. Angelyn handed me $31.

****

Sunday morning, the last day of CFD, came quickly. The small crowd surged as the rodeo let out. The locals had to work on Monday, and many tourists had either left for home or run out of money.

Amber called in sick and arrived late in the afternoon. I noticed her working another joint across the way and worried I had encroached on her balloon dart game turf.

Anice and I spent the morning chatting between rushes. Religion dominated our conversation. She enjoyed evangelizing at the carnival, especially on Sundays.

By this time in my mainstream Presbyterian life, I talked about my offbeat spirituality but didn't wear it on my sleeve. Church services around town must have ended because business picked up around lunchtime. I pushed both sizes of a Shroud of Turin mirror.

"What do you think about UFOs?" I asked, out of the blue.

"Like Aliens? They are the devil," she said without hesitation. "They are the messengers of Satan."

I recounted my flying saucer experience from when I lived in Gillette and camped with friends at the Morton Pass Farm, a few miles north of Laramie. I explained to her that I had read Billy Graham's *Angels: God's Secret Agents* (1975), a book about angels as aliens. It places good and evil angels in context and mentions the UFO phenomenon, and I can't help but draw the same comparisons to what I saw.

Graham speculates that UFOs are God's angelic hosts who preside over the physical affairs of the universe, which would explain supernatural occurrences. Anice looked at me skeptically and said she'd do more research. I wrote down the book title for her, but we agreed to disagree.

****

The music stopped, and the carnival grounds ground to a halt at 2:15 a.m. on a dark Monday morning. The women who operate each joint are the informal crew leaders, and they begin taking everything down in a process called the "slough" (rhymes with cow).

"We'll see you next year," Dozer said, handing me a fistful of dollar bills. He hitched the dart game trailer to a panel truck and pulled out of the empty parking lot.

The $81.00 I earned during those three long, demanding nights left me tired yet gratified. As a souvenir, I bought a billiard stick from one of the carnival vendors. Compared with other sticks, billiard cues have a narrower shaft and a ferrule that holds the tip in place.

After writing this story, I went down to the basement to check whether I still had my carnival pool stick. I found it in the same box as the Lander Centennial poster, but I couldn't find my 9-ball stick.

I got a good deal on a Meucci "Sneaky Pete." Sneaky Pete is a high-end, straight pool cue that looks like a bar stick to avoid attracting attention when playing serious games.

When I get a beer at the Buckhorn, I half expect to run into Anice and Amber at the bar. A guy hustled me only once, for what it's worth. We played for a shot of whiskey at the Buckhorn Bar & Parlor in Laramie. Before I knew it, my opponent had blocked every pocket and then ran the table. I owed him a shot of Jack Daniel's on the rocks.

****

When I decided to move out of the Downtown Lander apartment above the Ace Hardware Store, I became a long-term housesitter for another Alan. He taught wilderness survival courses for the National Outdoor Leadership School (NOLS), which has its international headquarters in Lander.

Alan expected me to keep up the place while NOLS assigned him to lead NOLS courses for months at a time. He constantly studied the Bible as a devout Christian, a lay biblical scholar, and a student of Harold Camping. Camping later lost credibility when his prediction of the end of the world failed to materialize.

I had maintained much of Christianity's basic premise that I had learned in Sunday School, but scriptural subtleties or literal interpretations didn't interest me. He introduced me to the Evangelical Free Presbyterian Church (E-Free), which differed from my upbringing in the UPC.

The E-Free movement emerged in the 1980s, when the UPC became more spiritually liberal. In the early 1970s, its Council on Church and Race granted $25,000 to the Black Panthers and $10,000 to the Angela Davis defense fund.

Those stances split the Cheyenne UPC, prompting conservative members to break away and found the Highlands Church near the Buffalo Ridge Addition in North Cheyenne. My parents stayed with the UPC. The more biblically literal E-Free led to an "Aha" moment that, strangely, made my Christian belief system feel more tangible.

****

I must have been coming from or going somewhere when I ended up in Cheyenne. I read a newspaper ad announcing that Billy Graham would give a free presentation at Frontier Park on September 17, 1987, as part of his American Crusade tour. I went over to listen. I had no idea that 25,000 people would fit in and around the venue. I sat in the East Stands over the rodeo chutes. Those are normally great seats during CFD, but not so good for watching Graham from over his shoulder.

I hadn't attended a major religious event like this. I later saw Pope John Paul II at Cherry Creek Reservoir in 1993. Talk about enormous crowds. I've taken Catholic communion only once, at that papal mass.

Rev. Graham didn't speak about angels or UFOs, but he's an inspiring speaker. Rather than Bible-banging and fear-mongering, he used the "think method" to encourage attendees. With God's help, they could nurture an innate ability to overcome their life problems.

Graham could relate to ordinary people. He told us he'd broken nine of the 10 Commandments, except for adultery, and didn't expect perfection from anyone. His Cheyenne appearance occurred when TV evangelist Jim Bakker fell from grace after sleeping around on his wife, Tammy Faye.

I gave a few bucks when his minions passed the hat. Back then, Graham's church had to issue a receipt if the donor requested a tax deduction.

A few weeks later, Jim Urish, the pastor of Lander E-Free, and his wife, Ann, both young and personable, invited me over to talk about my faith and related topics. The Billy Graham organization informed Jim that I had attended the Cheyenne gathering.

I had forgotten that I had listed E-Free as my home church on the offering envelope. I'm not the overly zealous type, and my listening to Rev. Graham surprised them. Our small talk turned to Graham's book on angels, and I told them my story about aliens as messengers of God. They knew Graham's book and looked at me as if Satan himself had possessed me. The topic didn't come up again.

The following summer, the Bill Hames Show contracted with Pioneer Days in Lander for the July 4th weekend. I asked if I could speak with Dozer. He and Angelyn had joined another branch of the show at the Colorado State Fair.

****

One Saturday morning, Tom Stromme, the WSJ photographer, pulled up in his treasure-filled van and pounded on my door. Tom scrounged around at yard sales on the weekends.

"I think you should buy this violin I saw." We went over, and the fiddle still sat in its case, and I bought it.

"You should take lessons," Tom said, referring to the instrument's provenance. The instrument once belonged to local fiddler Quentin Roberts.

I wrote a newspaper story about Becky Murdock's local Suzuki violin school. I contacted her about enrolling in classes. I knew about her Suzuki teaching method, which resonated with me.

I felt at ease learning about Shinichi Suzuki. Dr. Suzuki based his teaching method on the idea that if kids in Japan can learn a complex language like Japanese, they can learn to play the violin. I credit my traumatic piano lessons, which forced me to read music, for how quickly I learned.

The Suzuki method incorporates several principles and practices that reflect Zen philosophy. These principles emphasize mindfulness, the process over the outcome, and holistic development.

In the mid-1980s, Becky and her husband Mike moved to the Pacific Northwest. She asked if I could take over her teaching practice. I agreed and ended up with a dozen or so of her students, along with some of my own. I taught in my living room, but as the business grew, I rented a studio downtown.

I eventually became too busy with my real job and returned the business to Becky, but I kept playing. By then, she had formed an orchestra, and a few of us would occasionally perform at a local bar called the Hitching Rack, where members of the Lions Club hung out after their meetings.

Once a month, on Wednesday evenings, my string trio, consisting of two violins and a viola, enraptured the otherwise rowdy crowd with Mozart. Since then, I have brought art forms to places patrons wouldn't typically expect.

I became more self-aware and *Zen*-like by becoming a Music Man and teaching Suzuki violin lessons using the "think" method, shifting my focus from outcomes to the process, going with the flow, and letting life play out. That included a last-minute trip to Peru in 1983.

29

Primos Peruanos

Half of my mom's family is Peruvian. On the surface, my Japanese-Peruvian relatives may seem unusual, but Peru became the first Latin American country to establish diplomatic relations with Japan in 1873. Grandma married my grandfather in Japan and later moved to Wyoming. Her brother immigrated to Peru.

Grandma Sakata planned a big family trip to Lima for the ceremony in October 1983. The business community in the nearby town of Supe (soo-peh) honored her brother. Peruvians are big on awarding medals.

My mom pressured me, a chronic overachiever, to take little time off work, other than a day or two around legal holidays. I felt guilty about leaving the office, but changed my mind, thinking this would be a good adventure into the unknown and good story fodder.

When Ernest Hemingway needed inspiration, he enlisted in World War I. Thanks to one of my Lander friends, the late Dave Raynolds, a retired U.S. Foreign Service diplomat, my trip to Peru would give me a taste of Latin American politics and reconnect me with my cultural past and family roots.

Peru severed relations with Japan during World War II. It considered an internment program but chose to deport over 1,000 Japanese

Peruvians to the United States, primarily to three Detention Centers in Texas near the port in New Orleans.

Unlike the WRA-managed Camps, the Immigration and Naturalization Service (INS) constructed and administered the Detention Centers in Texas at Seagoville, Kenedy, and Crystal City.

Latin American countries deported Japanese and Germans to the United States. The INS sent women and childless couples to the Seagoville Center, families with children to the Crystal City Center, and men to the Kenedy Center.

In 1903, Congress transferred the Bureau of Immigration to the Department of Commerce and Labor, which is now a separate department. The U.S. government sought to keep immigration in check to protect American workers from lower-cost foreign labor.

Congress established the INS in 1933 and transferred the Service to the U.S. Justice Department in 1940 to address potential enemy aliens as the United States moved closer to involvement in World War II.

The American Red Cross monitored the INS to ensure that the Detention Centers met the standards set forth in the Third Geneva Convention of 1929, Relative to the Treatment of Prisoners of War. The Geneva Conventions set standards for food quality, the size of living quarters, and the quantity and type of clothing detainees may possess.

Like the WRA, the INS designed its Centers as stand-alone communities with food stores, auditoriums, medical services, places of worship, and post offices. The Centers also offered retail storefronts, including bakeries, barbershops, and beauty parlors, as well as school systems. Japanese *sumo* wrestling rings and German *biergartens* added culturally appropriate touches.

******

In April 1942, the U.S. Army Transport (USAT) Etolin departed Callao, Peru, carrying nearly 150 Japanese men. The Etolin picked up Japanese deportees from Colombia before heading to San Francisco.

The INS denied them visas and passports, classified them as enemy aliens, and detained them at Assembly Centers alongside domestic incarcerees.

Other ships, including the Swedish charter Steam Ship (SS) Gripsholm, the SS Shawnee, and the SS Frederick C. Johnson, transported Japanese from Peru to Panama before sailing to the United States. The ships docked in New Orleans.

In April 1942, the INS took over a women's prison in Seagoville, Texas, and converted it into a Detention Center 20 miles southeast of Dallas, where the INS sent women and couples without children.

In July 1942, the Seagoville Center detainee population consisted of a handful of German men and 40 German and Japanese women. The number of detainees grew in the months that followed.

The INS considered it "voluntary" because they agreed to join their detained husbands. Regulations permitted women to possess personal items such as hot water bottles, clothing, and sewing supplies, as well as creature comforts like rugs, curtains, and cushions, and small electric appliances like irons.

The number of occupants in Seagoville decreased because of the deportation of detainees to Germany and Japan. In June 1942, the U.S. Department of State (DoS) deported 1,500 Japanese. By August 1944, the Center's population had dwindled to about 380, mostly Germans.

In March 1942, the INS repurposed a 22-acre Great Depression-era Civilian Conservation Corps (CCC) site in Kenedy, Texas, in Karnes County, 60 miles southeast of San Antonio, into the Kenedy Detention Center.

The CCC, part of FDR's New Deal and an essential public-works relief program, provided manual-labor jobs to unemployed, unmarried men from 1933 to 1942 during the Great Depression.

Workers conserved natural resources and built public works projects for federal, state, and local governments in rural areas. Many CCC projects in Wyoming included roads in Yellowstone National

Park, facilities at Glendo State Park, and countless other public works projects across the state. The U.S. Congress ended the program in 1942. The need for the massive work-relief program declined with the onset of the World War II military draft.

Latin American countries deported 2,000 Japanese, Germans, and Italians and processed them at the Kenedy Center. The initial wave of detainees arrived in April 1942 from Latin America and included more than 650 Germans and Italians. Over the next two months, 600 additional German and Japanese detainees arrived. Over time, the detainees at the Kenedy Center divided into ethnic "clans," such as the Germans from Guatemala, the largest clique. Conflicts among the groups intensified.

At its peak in May 1956, the U.S. Army and the INS guarded 426,000 PoWs held in the U.S.: 372,000 Germans, 50,000 Italians, and 4,000 Japanese. Congress gave the INS greater authority to house potentially dangerous enemy aliens and American citizen Axis sympathizers in WRA incarceration camps and INS detention camps.

In September 1944, Kenedy released, repatriated, or transferred detainees to free space for a German and Japanese PoW Camp. Seagoville authorities deported nearly all Japanese Latin Americans to their home countries, with some families transferred to the Crystal City Center. The Seagoville Center closed in May 1945.

INS leased 200 acres of land in Crystal City, Zavala County, 50 miles from the Mexican border, to build a third detention center. Crystal City, originally a migrant labor facility established in the 1920s, boomed as migrant farm laborers crossed the border to work on local farms.

The Center detained Japanese and Germans deported from Latin America and incarcerated Japanese Americans transferred from other WRA assembly centers to Crystal City. By the end of 1945, the Center held 3,400 Japanese and German incarcerees.

****

Peru developed a strong relationship with the United States during World War II. Capitalizing on anti-Japanese sentiment in Peru strengthened its defense in the Western Hemisphere. The relationship prompted American banks to approve loans to finance a Peruvian steel-processing plant. In exchange, Peru allowed the U.S. military to operate an airbase at Talara, a strategic location for defending the Panama Canal.

I have Peruvian cousins named Carlos, Juan, and Pedro. Pedro moved to the United States and now lives in Florida. Recently, he came to Colorado for a job-related conference. We met up briefly and took a whirlwind drive to Estes Park. We're in touch on Facebook.

Pedro didn't know why the Peruvian government allowed his family to remain in Peru rather than deport them. He still owns the property in Supe, Barranca Province, on the Pacific coast. In 1983, Supe lacked running water, and domestic electricity use easily overloaded the rudimentary electrical circuits. When the Peruvian economy declined, some of my cousins not born in Japan emigrated to Japan, where they faced discrimination.

The adults all knew at least a little Japanese. We asked our bilingual relatives questions in English or Spanish, and they translated them into Japanese. Then the response would be in either English or Spanish.

I liked the food. My *Tias* prepared Japanese-style Peruvian dishes. We had a lot of *ceviches* (raw fish marinated and cured in lemon), including versions with *shoga* (ginger) and shoyu. Chinese restaurants are called *chifas*. I've read that there are now Japanese-style *nikkei* Peruvian restaurants.

****

In 1983, the Communist Shining Path guerrilla fighters terrorized the mountainous regions and slaughtered hundreds of native people.

Dave Raynolds often visited me in my office. He, his wife, and their daughter owned a bison ranch in Sinks Canyon. I told him I'd be away in Peru.

"When you're on one of those Peruvian buses, sit next to someone with a chicken. If a terrorist gets on board, grab the chicken and blend in with the rest of the passengers," he advised.

I didn't encounter any chickens on the bus, but while flying to Iquitos on a side trip to the Amazon River headwaters, the Fawcett Airlines jet stopped on the taxiway to let a passenger board, lugging a box full of peeping chicks. The passenger sat in my row.

"I have a friend, Frank Ortiz, who works at the U.S. Embassy in Peru. I'll call ahead and let him know you're coming," Dave said on his way out the door.

The chaos in Lima and the long lines of would-be asylum seekers stretching around the U.S. Embassy looked like a scene from the 1982 film *Missing*, starring Sissy Spacek and Jack Lemmon as Beth and Edmond Horman, the parents of a journalist who disappeared during Chile's 1973 overthrow of President Salvador Allende.

I escorted my family to the Embassy, where we checked in as a precaution. We cut to the front of the long line. A young Marine behind a foot-thick pane of glass greeted us. He buzzed us in to meet Frank Ortiz.

President Ronald Reagan appointed Frank Ortiz as the U.S. Ambassador to Peru. We arrived to find him and his staff frantically packing and preparing to leave amid the domestic chaos. We had only time for small talk before the Embassy staff ushered us out. The next morning's lead story reported that the U.S. Department of State had recalled Frank Ortiz from the soon-to-be-closed Embassy because of the political and social unrest.

******

The AeroPeru flight to Miami had worn me out. I landed late, booked a room at an airport hotel, slept a few hours, then boarded a domestic flight back to Denver and a commuter flight to Riverton. That's the same route I took when I met Mrs. Honkawa.

My friend and newspaper colleague Diana, who accompanied me to the Heart Mountain Camp the first time, picked me up at the Riverton airport. I didn't have jet lag from the three-hour time change, but returning to my daily frenetic grind turned out to be very relaxing.

30

I'm a Japaho

Dave Raynolds debriefed me on my refreshing visit to Peru and my frantic meeting with Frank Ortiz. He updated me on what I had missed, including the ongoing struggle to address the closure of the U.S. Steel taconite mine. The Lander Centennial Committee had the celebration planning well underway, and it had a life of its own, renewing optimism during the economic bust cycle.

After returning from Peru, I became involved in an environmental justice project when Gov. Ed appointed me to the Uranium Mill Tailings Task Force. The Uranium Mill Tailings Radiation Control Act (UMTRCA) of 1978, administered by the U.S. Department of Energy, authorized the creation of a community Task Force to gather public input. Environmental pollution and hazards have historically affected marginalized communities, particularly those living in poverty and people of color, a pattern now known as environmental racism.

During the height of the Cold War in the 1950s and 1960s, the U.S. government promoted uranium mining for nuclear weapons production.

From 1958 to 1963, Western Nuclear transported uranium ore from its mines near Jeffrey City to the Susquehanna-Western, Inc. mill near Riverton and the Wind River Reservation.

The facility processed more than 800,000 tons of uranium ore trucked from the Gas Hills mining district, converting it into yellowcake. When the mill closed, Western Nuclear left behind a 70-acre, unlined pile of nearly 1.8 million cubic yards of radioactive waste.

Our Task Force had many concerns about mill tailings removal, containment, and long-term monitoring, in collaboration with the DOE and other agencies, including the EPA.

I befriended one member, Northern Arapaho Business Council Chair Gary Collins. My friendship with him and the connections I later made with the Northern Arapaho Tribe would, in a roundabout way, reconnect me with my Japanese cultural roots.

The Task Force held public meetings. Residents experienced health issues linked to the contamination, such as cancer and other radiation-related illnesses.

U.S. Senator Al Simpson played a significant role in addressing the uranium tailings issue. He advocated for federal funding to mitigate environmental damage across the United States. I arranged a meeting with Senator Al Simpson on behalf of the Task Force. A local politician and a constituent stumbled into the meeting, and the good Senator chewed them out for disrupting the meeting.

Afterward, the gatecrasher took credit for organizing the mill tailings meeting. Years later, when we ran into each other in a parking lot before a UW football game, he apologized to me for that. He described it as a political lie that got out of control. At least he felt guilty about his microaggression.

Microaggressions are subtle actions or comments that convey prejudiced attitudes toward marginalized groups. These can include seemingly innocuous remarks or behaviors that perpetuate stereotypes or dismiss the experiences of those who face systemic discrimination.

I felt that I had reached the top of my game and began thinking about what might be next. The public sector had lost its challenge, and a mayoral change in 1987 reinforced that. The new Head of State asked her top carryover staff members to submit letters of resignation and would let us know who she would hire back. I didn't need to deal with the new power-and-control leadership style, so I decided to give free enterprise a try.

****

A business I helped establish in Lander had an opening in its finance office, so I signed on with them. They manufactured steel parts on a just-in-time basis for an exercise equipment company. After a promising start, the company became unstable and eventually went out of business.

The revolving door of jobs would be the story of my life after I left the steady public sector. Because of my Music Man ability to pick up pieces, floundering groups hired me to resurrect projects and develop new approaches, but when all the money that once flowed had dried up.

I'd always been on an even keel, but encountered rough seas when I weathered an unfortunate marriage with a business partner, which proved that I'm better at helping others get started from the outside than at working with people who think they know what they're doing from inside their business.

****

Around that time, I received a life-changing phone call from Ernie Sun Rhodes, chair of the Northern Arapaho Economic Development Commission (EDC). He asked whether I'd be interested in working for the EDC. After a few false starts, I began my role as the Economic and Community Development Director for the *hinono'eiteen* (Northern Arapaho Tribe).

Every morning for four years, I made the 16-mile commute from Lander to the tribal offices in *Ethete*, which means "good" in Arapaho.

The cultural upheaval the Japanese experienced during and after World War II is minor compared with the impact of Manifest Destiny on Native Americans. I learned about Manifest Destiny in my high school American History class taught by Mr. McIlvain. I didn't have a practical understanding of it until I worked for the Northern Arapaho Tribe and, by association, the *sosoni'iiteen* (Eastern Shoshone) tribe. Both tribes share the Wind River Reservation.

Federally recognized tribes are sovereign nations with a direct relationship to the U.S. government, as spelled out in the U.S. Constitution. Federal funds, for example, flow directly to the tribes and don't pass through state governments. Article I, Section 8, Clause 3, known as the "Commerce Clause," affirms the sovereignty of Native American tribes and their separation from national and state jurisdictions.

After the Sand Creek Massacre in 1864, the U.S. Government sent the Southern Cheyenne and Southern Arapaho to a shared reservation in western Oklahoma, established under the Medicine Lodge Treaty of 1867.

The Northern Arapaho did not initially move to Wyoming after being displaced and moved to various locations, including Nebraska and Kansas. In 1878, the BIA forced the tribe into Wyoming.

Shoshone Chief Washakie granted the Arapaho permission to temporarily reside on the Shoshone Reservation. The Northern Arapaho had no official treaty approving their placement there.

The BIA thought otherwise and established the Wind River Reservation, where the two tribes remain at odds. The Shoshone and Arapaho tribes have separate tribal governments but jointly manage the reservation. They didn't get along before the Indian Appropriations Act of 1851, which set aside land for reservations, and still don't.

****

During my tenure, the tribe proposed several controversial projects, including Monitored Retrievable Storage (MRS). In 1991, President George H. W. Bush appointed David H. Leroy as the DoE's first and only Nuclear Waste Negotiator. Congress created Leroy's position under the Nuclear Waste Policy Amendments Act of 1987.

Leroy negotiated with states and Native American tribes to identify a suitable location for the MRS nuclear waste repository, where power companies would ship spent nuclear fuel rods by rail for storage.

The Northern Arapaho Tribe submitted a unilateral proposal to site the MRS on private land. Prospective MRS hosts attended workshops on how to plan for the future, thousands of years from now, when culture and languages will change.

The slight possibility of a radioactive environmental catastrophe halted the project, which would have created a steady labor force for 24,000 years, the half-life of Plutonium-239.

A group of private businessmen, including my mill tailings meeting gate-crasher, picked up the MRS pieces but didn't get very far with the idea either. A friend from Gillette, the DoI Solicitor General, helped move the project through the bureaucracy until January 20, 1993.

Democrat Bill Clinton defeated President George H.W. Bush and third-party candidate Ross Perot, which meant my friend lost his job when the guard changed.

MRS, a major long-term project, would have diversified Wyoming's labor force. The state's economy has primarily been pass-through: value added to fossil fuels at out-of-state power plants, livestock finished in out-of-state feedlots, the Transcontinental Railroad moving people across and out of Wyoming, and unused water flowing out of the state.

******

In 1989, the SCOTUS upheld a Wyoming Supreme Court ruling, awarding the Eastern Shoshone and Northern Arapaho tribes 500,717 acre-feet of water under their 1868 pre-territorial rights—the most senior rights.

While working for the Northern Arapaho, the Tribal Business Council instructed staff to use water and conserve it as much as possible within the reservation's boundaries. We established the 600-acre

Arapaho Farm. The enterprise consisted of fallow ground plowed and hand-irrigated.

Before that experience, I identified as a farmer. One summer, my sister and I spent a month irrigating sugar beets on the Shinmori farm near Orpha. That's how I got to know their kids, Bobby, Kathy, and Jay, who taught me how to hand-irrigate. Early each morning, we moved water across the fields using arced plastic tubing of various diameters, relying on the siphoning effect. I filled each tube with ditch water to remove air, covered one end with the palm of my hand, and lifted the tube over the ditch berm into the sugar beet furrow.

Spreading irrigation water became a life skill for me. I surprised the Arapaho Farm Manager when he watched me hand-irrigate. We created jobs by hand-irrigating rather than using more efficient Poly Vinyl Chloride (PVC) gated pipes with linear holes that squirted water into the crop furrows.

In addition to the tribal farm, which added value to water, the bison reintroduction project also required water. The first efforts began with a traditional bison ceremony in 1993, coinciding with a tribal summer school camp.

****

That summer, the tribal insurance agent, Ed King, and I hauled a horse trailer behind his pickup to Lame Deer, Montana, to pick up a bison the Northern Cheyenne Tribe had promised to deliver.

"He roamed back into the hills," the herd manager explained. "I had him here yesterday."

I called the Crow Tribe Bison Program, and we headed to Crow Agency.

"They must have a sixth sense. The herd retreated into a canyon. You're a little late," the program administrator told us after driving an hour and navigating dirt roads to the bison pasture.

We rambled back to Lander, where we started, and purchased a bison from Dave Raynolds, my retired diplomat friend.

"What we're missing in our cycle of life is the buffalo," tribal elder Ignacious "Iggy John" C'Hair said. "The kids need to learn about this."

One of the tribe's top priorities is reversing the effects of assimilation by reviving the tribal language and ceremonies. After our wild buffalo chase and successful "hunt," the Arapaho Entertainment Committee transported the bison carcass to the Blue Sky Hall gymnasium, a tribal community meeting space.

The Arapaho elders presented a traditional ceremony at the summer camp, which *National Geographic* photographer Sarah Leen photographed, documented, and published in 1994.

****

Toward the end of my formal employment with the Arapaho Tribe, a tribal elder and artist, Eugene Rigdely, Sr., approached me about a project involving tribal artists. In 1992, the 500th anniversary of Columbus's arrival in the "New World," I commuted between Lander and Boulder, Colorado, to assist with a cultural exchange program. Since then, the Boulder community has placed me in the role of a minority advocate.

If you haven't had the chance to spend time among Native American tribal members, it's an experience everyone needs. The Arapaho are collaborative, and reaching consensus among several interests, including spiritual leaders, elected officials, and the tribal members-at-large, known as the General Council, takes time.

I served as the liaison between the Northern Arapaho artists and the local nonprofit The Next 500 Years (N5Y). Many art gallery owners on the Pearl Street Mall contributed by offering wall space for Northern Arapaho artwork.

Thinking the cultural conduit would be a way to earn a few bucks, I decided to move to Colorado. That didn't happen because one of the N5Y founders allegedly stole a Rolex wristwatch donated by another volunteer. Its sale would have raised enough money to keep N5Y going.

"You watch out," an Arapaho elder warned me. "You're more like us than them," he said, referring to my skin color. "You know our tribe's history and the Sand Creek Massacre. Don't let them use you."

I kept the cultural pipeline viable for two summers, but couldn't sustain it through volunteer efforts. Plus, I didn't make the winter commute, and several Boulder galleries had closed their doors.

Some positive developments have occurred since Eugene first envisioned the cultural conduit. While not ideal, the City of Boulder is developing a Fort Chambers management plan with the Arapaho to permit ceremonial use of the parkland. The sod fort, built in the wake of tribes defending their homelands, became a place where Boulder volunteers trained and participated in the Sand Creek Massacre.

It's been a struggle, but my job transitions have led to a 40-year relationship with the Northern Arapaho Tribe that endures today.

The cultural conduit developed into a story about the Arapaho connecting their language and culture to the land, told through two documentary projects. *Beyond Sand Creek* (2022), which aired on PBS, focuses on tribal efforts to reclaim land in northern Colorado and to educate students about the language, ceremonies, and culture, linking them to the land base. *The Arapaho Covered Wagon Redux* (2024) challenges negative stereotypes of Native Americans through an original soundtrack performed by the Northern Arapaho Eagle Society drum and the Boulder Symphony.

****

In 2016, I, along with Gary Collins and other tribal members, organized another bison ceremony for the two documentaries. Rather than chasing around the country, hoping a tribe would share an animal, I took a different approach and worked with the State of Wyoming Parks Division.

By the late 1880s, hunters had nearly driven bison to extinction, with fewer than 100 animals remaining in the wild. Finding one critter for this tribal ceremony became a bureaucratic nightmare.

Wyoming is home to three public and sort-of free-ranging public bison herds.

The most well-known herd roams throughout Yellowstone National Park. The bison range should be much more extensive than the current park boundary. The herd's population grows faster than the USNPS can control through natural mortality and predators.

They wander out onto non-federal lands, causing conflicts among state wildlife and agricultural agencies, environmentalists, and ranchers who fear that a bacterium called *Brucella abortus* will infect their herds and cause spontaneous abortions. According to the USNPS, there has been no documented case of *B. abortus* transmitted between bison and cattle.

The Interagency Bison Management Plan guides representatives from various federal, state, and tribal agencies working together to manage the bison population, particularly their migration outside Yellowstone National Park.

Between LaPorte and Fort Collins, Colorado, the USDA Animal and Plant Health Inspection Service (APHIS) culls Yellowstone bison that test negative for brucellosis to seed and expand Great Plains tribal herds. APHIS manages a small quarantine facility that has produced a herd that roams the Soapstone Prairie Natural Area, managed by the City of Fort Collins, and the Red Mountain Open Space, managed by Larimer County.

APHIS manages birds at airports to prevent collisions with airplanes. The agency uses plant- and animal-sniffing dogs to monitor passenger check-in lines for illegal animals and vegetation smuggled in and out of the United States. APHIS also has a research branch that developed a way to keep prairie dogs from chewing on underground nuclear missile silo wiring.

Had they been in place, APHIS Airport Wildlife Services bird-mitigation protocols might have prevented a U.S. Air flight from crash-landing on the Hudson River in New York City, now known as the "Miracle on the Hudson."

The State of Wyoming manages herds at Hot Springs State Park in Thermopolis and at Bear River State Park near Evanston. We received word of a "dry" cow from the Thermopolis herd. She could not reproduce, and the Park would eventually sell the bison at auction.

"I'll take her," I told the Hot Springs State Park Superintendent, Kevin Skates, one of my Political Science 101 class students at UW. "What do I do next?"

Former Wyoming Arts Council folklorist Annie Hatch came to the rescue. She grew frustrated working through channels and arranged a 10-minute meeting with some state government higher-ups.

That whirlwind meeting secured the bison cow for our ceremony. The agency agreed to donate the animal for the ceremony and to forgo the $1,000 it would have realized at auction. The goodwill value offset the revenue loss.

****

The Transcontinental Railroad enabled more settlers to move further west, and with that, bison numbers declined because the railroads wanted bison eliminated. Herds of bison standing on the tracks damaged locomotives when trains failed to stop. Bison could delay trains for days.

During the Manifest Destiny period, the railroads and the government treated bison as commodities. The U.S. Army condoned their mass extermination. Herds roamed and lingered in pastures to graze, making them easy targets for hunters more interested in their body parts than in their spiritual significance.

Railroads hired commercial hunters, including William "Buffalo Bill" Cody, to shoot bison, which also served as a food source for their laborers. Bounty hunters soon arrived in large numbers. Hunters pointed their rifles out the windows and climbed onto the railcars, knocking over 150 or more animals.

Hunters left animal carcasses on the prairie for scavengers, including coyotes, wolves, and raptors. Traders loaded massive quantities of buffalo hides and bones onto railroad flatcars. They shipped them back east for processing into clothing, carbon black, fertilizer, and powder used to manufacture fine bone china.

Fewer bison also meant more range for cattle driven up from Texas. The U.S. government removed the Great Plains tribal members' primary food source and the center of their spiritual life.

Gary Collins and I discussed the status of the bison to avoid further bureaucratic delays. Would the Wyoming Department of Agriculture classify our bison cow for the 2016 Arapaho ceremony as a "wild animal" or as "domestic livestock"? Will the Game and Fish Department require the bison to receive Brucellosis inoculations if they classify it as wild?

It didn't matter.

On the day of the ceremony, an early-model Wyoming state government pickup truck hauling an ancient, desert-khaki-painted Bureau of Land Management (BLM) surplus horse trailer kicked up dust as it rambled slowly along the dirt road toward the Ethete Rodeo Arena.

The driver backed up to one of the catch pens, and his helper, an East High School classmate of mine named Roger Shanor, unloaded the animal. I signed for her on a scrap of paper.

I contacted all the reservation schools about the event, mostly as a courtesy. Much to my surprise, soon after the bison arrived, a caravan of Yellow Dog school buses arrived from two directions and converged at the rodeo grounds. Chaperones disembarked hundreds of schoolchildren to take part in the sacred event.

The night before the ceremony, Harvey Spoonhunter, another former Northern Arapaho Business Council chair, invited me to his house and to the sweat lodge. Officiants cover domed sweat lodges with blankets and tarps to keep in heat.

He and his brother, Marlin, placed round river rocks in a fire pit and heated them with red-hot embers. Harvey carried the hot stones into the sweat lodge on a shovel blade and dropped them into a pit.

"We have an important ceremony tomorrow," Harvey said before the sweat began. "A bison will give her life to make our tribe stronger."

He blessed a container of water, ladled it over the rocks, then closed the door, creating a dark, humid atmosphere.

The next day, Iggy John, the tribal elder, presided over the bison ceremony.

"Alan, killing a buffalo is on my bucket list," he told me. "Can I have the honor?"

After Iggy John offered a blessing honoring the bison and the Eagle Society sang, my colleague, Gary, instructed him on where to aim his .30-06-caliber long gun. He squeezed the trigger. The rifle cracked, and she dropped in her tracks. A designated woman, a tribal elder, oversaw the butchering of the bison in the traditional way.

As a non-tribal member, I found the event uplifting. Busloads of students gathered around Iggy John and the bison to see and hear the elders dress the bison for subsistence and ceremonial purposes.

The state of Wyoming and the U.S. Government imposed more regulations on this one bison cow from Hot Springs State Park than on the 30 million slaughtered in the 19th century.

I've been working with many of the same tribal members to restore bison to the Northern Arapaho Tribe. The restoration began in 2019, when the National Bison Refuge in Montana released 10 animals into a pasture near the Eastern Shoshone tribal land on the reservation's western edge. I've heard that talks are underway to decommoditize the animals and merge the two herds.

****

The United States boomed because of westward expansion. Mass European emigration led to growing public support for standardized education based on cultural values and norms presumably held by all citizens, including Native Americans.

Between 1790 and 1920, the U.S. government subjected tribal members to its Americanization policies and forced Native Americans to adopt Anglo-American culture.

President George Washington had an assimilation strategy to manage relations with Native American tribes and to expand the United States into tribal territories.

Washington's approach encouraged Native Americans to adopt Christianity and European-style education. It promoted farming over the traditional hunting-and-gathering lifestyle and encouraged the adoption of European-style governance and social structures within Native American communities.

His paternalistic policy goal would integrate Native Americans into the dominant new society, making them more "civilized" and compatible with the expanding United States.

President Andrew Jackson institutionalized Washington's goal when he signed the Indian Removal Act in 1830. The wars against the tribes ended in the late 19th and early 20th centuries. The Bureau of Indian Affairs outlawed traditional religious ceremonies. Many books and movies depict Native American children being forced to enroll in boarding schools. The BIA required them to abandon their traditions, learn English, and attend a Christian church.

The Dawes Act of 1877 transformed the traditional collaborative tribal structure into rugged individualism aligned with the American Way. The Act granted each tribal member U.S. citizenship and an allotment of reservation land, theoretically fostering a sense of ownership and turning nomadic people into sedentary farmers.

****

Americans have become more civilized, yet the national goal of racial homogeneity has remained unchanged for centuries.

After working with the Northern Arapaho tribal elders, I came to understand their challenges in reviving their language through reverse assimilation and in reclaiming their traditional homeland. I realized how my parents tried to protect me from racism by complying with the American Way.

After 40 years of contact with the Northern Arapaho, the curious often ask me how I've maintained a strong relationship with the tribe.

"I look Arapaho, I'm not related to anyone, and I can't vote," is my usual response. "I'm a Japaho."

31

Evolving Traditions

Superman celebrated his birthdays in Smallville. He sat around holiday tables with his adoptive parents, Jonathan and Martha Kent, and learned Kansas values from the only parents he ever knew.

They told him he had come from somewhere else, but they couldn't tell him much about that distant place called Krypton. Like many children of immigrants, Clark grew up knowing he had roots elsewhere while feeling completely safe and comfortable in his home.

When Jonathan and Martha passed away, Clark lost his parents and his last living connection to the traditions that had shaped him. The values remained, but he had to decide what to carry forward and what to leave behind.

My move from Lander to Boulder stirred up a similar question. As a relatively big fish in the small Wyoming pond, Colorado challenged me as I reinvented myself, something I never imagined doing while growing up in Wyoming.

I lived in Wyoming from my birth in 1953 until roughly 1993. The exact departure date is fuzzy. I kept an apartment in Lander, continued working there, and commuted regularly to Boulder and Bozeman for projects in the Greater Yellowstone Ecosystem. Unlike a graduation, retirement, or wedding, I had no single moment when I could say I had officially left Wyoming behind.

My address and perspectives changed. Colorado opened my eyes to a cultural heritage I had largely ignored. Beyond my tunnel-vision experiences growing up in Cheyenne, I paid little attention to the history of the Japanese American community that had quietly shaped my family and my hometown. Researching this memoir sparked a cultural renaissance, bringing back memories, questions, and more than a little angst.

My Nisei parents, aunts, and uncles gradually westernized their lives after the Issei generation passed away. Today, none of those elders are alive. My sister and I, our cousins, the generations that follow will carry on the family legacy. We've scattered across the country, built private lives, and created our own traditions. Like Clark Kent looking back toward Smallville, I find myself wondering which parts of the past deserve preservation, which should grow, and how a family honors its history after the people who carried it are gone.

After spitting into an ancestry.com tube, I learned I have four close second and third cousins and several distant relatives from my Grandpa Ohashi's family.

I visited my cousin Milton in San Francisco for Memorial Day weekend 2017 and visited the graves of Auntie Rose, Uncle Vince, and cousin Carolynn.

We toured some haunts from our younger years on the streets of San Francisco. I ate *nigiri sushi,* small wads of rice topped with fish or crustaceans, for the first time over New Year's in 1981 at Godzilla Sushi. The *sushi* chefs colored the rice in various colors: rainbow rice. During that same trip to San Francisco, I tried my hand at rolling *sushi* the size of hockey pucks.

In 2017, Godzilla Sushi discontinued serving multicolored rice, opting for traditional white, sticky rice instead. The restaurant displayed its funky, historical artwork in the back hallway.

Milton took me to my first strip club in 1981. The overly buxom Carol Doda and her Condorettes made the Condor Club famous. In

Dirty Harry (1971), Clint Eastwood cruises down Broadway and slowly passes by the Condor Club.

"No cover. Two-drink minimum." The sidewalk barker waved us through the door. Milton introduced me to Galiano Stingers: Galiano and peppermint schnapps on the rocks at that bar.

The Condor Club remained the same in 2017, except that only photos of Carol Doda hung on the walls. She died in 2015. Carol descended from the rafters on a white grand piano, which is now displayed on the floor in front of the stage.

When I'm with family, I always talk about a cousin reunion. I sorted through some photos of Milton and his siblings from Auntie Elsie's box of pictures, which brought up many memories.

All but three of my Sansei-generation first cousins are still on the right side of the grass, but nobody wants to help me organize a get-together. The surviving cousins and their families live scattered across the country, including Hawaii, Washington State, California, Utah, Wyoming, and Kansas.

For starters, I'd like to meet some of my long-lost relatives. Rather than a face-to-face meet-up, we could have a virtual reunion on Zoom, my preferred live-stream conferencing service.

Auntie Joan and Uncle Tom both passed away in their 80s in Greeley. I missed Joan's memorial but drove to Tom's service near Loveland in 2019. I didn't know anyone at Tom's service besides my cousins, since the attendees included mostly his millwright colleagues and friends.

I'd been out of touch with my cousins for the most part. I met a few of their children. Now they're adults. Cousins Margo and Gary are still in Greeley. Even though they are only an hour away, we have grown apart on a day-to-day basis. Sisters Bobbi lives in Hawaii, and Kathy is in California.

We share our childhoods and memories of growing up in a close-knit extended family. Those big-picture experiences helped shape who we are today. Our recollections of the good old days keep us connected when we meet.

"Now we're orphans and the family elders," Bobbi lamented. "How did that happen?"

I think all Baby Boomers share similar views on generational succession. I knew I'd get older, but I didn't expect it to happen this fast.

****

My family always had a big Thanksgiving get-together at our place in the Cole Addition. Grandma Ohashi put out a spread on the Southside. We never ran out of turkey. Since my emancipation and leaving town for college, I haven't found a new Thanksgiving groove, nor have I for any other holidays, for that matter.

Since college, Thanksgiving has been a second-tier holiday for me. At Hastings College, classes ended on Wednesday, and the school would let out for the long Thanksgiving weekend. I stayed on campus for two Thanksgiving breaks, visited a classmate's home for another, and carpooled back to Wyoming once with Randy, my only Cheyenne classmate with a car.

I liked being on campus during breaks because most of my classmates had returned home. I had the place to myself. Now that I've realized I'm an introvert, that makes perfect sense.

I remember planning to drive from Gillette to Laramie one Thanksgiving. A big snowstorm in eastern Wyoming shut down I-25 and stranded Tom and me at the 3003 Club. We went to the 7-Eleven at the bottom of the hill to pick up frozen steaks and other convenience-store food to round out our feast, which irritated Tom because we didn't celebrate properly.

****

These days, floundering around holiday traditions has become even more prevalent since my parents died. My partner, Diana, and I visit one of her daughters, Amanda, her husband, Tony, and their son, Mason. That's been a little different each Thanksgiving.

Tony is from New Zealand, and he prefers beef steaks to turkey. Maybe variety is a sign of the times. I roast a turkey earlier in the week to satisfy my craving and to have plenty of leftovers for sliced turkey sandwiches, my Hitching Post staple.

Christmas is still my favorite holiday. The great thing about living in America is that everyone can celebrate Christmas however they like. My parents, especially Mom, taught my sister and me our family traditions.

We put up a tree, but not on a particular date. We hung delicate hand-blown glass pieces from Germany and carefully placed the tinsel strands, made from a lead alloy, one piece at a time on each bough.

Shortly after New Year's, I dreaded the tedious chore of disassembling the tree, including putting away the tinsel, one strand at a time, in the original box for reuse the following season.

As adults, Dad carved a standing prime rib roast dinner, our new Christmas Eve tradition in Laramie. Dad loaded us into the car, and we drove to the midnight service at the Presbyterian Church. We didn't open presents that night. Everything waited until the big morning.

One Christmas Eve, as I slept, waiting for Santa Claus, he turned on the carport light at the Shermans' house next door. The beams shone directly through my bedroom window, signaling that Santa had finished his visit to our house.

I began inspecting under the tree at 3:00 a.m. Dad came out and reminded me that the action wouldn't start until 6:00 a.m. and that I might as well go back to bed. When I did, I lay there in anxious anticipation. Luckily, I had a high degree of delayed gratification.

In future years, Dad covered my bedroom window with a large cardboard Coca-Cola advertisement to obscure Santa's roaming around the neighbors' houses in the wee hours of the morning.

The stocking stuffers always included a navel orange that had worked its way down to the toe. I still have the sock my mom knitted. A small Cutie orange now rolls down to the toe: shrinkflation. I didn't feel right asking for specific presents, and always happy with what I received, even underwear.

After picking up the living room, we trekked to my grandparents' to round out the day. I recall firing my bazooka rockets around, which my grandmother didn't like.

Neither my sister nor I had children. Mom held onto the family traditions as long as she could. I didn't realize how young children help shape traditions, especially around the holidays. Shortly after my parents died, my sister sorted through the Christmas decorations and split them up, signaling the end of an era.

As an adult living in Lander and Gillette, I had to plan for blizzards that snowed me out more than a few times. Both drives took four hours in good weather to reach southeastern Wyoming. I moved to Colorado to be closer to Wyoming. The trek from Boulder took 90 minutes. U.S. Highway 287 rarely closed between Fort Collins and Laramie during the worst storms.

Diana and I also celebrated Christmas Eve at Amanda and Tony's place. They observe New Zealand customs, like a pillowcase stuffed with way more loot than a stocking. I enjoyed watching Mason get into the Christmas spirit. He's older now, and the cuteness of Christmas morning has worn off.

****

Japanese celebrate New Year's Day with extravagant parties. The TV blared with college football games when the main post-season attractions included the Rose, Sugar, Orange, and Cotton bowl games. Three original bowls had the best names, referencing actual containers. The cleverest name is the Cotton Bowl (Boll).

Wyoming played in the Sugar Bowl before the Black 14 incident and in minor games with absurd names like the Gator and Sun bowls. Who has ever seen a Gator or the Sun in a bowl?

We snacked on big spreads of *maki sushi*, a steamed clawless Pacific lobster, sipped good-luck *sake*, and slurped down New Year *ozoni* (good-luck soup) served with globs of unsweetened *mochi* prepared by the Grandmas, who spent days in the kitchen.

I still make a pot of *ozoni*, but that tradition hasn't gained much traction, except with my next-door neighbor, Henry. We used to meet at the New Year's Day *mochi*-pounding *mochitsuki* celebration at Sushi Zanmai, the longest-standing Japanese restaurant in Boulder.

****

After Grandparents Sakata and Auntie Hisako passed away, my mom used part of her inheritance to organize a family pilgrimage to Japan in 1993. A tour company arranged the itinerary, including hotels, meals, and visits to must-see attractions. When the tour ended in Tokyo, one of Mom's cousins showed us around the city.

My Dad developed a lung disorder and had pronounced shortness of breath when he couldn't walk up a steep staircase in a tall temple we toured. His lungs deteriorated over 10 years until he died in his hospice bed in Cheyenne.

I suspect this is the same disease that made me sick shortly after I turned 60. Work and travel took a toll on me in 2013, and I ended up flat on my back for six weeks in the hospital and in rehab. I went to the emergency room, and the doctor admitted me to the hospital in mid-December.

I thought I'd be bedridden for a couple of days, but I spent Christmas and New Year's Day with the second-string staff at the Good Samaritan Hospital, 30 miles from Boulder.

The hospitalist finally diagnosed me with a septic ulcer and wheeled me into the operating room for emergency surgery. Hospitalists are MDs who treat on behalf of primary care physicians, freeing those physicians from having to wander the halls looking for their patients.

The following week, I underwent another surgery, this time a Video-Assisted Thoracic Surgery (VATS) procedure. The pathology lab sent my tissue samples to several laboratories. The one at the University of Michigan determined that I had fungal Pneumocystis pneumonia (PCP), the same disease that killed 100,000 Acquired Immuno-Deficiency Syndrome (AIDS) patients between 1981 and 1990.

I readjusted my outlook on life after recovering from my deathbed illness in January 2014. I've been more intentional about getting my various "bands back together," including reconnecting with my family roots. That experience put me on the path to writing this book.

Maybe my genetics predisposed me to a similar disease that took Dad's life a decade earlier. I'm pretty sure he would have received a different diagnosis and treatment for his lung disease if VATS had been available.

Mom and Lorinda took some time off from the hospital, which gave Dad and me some time together. I won't call it quality time. Over the years, I made frequent trips to Laramie for holidays and family events, but also popped in when my parents invited me to UW sporting events or when I had meetings in Cheyenne.

During those visits, I spent time with my parents. I consider those visits quality time, not guilt-driven time. The last thing I want is for the hospice nurse to heavily sedate me on my deathbed while people stop by to see me. Why didn't they visit when I still had it together?

****

My move from Lander to Colorado *circa* 1993 took several years to establish myself as a fundraising expert. After working as a consultant on a series of gigs, two nonprofits hired me for full-time positions.

First, I worked for Project Safeguard, a domestic violence (DV) prevention organization, and then returned to graduate school at the University of Colorado Denver (CU-Denver). I earned a Master's in Public Administration (MPA) with a focus on nonprofit management and DV prevention. The MPA has helped me write grants to fund my creative projects.

My CU-Denver classmate and colleague, Randy Saucedo, asked me to document his DV and sexual assault survivor panel presentations, so I continue to be part of the DV industrial complex as a volunteer.

The woman who hired me decided to retire. Her replacement had little supervisory experience. Project Safeguard laid me off in June 2003, in the wake of 9/11.

Assets for Colorado Youth, a positive youth development nonprofit, hired me when my unemployment benefits expired. The Saturday before my job began, I visited my dad and told him that Monday would be my first day on the job. I offered to stay, but he insisted I return to Colorado.

"I'm not going anywhere," he said. "Get yourself a new pair of shoes."

"I'll be back after work," I responded. My sister called to say that Dad had passed away on Monday, August 18, 2003. His death marked a rite of passage for me. The rituals of carving the turkey at Thanksgiving and the standing rib roast at Christmas became my responsibility.

On my first day, I learned that the woman who had hired me had resigned and taken a job in Mayor John Hickenlooper's administration. Her replacement had little management experience. We had different fundraising approaches, and she laid me off in 2005.

During my unemployment, Mom didn't live to see Christmas. She died on December 2nd at home in Laramie from a brain aneurysm, ending the O'Hashi family traditions as I knew them.

I grew tired of working real jobs.

"I'm as incompetent as my supervisors," I thought. "I might as well supervise myself." I wrote *The Zen of Creative Imperfection* (2025), recounting how I resurrected myself as a creative entrepreneur. If you want to find out how I ended up writing this book, read it.

As for the winter holidays, I still put up a small tree in our miniature condo and go through the motions of Christmas, more out of habit than anything, to reminisce. My movie-making colleague, Michael Conti, suggested I try oyster stew on Christmas Eve. "It has something to do with Catholics not eating meat on Fridays," he explained.

****

When I turned 19, the legal age at the time, I started a new holiday tradition that appealed to my friends. My birth on May 2, 1953, fell on the 79th running of the Kentucky Derby, the first Saturday in May. Dad had his money on the favorite, Native Dancer. Long shot Dark Star, ridden by Henry Moreno, won the race.

Diana and I flew to Louisville, Kentucky, to celebrate my 50th birthday at the Derby. The inexpensive infield tickets surprised me. The hoopla didn't disappoint, with women wearing enormous wide-brimmed hats and mint juleps flowing all day.

The infield offered the best Derby viewing experience. We stood right at the wire, where the races ended. A guy in a tuxedo had passed out in front of us and lay on the grass. He came to just as the horses neared the finish. He got to his knees and stood as Funny Cide, a 13-1 long shot, won the 2003 Derby by one and a half lengths over the favorite, Empire Maker.

Since I graduated from college, I've celebrated my birthday on Derby Day with mint juleps and some off-track betting. Mint juleps are cocktails made with bourbon, simple syrup, mint, and crushed ice. Online betting is now allowed, so watching the race at an off-track betting parlor is unnecessary.

My birthday occasionally falls exactly on Derby Day, so I plan a big celebration with funky hats, BBQ, Derby pie, and horse-race gambling. The two dates coincided in 2020 during COVID. I had a Zoom call and invited friends and family from around the country. I had a fun time catching up with people, even for a few minutes. In 2026, my birthday fell on Derby Day. I hosted a big potluck dinner and betting pools.

****

The Skyline Nisei Club organized the Memorial Day picnics, the Cheyenne version of the *Bon* Festival, before we headed out to decorate the Japanese graves in the segregated section of the Lakeview Cemetery, the Buddhist version of the Day of the Dead. It finally occurred to me that the main reason my parents took me, even though I always had a good time, those Club activities provided safe places where Japanese friends and families could interact. They never explained to me that nonwhites had to bury their dead segregated from Caucasians.

Although we didn't have any of the music, drumming, or dancing, the picnic fare included American standards like hot dogs, hamburgers, and potato salad, as well as Japanese food. The moms prepared New Year's Day food in the summer.

Tupperware boxes contained all kinds of *maki sushi* rolled with fancy fish, like *unagi* (eel). I didn't try *nigiri sushi* until I went to Godzilla Sushi. Raw fish didn't meet the "working class" standard because it required refrigeration and not practical for a *bento* (lunch) boxes.

The moms made specialty items like inari, made from *abura age* (thinly sliced deep-fried tofu pouches) and stuffed with seasoned rice. These are very labor-intensive.

Each family had their secret *teriyaki* chicken marinade: some sugary, some with ginger, some thicker, and some thinner. My mom made thinly sliced *teriyaki* flank steak, a cheap cut at the time that is now expensive.

I learned to make *musubi* (rice balls) with a bit of *umeboshi* (pickled plum) in the middle. As an adult, I developed a taste for SPAM *musubi.* SPAM is chopped-up, reconstituted pork in a rectangular can, a food staple included in C-rations during World War II. I read that soldiers consumed 150 million pounds of SPAM during that time. I keep a can of SPAM around for emergencies.

****

The Japanese community, including my family, transitioned in the 1970s. The Skyline Nisei Club became less active as the Issei generation passed away, along with traditions like the summer picnics and gatherings at the cemetery.

Progress changed things when the Memorial Gardens opened on the east edge of Cheyenne, where my family bought in as charter members. It's one of those headstone-less urban-sprawl cemeteries that sprang up all over the West on the outskirts of towns. Grounds crews could mow over the flat grave markers.

All my family members' plots are out there. Our move from the urban Lakeview Cemetery coincided with the scattering of Cheyenne's Japanese community, particularly from downtown.

The family cemetery plot on the eastern edge of Cheyenne is one thing that will keep me coming back. Very few out-of-town cousins visit Cheyenne anymore. Jake and Jeanne's daughters, Alison and Leslie, are the only cousins who live in Cheyenne.

For the record, if I don't get around to updating my will, I want some of my ashes scattered in Crow Creek on the east side of Central Avenue, which runs alongside I-80. Crow Creek, the original military settlement, became Cheyenne. Dad and I hiked around the sandstone cliffs and explored animal dens. My heirs can scatter the rest of my ashes atop Devil's Tower and at Yankee Stadium, or bury them in the family plot in the Memorial Gardens.

The only time I see my cousins these days is at funerals. I told them we need to have a reunion before funerals become too frequent. Soon, those will be our memorial services.

My Kentucky Derby Zoom call reunion got the cousins out of the gate. Maybe we'll get around to it next year, or in three years at the latest. Event planning takes up what little discretionary energy I have left. I need an intern.

In the meantime, do what you can to keep your stories and traditions alive. As I've sorted through papers and boxes, the information has provided good fodder for this book. I mentioned that Uncle Jake sent my *Wyoming Graffiti* manuscript, an anthology of my newspaper columns, to The Portfolio Publishing Company of Texas, Inc.

"Should you wish to publish it on your own, we may be able to market it with our publications or do the production on a cost basis," President Susannah S. Borg wrote in a rejection letter on December 20, 1988. I should have contacted her earlier about the rewritten version. Unfortunately, she died in 2021.

Like the "Beyond Heart Mountain" newspaper column I wrote about Mrs. Honkawa that sat on a shelf since 1988, many of my other stories have universal punchlines, too.

Maybe I'll base a book on the column about why I eat my "last meal" as often as possible. You know, the meal I'd order on death row before the prison guard declared me a "dead man walking."

32

Cultural Competency

What if becoming culturally competent begins with examining the life recordings playing in our heads?

Those recordings start early. Parents, relatives, teachers, friends, churches, schools, television, comic books, and communities all help form our perceptions of people who look, speak, worship, or live differently from us. Over time, those experiences become assumptions. Some are helpful. Others deserve a second look.

In a 1960 Superman cartoon titled *Lend a Friendly Hand*, published for the United Nations Year of the World Refugee, two American boys want to play with an immigrant named Sandor. They feel awkward because they don't understand him. Rather than lecture them, Superman flies the boys to a foreign land and shows them a refugee camp.

Superman explains that war, politics, or disaster may have forced Sandor's family to leave their home. Global institutions have helped refugees to rebuild their lives. Superman says ordinary people can assist, too.

He tells the boys to learn about Sandor's background. Superman possessed and practiced cultural competency well before the phrase became fashionable. He encouraged an inquiring mind rather than fear, understanding others rather than drawing assumptions about them, and building relationships rather than stereotyping people.

If you search Google, you'll find dozens of definitions of cultural competency. For my purposes, I define cultural competency as a process. In my workshops, participants recall their experiences, reflect on them, and renew their perceptions of those who differ from themselves. The goal is the willingness to revisit old assumptions and see people more clearly.

Like Superman, I've spent much of my life learning that appreciating another person's story often begins by reexamining my own.

I started the story by recounting how my aunt experienced December 7, 1941, and my mom's observation about the backlash Muslims would face after 9/11. True dat. As happened to the Japanese in 1941, in the days, weeks, and years following 9/11, elements of American society turned against Muslims and people who looked like Muslims, including Asians.

Shortly after the 9/11 attack, the U.S. government detained more than 1,000 Muslims and Arabs without charge. As happened after the attack on Pearl Harbor, the U.S. Executive Branch reorganized its immigration and national security agencies and implemented new laws and policies.

People of the Muslim faith have a long history in the United States, longer than that of Asians. Transatlantic enslavement brought 388,000 Africans to the Americas from the 16th to the 19th centuries.

Precise numbers are difficult to determine due to the lack of complete records, together with the diverse regions where traders captured Africans. Historians estimate that Muslims accounted for 10 to 15 percent of Africans brought to colonial America.

There are records of Muslims who fought on the American side during the Revolutionary War. One well-known figure is Bampett Muhammad, an African Muslim who fought for the American blue coats.

The exact number of Muslim soldiers in the American Civil War is not well-documented, as the Department of War didn't record soldiers' religious affiliation. Based on the demographic patterns of the African and Arab populations in America at the time, historians estimate that close to 300 Muslims may have served in the Civil War.

A former enslaved African who served in the Union Army, Mohammed Ali ben Said, also known as Nicholas Said, wrote an autobiography detailing his experiences.

No federal laws limited Muslim immigration based on their long history in America. Compare that to the Immigration Act of 1924, which limited the number of Asians allowed to enter the country.

****

Wyoming isn't without its conflicts involving Muslims. The Powder River Basin is home to nearly 200 residents who identify as Muslims, including 30 who live in Gillette, my former stomping grounds.

I can't say I ever came across any Muslims when I lived in Gillette. Northeastern Wyoming has a long history of Muslim immigration dating back to 1909, when Zarif Khan moved to Wyoming from Afghanistan.

Many accounts chronicle Khan's experiences as "Hot Tamale Louie." He sold steamed cornmeal snacks on the street to passersby and eventually opened a storefront in Downtown Sheridan. Louie's customers respected him and his business, and supported his application for naturalization as a United States citizen.

The 1924 Act prompted lawsuits seeking to revoke the citizenship of previously naturalized people, including Louie. In 1926, immigration authorities stretched the 1924 Act to its limits, declared Louie Asian, and reversed his status. In 1954, he reapplied and received significant community support, leading to his renaturalization.

Most of the Muslims in Gillette descended from Khan. In 2015, a group of local Muslims decided to purchase a home and convert it into a mosque. That decision sparked an uproar among the locals and a local movement called "Stop Islam in Gillette."

The protests and rallies raised eyebrows among law enforcement agencies, including the FBI. The Stop Islam group's advocate, Matt Colvin, and the mosque organizer, Aftab Khan, eventually reconciled.

Wyoming Public Radio, the state's National Public Radio affiliate, hosted a conversation for a segment titled Time Heals All Wounds: Breaking Bread, Finding Common Ground After Angry Mosque Incident. The two advocates agreed to disagree. The short-lived conflict left Gillette boiling. Now, the aftermath is simmering. Colvin and Aftab Khan came to understand one another's positions.

Intentional actions like the WPR radio program brought people with divergent perspectives together and institutionalized civility in the public discourse of controversial issues. The challenge is for individuals to reimagine Superman's American Way by becoming more culturally competent.

Oppression toward Muslims and people who look like Muslims has continued since 9/11. Based on the Japanese experience in World War II, xenophobic American history has repeated itself. The facts are different, but the cultural pushback is similar.

The Islamic State of Iraq and Syria (ISIS) carried out a terrorist attack in Paris on the evening of November 13, 2015, involving shootings and bombings, resulting in 130 deaths and hundreds of injuries.

U.S. authorities believed that terrorist threats had grown in several Muslim countries. Donald Trump, a week after his 2017 inauguration, gave himself a legal remedy to discriminate when he issued EO 13769, Protecting the Nation from Foreign Terrorist Entry into the United States, the first in a series of EOs banning Muslims from entering the United States.

President Joe Biden rescinded Trump's orders, but rhetoric widened the cultural divide, evidenced by nationwide demonstrations in favor of and against the institutionalized xenophobia toward Muslims.

******

Racial strife reached a crescendo during the COVID-19 pandemic in the summer of 2020, when anti-Asian and anti-Black sentiments surfaced. Anti-Asian elements in society politicized the pandemic and blamed COVID-19 on China because the disease originated there. They hurled racial epithets and committed random and intentional acts of violence against Asians of any ethnicity.

The Stop Asian American Pacific Islander Hate Center reported nearly 1,900 hate crimes against Asian Americans, of which 69 percent involved verbal harassment.

"I was standing in the grocery store line, and I hear a voice behind me. 'You know the Chinese caused all this (COVID-19) to happen,'" said Carol Lou Kishiyama Hough in an interview for my documentary, Beyond Heart Mountain. "Here I am in my 70s, and I still have to put up with this."

While in police custody, Minneapolis law enforcement officers killed African American George Floyd. The incident sparked nationwide riots and protests.

Chaos theory is my explanation for the violence. In Jurassic Park (1993), mathematician Ian Malcolm (Jeff Goldblum) argues that human involvement cannot fully control the cloned dinosaurs in a natural environment.

I think that chaos theory gives a structure for understanding the violence that occurred during the COVID-19 pandemic, highlighted by the murder of George Floyd and the scapegoating of Asians for causing the pandemic. Self-isolation created a volatile and uncertain environment in which minor stressors and small disruptions led to social turmoil and violence.

Economic instability, social isolation, and health anxieties triggered emotional and psychological stress during the pandemic. These upheavals spread through vulnerable communities, leading to unpredictable and violent outcomes.

Unstable systems mirror the uncertainty of human behavior under extreme stress. The murder of George Floyd and the violence toward Asian women in Georgia may appear random, but they are elements of broader patterns of social instability influenced by the pandemic.

I think chaos theory explains the Tule Lake Camp uprising during World War II. Interconnected stressors of separation from familiar environments, harsh living conditions, and unfair treatment contributed to violent behavior. The WRA police responded similarly.

Can we examine the root causes of racism and xenophobia by learning from the Japanese incarceration during World War II and reimagining Superman's American Way?

****

Over more than three decades, I've been conducting diversity and cultural competency training. The need for such training resurfaces every few years. Social, cultural, and political tensions arose during the 2016 election cycle.

Over the years, I've observed that people in the dominant culture are complacent. They don't think they are racist because they don't wear white pointy hoods or burn down churches and disregard their historical White Privilege.

Is there a will among dominant culture members to become more culturally competent by better understanding our personality tendencies and life influences that constructed our views about race and ethnicity?

"What type of bread did you eat growing up?" is an icebreaker I use. The answers are more diverse than you might think, based on region, race, and ethnicity. My answer is white bread and tortillas. I tell the story of how my mom learned to make them from her Mexicana friends in Orpha.

"What did you learn from a caring adult other than a family member who influenced you as a child that sticks with you today?" My response has been about my basketball coach, Mr. Goff, who substituted me into a game when Husty and Bobby had off nights.

"What childhood holiday do you still favor, and is there a new celebration you observe as an adult?" Then and now, it's Christmas. When I turned 19, the legal age at the time, I began partying on Kentucky Derby Day.

Keep the time connecting the past and the present as close as possible. That makes it easier to reflect on how to create a better future in the moment.

Remember the climax of The Wizard of Oz (1939), when Dorothy gets herself back to Kansas? Glinda, the Good Witch of the North, gives Dorothy the glittery Ruby Slippers after her house kills the Wicked Witch of the East. She later learns that she can return home by clicking her heels together.

Like deciding which Yellow Brick Road fork to take and how to defeat the Wicked Witch of the West, cultural competency requires work to overcome difficult obstacles so that each of us can realize that we possess the inherent ability to understand ourselves and to engage our allies.

Sometimes we need support from our Lion, Tin Man, and Scarecrow.

****

Why is cultural competency different from learning about diversity? First, some history. Affirmative Action began in 1961. President JFK issued EO 10925, which directed federal contractors to take "affirmative action to ensure that applicants are treated equally without regard to race, color, religion, sex, or national origin."

Affirmative Action led to workplaces with more people of color and, along with the Civil Rights Act, signed into law by President LBJ in 1964, which prohibited employment discrimination by large employers.

The need for "diversity training" to define the various cultures emerged when workplaces became more diverse. More information would lead to greater acceptance within the dominant Caucasian culture without institutional changes.

Defining "diversity" became unworkable. For example, greater awareness of Asian Americans led to further definitions, such as Asians being broken down by country and separated by tribes and languages.

Diversity included race and ethnicity. I define ethnicity as a person's place of origin. My race is Japanese, and my ethnicity is American.

Some Asians settled in South America and had a different sense of identity than those who ended up in the United States.

Diversity training defines and describes demographics, which developed into "cultural competency."

****

Becoming more culturally competent calls for understanding ourselves and changing our perspectives on others. At any given moment, individuals, groups, and communities possess varying levels of cultural awareness, knowledge, and skills necessary to interact with others, guided by their histories and experiences.

"I think 'all lives matter,' not only Black lives," a guy in a Wyoming-based Zoom meeting said. My home state is very conservative.

I responded with a story about growing up in the Cole Addition, my idyllic Mid-Century Modern neighborhood in Cheyenne. My oddly diverse community included several Japanese and Greek families, all within a block or two of each other. We had close-knit extended families.

We all knew each other because every kid attended the same school. In the summer, backyard barbecues rotated from house to house.

One day, my next-door neighbor, Alex, rang the bell to ask to talk with my parents. I asked if I could relay a message. Later, I learned that his brother, Gus, had died. Three generations of his family lived together, including a grandmother called Yaya and Alex and Joanne's son and daughter.

My mom and the other neighbors brought over a covered dish. We all mourned for Alex and his family.

Most of the time, all neighbors matter. During Alex's time of mourning, however, his family mattered more than any other neighbors. It may seem self-interested when a neighbor brings forth an emergency, but it's how communities unselfishly offer support that matters.

****

All our experiences are different. "I'm color-blind and don't see racial differences" is a comment I hear from Caucasian people.

On the surface, that statement seems to be about social awareness. Observations like that discount everyone else's personal histories and experiences, assuming that others share your worldview and don't have one of their own.

My cultural competency presentations begin with each participant recounting their personal journey by thinking about their history and developmental influences, and how those experiences influence our perception and understanding of others.

Diversity, on the other hand, encompasses many groups. Learning all aspects of diversity is daunting because there are so many religions, languages, races, and ethnicities that the list is nearly endless. It's not practical to learn all aspects of "diversity," let alone specific cultural characteristics and practices.

When I worked for the DV prevention agency, I recall a story told by a victim advocate who responded to a crime scene. A bad guy had murdered an Asian woman. One of her family members began repositioning her body.

A law enforcement officer on the scene restrained the family member. The advocate intervened, unaware of the crime victim's exact race and ethnicity, but knew that rearranging the body is part of ritual practices in some cultures and explained this to the officer, who then understood.

Participants in my workshops at least begin to recognize that it is possible to shed behaviors, recognize privilege, and understand the need to make personal sacrifices for the good of the whole.

If you seriously begin to make personal change happen, you may lose friends but make better ones, and it takes time. If you desire to relate to people different from yourself, be willing to change your worldview by clicking your heels together.

"There's no place like home."

The Immigration and Nationality Act of 1965 eliminated discrimination against immigrants on paper. Laws changed more quickly than attitudes. Many Americans continued to cling to the idea of ethnic homogeneity even as newcomers from Latin America, Asia, and Africa redefined our nation into a diverse tossed salad dressed with new interpretations of the American Way.

What if Superman's message becomes stronger as the world changes?

In 1960, Superman taught two boys to understand an immigrant named Sandor by learning his story. More than half a century later, in *Action Comics* #987 (2017), Superman confronted a far different challenge. As immigration and xenophobia became flashpoints in American politics, a man attempted to attack a group of immigrant workers whom he blamed for his economic struggles. Superman intervened, shielding the workers from violence and confronting the attacker.

In 1960, Superman expressed his curiosity over fear. In 2017, he defended the same value. Superman stood firm with those whom society had judged not by their character, but by their immigration status.

Cultural competency begins for me with examining my life recordings. It matures when I challenge my old assumptions, listen to unfamiliar stories, and recognize our mutual humanity. Young Superman introduced Sandor to his classmates, and the older Superman protected immigrant workers from violence, both reflect the same truth. Understanding others is harder than fearing them, but it is also more rewarding.

As I learned more about my family's history, Heart Mountain, and the experiences of Japanese Americans, I replayed and edited my life recordings. Cultural competency challenged me to see my past more clearly. Like Superman, I measure my strength by how willing I am to stand with those who are different from me.

Afterward: Multicultural Superman

There's nothing wrong with Superman's American Way. As a child growing up in Cheyenne, Wyoming, I embraced it wholeheartedly. Work hard. Play by the rules. Earn your place. Become American enough, and you belong.

For generations, that formula carried an unspoken assumption: success came through competition, assimilation, and individual achievement. The strongest prevailed. The winners advanced. Newcomers fit in by becoming more like everyone else.

Superman reflected the times in which he lived. During World War II, he battled America's enemies: Germany, Italy, and Japan. During the Cold War, he became a symbol of Truth, Justice, and the American Way. Yet as America changed, so did Superman. The Man of Steel gradually became less a champion of conformity and more a bridge between worlds. After all, he emigrated from Krypton, grew up in Kansas by two Earthlings, and lived comfortably between cultures.

That evolution mirrors my own.

What if the American Way is not about winners and losers? What if we measure strength by collaboration rather than domination? What if belonging comes not through assimilation, but through the intentional work of understanding and accepting one another across cultural divides?

Those questions followed me long after I left Wyoming. They shaped my understanding of what it means to be Japanese American, and ultimately led me to reimagine the American Way for myself.

Comic books, while popular among young people, had a poor reputation. Parents classified comics as the decadent video games of their day. The culture police blamed comic books for juvenile delinquency.

I read a blog post on the Detective Comics (DC) website about how, in 1949, Superman's publisher created public service announcements (PSAs) to counter negative public perceptions of comic books.

The NSWA Committee on Japanese Americans responded to the backlash following the World War II incarceration of Japanese Americans. NSWA published bulletins on conflicts over employment rights, housing availability, and state legislation that codified discrimination, including the Alien Land Acts enacted nationwide, which prohibited Japanese property ownership.

In 1959, the NSWA partnered with DC to create PSAs featuring Superman, who reminded us of his civil and culturally inclusive American Way.

". . . and remember, boys and girls, your school—like our country—is made up of Americans of *many* races, religions, and national origins. If you hear anyone talk against a schoolmate or anyone else because of their religion, race, or national origin—don't wait. Tell them *that kind of talk is un-American!*"

Public relations efforts, such as the NSWA-DC partnership, raise awareness, but youth need skills to change their attitudes and behaviors toward students who differ from them.

****

I've read that a new Superman may have brown skin. Changing Superman's skin color can be a powerful symbolic gesture that challenges traditional superhero representations and fosters inclusion for marginalized communities. Seeing a superhero who looks like them can empower people of color, particularly youth.

Such efforts must be part of a broader effort to promote cultural competency and address systemic inequalities. Social change comes from a combination of symbolic actions, substantive changes in individual behavior, and changes to institutional power structures. How might a reimagined Superman remind us of a more inclusive American Way?

Individual civility: On a personal level, the only person I can change or control is myself. I've set my social-change bar at the "grocery store line" standard. That means that when I wait in line to check out and hear an offensive or disrespectful remark from a fellow shopper, I turn around, confront the perpetrator, and become an ally to the victim who withstood the taunt.

Conversations about race and ethnicity are difficult because the dominant culture has instead normalized discomfort around race and ethnicity. I hesitate to confront anything I hear, for fear of making inappropriate remarks or references.

Psychological research has found that biased views about race and ethnicity result from lifelong socialization. Regardless, the United States population continues to become more diverse and multicultural, projected to be a majority-minority population by 2045.

In 2015, the Pew Research Center administered an Implicit Association Test (IAT). The IAT quantifies hidden biases by measuring how individuals relate positive and negative words to races and ethnicities.

The Pew study investigated the subconscious biases of Caucasians and Asians toward one another. Half of the Caucasian sample preferred Whites over Asians, while 38 percent of the Asian sample favored Whites.

Bringing about social change is challenging work, mainly because the dominant culture continues to cook racial homogeneity into the American Way oatmeal. It's a vulnerable place, but individuals must be willing to change. If I'm unwilling to get out of my comfort zone, I can't expect others to do so. I try hard to walk my talk.

It's challenging to unwind the recordings in your head and reflect on how Superman's American Way influenced who you are and why you became who you are today. It's okay to make mistakes as you change your perspective on folks who differ from yourself.

Getting to know people different from me is both a challenge and a way to create a quiet movement that engages people civilly, one person at a time, rather than reacting to what you may experience. Social change doesn't happen by "liking" posts on Facebook.

Ranting, chanting, raving, and waving signs at rallies make for good photo ops. After the signs are in the dumpster, what then? Rather than yelling at the TV, be proactive by talking to an ally about the topic and building your counter-movement, one person at a time.

Individual change is an ongoing march. Take small steps. Who do you sit next to in church? Sit next to a stranger. Who do you invite for coffee? Go out of your way to ask someone you haven't seen in a while.

Neighborhood civility: Urban sprawl normalized assimilation. I don't think it's hyperbolic to say that African enslavement led to Manifest Destiny, the genocide of Native American tribes, and the Japanese prison camps.

Discrimination and racism toward the Japanese and other brown-skinned people became intended consequences. The West 17th Street Japanese community in Cheyenne experienced a cultural shift between 1924 and 1944. Over time, the dominant culture normalized assimilation and the Model Minority label, which grouped all Asians under the same Perpetual Immigrant stereotype.

The displacement of the Japanese because of discriminatory laws that erased the community's culture led to the decline of Downtown Cheyenne. Couple that with public policy that enabled communities to raze historic buildings and their untold or forgotten stories.

Even if developers tear down buildings, you can advocate for and preserve your community's character by remembering the stories of the people who live in the neighborhood, as happened when the Dinneen brothers constructed the Lotus Townhouse community on West 17th Street.

National civility: Individuals with collaborative, synergistic living experiences like mine can scale a national movement. I advocate for intentional community housing arrangements and am particularly fond of the collaborative secret sauce.

Cohousing communities rest on the premise that they reinvent Superman's American Way by accepting individual differences, including all perspectives, making decisions by consensus, and working toward the good of the whole.

The National Cohousing Alliance (CoHoA) provides technical assistance and direct services to approximately 6,500 residents across more than 180 existing cohousing communities and to 5,600 people forming 140 groups.

Cohousers own or rent private dwellings and share and maintain common areas. Cohousing differs from a commune because there is no shared economy.

CoHoA assists community members looking to repurpose abandoned buildings or build on vacant property to create vibrant neighborhoods by collaborating with current residents and businesses to agree on a story that promotes acceptance of both current and new neighbors.

Good stories about your community's purpose, norms, expectations, and culture inform investors, architects, and builders about how their participation can revitalize, redevelop, or develop new neighborhoods.

I visited friends from Cheyenne who lived in the Cole Addition and later moved to Sun City West near Phoenix. It's an age-restricted community that reminded me of growing up in the suburbs, except that all the residents are older, with grown children, rather than young families with elementary school-aged kids. I may end up returning to my past in an older adult suburb if I don't watch it.

Cohousers are likely to be people who share a mindset for reimaging Superman's American Way. Write a community story, settle on a mission and core values, agree to participate in creating and maintaining your community, and make decisions by consensus.

If you don't want to be a formal cohouser, get to know your neighbors. Learn more from my book, *Aging Gratefully in Good Company:* Brewing with happiness, purpose, and connection adds life to our years and years to our lives (2023).

****

Get off the couch and SHARE, as I've been doing since I started my cultural competency journey.

- **Socialize**: I stay in closer touch with my friends and family and make more than small talk with people I meet in passing. I hope it doesn't take a deathbed experience to get you off the couch.
- **Help**: Lend a hand. I'm a lot better at asking for help and giving help. "If you need something, don't hesitate to ask," is what I used to say. "You're in the hospital? I'll stop by on my way home from the store," is what I say now, being intentional about my actions. Regarding charitable giving, I donate to my chosen nonprofits monthly, not one time at the end of the year.
- **Accept**: This has been the most difficult because it's ongoing. I have found it hard to stay at the top of my game all the time. I ask people about their backgrounds to avoid inaccurate judgments.
- **Reach Out:** Turns out, COVID or no COVID, I don't get out much, which I attribute to being an Introvert. A few weeks ago, I attended the CoHoA conference in Denver. I broke out of my comfort zone, met as many strangers as possible, and sat next to people I didn't know at meals and workshops. I collected contact information and will stay in touch with my new acquaintances.
- **Engage:** I've shifted from a mindset of winning over losing to one of collaboration. I advocate genuine acceptance of those different from me and reject acceptance by exclusion. I envision a future built on mutual respect and understanding. By doing good and avoiding harm, we can create a society that

thrives on the strength of its diversity and the power of its unity.

Superman has been one of my role models since childhood. I didn't realize then that my own life would become a journey between worlds. Growing up Japanese American in Wyoming, I straddled cultures without fully understanding them. That experience gradually taught me cultural competency, empathy, and the value of seeing the world through more than one lens.

As an adult, I finally learned about the wartime incarceration of Japanese Americans. I discovered that the Western Civilian Control Administration had imprisoned my grandfather and uncle in an assembly center for close to a year. That revelation changed the way I viewed my family, my country, and myself. It helped me see a world beyond Heart Mountain.

The boy who admired Superman believed in a fixed and unquestionable American Way. The man writing these words now sees it differently. The American Way is still rooted in truth and justice, but it grows stronger when it embraces many histories, many cultures, and many voices.

That's the lesson of a multicultural Superman. He doesn't abandon his origin story, nor does he reject the place that raised him. He draws strength from both. In a nation shaped by people from every corner of the world, a reimagined American Way is about learning how to belong together.

****

My vast store of general knowledge has limits. I've woven my experiences and recollections into the historical details of the four years and millions of dollars the U.S. government spent constructing and managing 15 assembly camps and 10 incarceration camps to contain 120,000 people.

As a news source, I consider an article 80 to 90 percent accurate to be close enough. As a journalist and writer, I strive for 90-95 percent accuracy. Please let me know if you have any concerns about my information, its accuracy, interpretation, or perspective.

One problem when discussing race and ethnicity is the lack of a common language, which is why references end up as derogatory slang terms. The Perpetual Immigrant stereotype also feeds into this lack of understanding. Japanese, Indonesians, Chinese, Koreans, etc., are all clumped under "Asian."

I researched, wrote, and edited much of the content for *Views from Beyond Heart Mountain* during the COVID-19 pandemic. I include information on how the pandemic reshaped Asian perspectives on the Perpetual Immigrant and Model Minority stereotypes that politicized the viral disease.

I consulted various sources and struggled with how to refer to them. I considered terms such as Indigenous People, American Indians, and Native Americans. I decided to use "Native Americans," even though some might interpret the term to refer to anyone born in America.

"Indian" is a misnomer, even though some of my Arapaho friends refer to themselves as being Indian. Indigenous People is too jargony. When possible, I referred to specific tribes rather than using the general term.

Much of the information about the 500 and 400 blocks of West 17th Street in downtown Cheyenne is from the original source material of the Japanese community chapter in *The History of Cheyenne*, edited by Sharon Lass Field in 1989. My mom, Auntie Hisako, and Auntie Elsie compiled the Japanese family histories that ended up in my inherited files.

Cross-checking those, I found inconsistencies and verified the information against online sources and conversations with family members.

The Special Collections Room at the Laramie County Library holds city directories and phone books spanning the past century, listing addresses for residents and businesses. The LeClercq Jones

Collection offers an excellent photographic record of downtown Cheyenne from the mid-1970s through the 1980s.

I can't forget Wyoming State Archives reference archivist Suzy Taylor. She can put her finger on any obscure file in the mysterious back room of the Barrett Office Building in Cheyenne.

I also drew on personal conversations with my cousin Milton Ichiyasu, my sister Lorinda, coattail cousin Carol Kishiyama Hough, high school friend Bob Walters, and childhood friends Randy Suyematsu, Brian Matsuyama, Terie, and Linda Miyamoto.

My *Beyond Heart Mountain* documentary included interviews with Carol, Bob, Brian, and Terie, which aired on Wyoming PBS in December 2021 and is available on PBS Passport.

I don't know whether many details would have surfaced without social media. I made several inquiries about the West 17th Street neighborhood on Facebook.

As for other information, being a seasoned journalist, I cross-referenced at least two credible sources on the World Wide Web to fill in details about events and people.

Ancestry.com and Newspapers.com are great resources for finding detailed information about people, places, and dates. If you don't think you have a digital footprint, think again. I'm amazed at how much data comes up, even with simple search terms.

If you have further questions about the Japanese internment that *Views from Beyond Heart Mountain* may have raised, the most comprehensive compilation of the Japanese American World War II experience is the *Densho Encyclopedia*, a publicly accessible, well-vetted website.

No matter what your memories are, I hope they are fond ones.

-30-

About the Author

Alan O'Hashi learned about truth, justice, and the American Way from Superman comic books. As an adult, he discovered that his place in the real world was far more complicated and interesting than any superhero story.

A Japanese American writer, filmmaker, and community media producer, Alan works with organizations, businesses, and storytellers to create culturally competent content that explores identity, belonging, and our shared humanity. His work examines the intersections of race, ethnicity, culture, nationality, and place, inviting audiences to see the world through multiple lenses and challenge their assumptions about themselves and others.

Through documentaries, books, and community storytelling projects, Alan captures the nuance and complexity of life in a pluralistic society. His stories often draw from personal experience, including his family's Japanese American history, the incarceration of his relatives during World War II, and his lifelong journey between cultures.

"Stories help us see beyond our own experiences," Alan says. "I want readers and viewers to encounter people they may never meet, consider perspectives they may never have imagined, and discover how much we have in common."

Like the multicultural Superman he writes about, Alan believes strength comes not from standing above others, but from understanding them. His hope is to contribute to a more equitable and fair society where people from all backgrounds can be seen, heard, and valued.

Alan lives in Boulder, Colorado, where he continues to write, produce films, and search for new ways to reimagine the American Way.

Abreviations

Views from Beyond Heart Mountain alphabet soup.

1917 Act – Immigration Act of 1917
1924 Act – Immigration Act of 1924
1965 Act – Immigration and Nationality Act of 1965
442nd IR – 442nd Infantry Regiment
442nd RCT– 442nd Regimental Combat Team
AA – American Airlines
ABC – American Bowling Congress
AIDS – Acquired Immunodeficiency syndrome
ARVN – Army of the Republic of Vietnam
BAPA – Boulder Asian Pacific Alliance
BCE - Before the Common Era (formerly BC)
BIA – Bureau of Indian Affairs
BLM – Bureau of Land Management
BMRR – Burlington and Missouri Railroad
BN – Burlington Northern railroad
BNSF – Burlington Northern and Santa Fe Railway
Board – Cheyenne Historic Preservation Board
BOS – Logan International Airport
Bosox – Boston Red Sox
BoR – Bureau of Reclamation
BSA – Black Student Alliance
BYU – Brigham Young University
CB&Q - Chicago, Burlington & Quincy
CFD – Cheyenne Frontier Days
CIO – Congress of Industrial Organizations
Camp – War Relocation Center
CCC – Civilian Conservation Corps

Center – Assembly Center, Detention Center, depending on context

CoHoUS – Cohousing Association of the United States

Committee – Fair Play Committee

CSA – Community Supported Agriculture

CST – Casper Star Tribune

DC – Detective Comics

DC – District of Columbia

DoD – Department of Defense

DoE – Department of Energy

DoI – U.S. Department of the Interior

DoS – U.S. Department of State

DV – Domestic Violence

DVD – Digital Versatile Disc

EDS Board - Economic Development and Stabilization

E-Free – Evangelical Free Presbyterian Church

EPA – Environmental Protection Agency

EHS or East – East High School

EO – Executive Order

F – Fahrenheit

FBI – Federal Bureau of Investigation

FDR – President Franklin Delano Roosevelt

Fort Warren - F.E. Warren Base

FSA – Farm Security Administration

GBSD – Ground-Based Strategic Deterrent

ICE – Immigration and Customs Enforcement

I-25 – Interstate 25

I-80 – Interstate 80

JACL – Japanese American Citizens League

JFK – President John Fitzgerald Kennedy

ICBM – Inter-Continental Ballistic Missile

IMHO – In my humble opinion

INS – Immigration and Naturalization Service

KB – KiloByte

Land Act – Wyoming Alien Land Act

LAX – Los Angeles International Airport

LCD – Liquid Crystal Diode

LDS – Church of Jesus Christ of Latter-Day Saints

LBJ – President Lyndon Baines Johnson

MP – Military Police

MRS – Monitored Retrievable Storage

NAACP – National Association for the Advancement of Colored People

NPS – U.S. National Park Service

NDEA – National Defense Education Act of 1958

NSWA – National Social Welfare Assembly

PCP – *Pneumocystis* pneumonia

PE – Physical Education

PF – Posture Foundation sneakers

PFC – Private First Class

PoW – Prisoner of War

PSA – Public Service Announcement

PTSD – Post Traumatic Stress Disorder

PVC – Poly Vinyl Chloride

Quakers – American Friends Society

RAM – Random Access Memory

RCT – Regimental Combat Team

ROM – Read Only Memory

RPG – Rocket Propelled Grenade

RPM – Revolutions Per Minute

SCOTUS – Supreme Court of the United States

Soviets – Union of Soviet Socialist Republics

SS – Steam Ship

UAP – Unidentified Aerial Phenomena

UFO – Unidentified Flying Object

UMTRCA – Uranium Mill Tailings Radiation Control Act of 1978

UP – Union Pacific railroad
UPC – United Presbyterian Church
U.S. – referencing the United States government.
United States – referencing the country (America)
USAT – U.S. Army Transport
USDA – U.S. Department of Agriculture
USNPS – United States National Park Service
USS – United States Ship
USSR – Union of Soviet Socialist Republics
UW – University of Wyoming
VW – Volkswagen
WAC – Western Athletic Conference
War – Capitalized, World War II
WCCA – Wartime Civilian Control Administration
WPA – Work Projects Administration
WRA – War Relocation Authority
WSJ – Wyoming State Journal
Wyoming State Parks – Wyoming State Parks and Historic Sites
WTE – Wyoming Tribune Eagle

Densho Encyclopedia Resources

The Densho Encyclopedia is a highly referenced source for information about Japanese Americans and World War II.

442nd Regimental Combat Team
https://encyclopedia.densho.org/442nd_Regimental_Combat_Team/

Amache Relocation Camp
http://encyclopedia.densho.org/Amache_(Granada)/

Gila River Relocation Camp
https://encyclopedia.densho.org/Gila_River/

Heart Mountain Relocation Camp
https://encyclopedia.densho.org/Heart_Mountain/

Jerome Relocation Camp
https://encyclopedia.densho.org/Jerome

Manzanar Relocation Camp
https://encyclopedia.densho.org/Manzanar

Minidoka Relocation Camp
https://encyclopedia.densho.org/Minidoka/

Poston Relocation Camp
https://encyclopedia.densho.org/Poston_(Colorado_River)/

Rowher Relocation Camp

http://encyclopedia.densho.org/Rohwer/

Topaz Relocation Camp
https://encyclopedia.densho.org/Topaz

Tule Lake Relocation Camp
https://encyclopedia.densho.org/Tule_Lake/

Pomona Assembly Center
http://encyclopedia.densho.org/Pomona_(detention_facility)/

Tulare Assembly Center
https://encyclopedia.densho.org/Tulare_(detention_facility)/

Seagoville Detention Center
http://encyclopedia.densho.org/Seagoville_(detention_facility)/

Kenedy Detention Center
http://encyclopedia.densho.org/Kenedy_(detention_facility)/
Crystal City Detention Center
https://encyclopedia.densho.org/Crystal_City_(detention_facility)/

www.ingramcontent.com/pod-product-compliance
Lightning Source LLC
LaVergne TN
LVHW031307150826
845672LV00010B/2659
* 9 7 9 8 9 8 9 4 2 1 3 2 9 *